Salon At Casa Guidi by George Mignaty, 1861   Courtesy of The Goewey Collection, Mills College Library

Elizabeth Barrett Browning's
Letters to
Mrs. David Ogilvy

Elizabeth Barrett Browning's Letters to Mrs. David Ogilvy 1849-1861

with recollections by Mrs. Ogilvy

edited by Peter N. Heydon and Philip Kelley

JOHN MURRAY

First published in Great Britain 1974
© Browning Letters, John Murray 1973
© Editorial Matter, The Browning
Institute, Inc. 1973

Printed in the United States of America
0   7195   3131   4

With deep appreciation the editors dedicate this volume
to
Ella Ogilvy Tomes, M. A., Oxon.
and
Herbert Frederick Collingridge, Lieut.-Colonel (Ret.)

without whose lively, affectionate, and knowledgeable interest in their grandmother's friendship with Elizabeth Barrett Browning, this edition of letters would not have been possible.

Acknowledgments

The Browning Institute and the editors of this volume are grateful to Mr. Bernard Barenholtz, Peter Croft, Esq., Mr. Herbert Nagourney, and Mr. Daniel E. Koshland for the part each has played in helping to acquire the manuscripts of these letters; to Mrs. Ella Ogilvy Tomes and Lt.-Col. H.F. Collingridge for their invaluable assistance in providing details about the Ogilvy family as well as their generous gifts to the Institute of their grandmother's manuscripts and relics; to the staffs of the Reading Room of the British Museum, and the Berg Collection of the New York Public Library, for their help in researching certain aspects of this correspondence; and to Ronald Hudson, Esq., Dr. William S. Peterson, and Signora Giuliana Artom Treves, for their keen editorial advice.

Permission to publish the letters from the Brownings to the Ogilvys and other Browning copyright material has been granted by Mr. John Murray. Permission to include Mrs. Browning's letter to her sister Arabel has been granted by the Henry W. and Albert A. Berg Collection of the New York Public Library. Permission to print a photographic copy of the George Mignaty painting, *Salon at Casa Guidi*, has been given by The Goewey Collection, Mills College Library, Oakland, California.

Contents

Illustrations

Introduction

I

The Sotheby Sale Catalogue for November 29, 1971 listed two lots, numbered 186 and 187, which held a very special appeal for Browning students and admirers alike. Described as a "Fine and extensive series of 28 A.Ls.s. (signatures cut from two), 2 A.Ls. and 6 incomplete A.Ls." from Elizabeth Barrett Browning to her friend Mrs. David Ogilvy, and being offered for sale by one of Mrs. Ogilvy's grandchildren, Lot 186 represented the first major series of Elizabeth's letters to see the public light since 1937. The sole letter in Lot 187 from Robert Browning to Mr. and Mrs. Ogilvy, "describing the last hours of his wife Elizabeth Barrett Browning," represented the logically concluding document in the friendship between Elizabeth and Mrs. Ogilvy which lasted for more than thirteen years until Elizabeth's death in June of 1861. When the Browning Institute's successful purchase of these letters was publicized in *The Times*, another grandchild of Mrs. Ogilvy's came forward with an offer of several remaining letters for sale to the Institute which complemented the other purchase and eventuated in the publication of the present edition of all thirty-nine letters.

The Browning Institute's special interest in this collection derives principally from its recent purchase of the Brownings' Casa Guidi apartment in Florence and its desire to establish there a library relating to the Anglo-Florentines of the nineteenth century. In these endeavors the Institute acts very much in concert with Elizabeth's own inclinations, as expressed in this correspondence: after visiting Petrarch's house she writes to Mrs. Ogilvy "It was very affecting—but then, you know, we have great organs of reverence & a taste for old slippers and such gear" (see Letter 8).

As the contents of these letters make clear, both Mrs. Ogilvy and Elizabeth are apposite exemplars of the Anglo-Florentine community, and it is therefore appropriate that this major collection will rest at Casa Guidi. Taken as a whole the correspondence reveals a substantial and intimate personal relationship between the two women on account of which, Mrs. Ogilvy records in a memoir published thirty-two years after Elizabeth's death, Elizabeth ". . . made me promise to keep her letters private, and I have respected her wish." Fortunately for Browning enthusiasts, Mrs. Ogilvy's heirs have recognized the wisdom of the letters' complete publication, for in this format it is possible to memorialize the dignity and sincerity of the women's friendship. Moreover, the light such correspondence throws on the creative personality standing behind the poetry "may be said to exceed that of any similar contribution," to quote Robert Browning's own words when referring to the Shelley letters in his *Introductory Essay* of 1852.

II

The letters themselves, Mrs. Ogilvy writes in her memoir, "were written in minute scratches no thicker than the hairs on a daisy stalk, on tiny note sheets, folded sometimes into tiny envelopes, the whole forming apparently a doll's epistle." Elizabeth often crowded her penmanship onto both sides of these note sheets of light-weight paper then used for foreign correspondence. They measure from 3-1/8" x 4-1/2" to 5-1/4" x 8" in size and range from 3 to 16 pages in length. Because the volume of Elizabeth's remarks frequently exceeded the bounds of the notepaper on which she was writing, she often concluded separate letters by crosswriting, squeezing words into the margins (see Plate I for a photo-facsimile of the first page of Letter 6) or by filling the space visible inside the envelope when the flap is opened. In one curious instance, Pen Browning, then not quite five, added "Penini's best love" in his own hand inside the envelope along with Elizabeth's complimentary closing (see Letter 24).

Elizabeth wrote and posted the letters in Florence, Siena, Paris, London, Bagni di Lucca, and Rome; they reached Mrs. Ogilvy, after being redirected in several instances, at Naples, Bagni di Lucca, London, Florence, Lyons (France), Edinburgh, Perth, Forfarshire (Scotland), and Lower-Sydenham. The correspondence as published in this volume is incomplete, however, since there are no extant letters from Mrs. Ogilvy to Elizabeth. It can be safely concluded that these letters were destroyed by Browning in 1887 when he moved his London residence from Warwick Crescent to De Vere Gardens, at which time it is known that he disposed of a number of similar mementos associated with the earlier years in Florence. Portions of the existing letters published here are missing, and it is possible that whole letters do not survive: the substantial lapse of time between Letters 28 and 29, as well as the way in which fresh topics are occasionally introduced (as, e.g., the mention of Henrietta's illness in Letter 33), seems to bear out the possibility. No presentation copies of the Brownings' poems remain in the Ogilvy family's hands, suggesting some earlier dispersal in which letters could have been included.

III

Mrs. Ogilvy's recollections published in this volume relate that the Ogilvys were given a letter of introduction to call on the Brownings in Florence by Elizabeth's cousin, Mrs. Martin Lindsay, when the Ogilvys and Lindsays were in Rome together in the spring of 1848. The first meeting, described in such comprehensive detail by Mrs. Ogilvy in her memoir, occasioned others in the months after the

Ogilvys had settled in Florence in July, 1848 (with their two-year-old daughter Louisa). The Ogilvys' first son, Alexander William, was born in Florence in September of 1848; the Brownings' only son, Robert Wiedeman Barrett ("Pen"), was born exactly six months later, prompting a closer association between the families. In the summer of 1849, the two families got together at Bagni di Lucca (then a fashionable resort for the English-speaking communities of Italy; see Letter 1), after which the Ogilvys returned to Florence and took up residence in the apartment one floor above the Brownings' at Casa Guidi.

There seems no doubt that the friendship between the two women ran the course of most friendships, vacillating between spirited intimacy and formal disagreement depending upon such vagaries as the conditions of their previous meeting, their moods, the passion of the position each of the two women adopted on various political, literary and moral issues, and the obvious inclination of each to be strong rather than weak in such matters. In short, no adjective can comprehend the qualities of their friendship at all times.

In a letter to Miss Mitford in April of 1850 Elizabeth speaks of the Ogilvys as "cultivated and refined people; ... [Mrs. Ogilvy] a pretty woman with three pretty children [Louisa, Alexander and Marcia Napier, born the preceding January at Casa Guidi], of quick perceptions and active intelligence and sensibility. They are upright, excellent people in various ways, and it is a loss to us that they should have gone to Naples now."[1] In a highly revealing letter to her sister Arabel on March 12, 1850 (published here for the first time), Elizabeth speaks more specifically of the Ogilvys as they were about to leave Florence for the extended trip to Naples, Capri and Sorrento (see Letters 2-7 addressed to these locations):

1. *The Letters of Elizabeth Barrett Browning*, ed. by Frederic G. Kenyon (2 vols.; London: Smith, Elder, and Company, 1898), I, 445-46.

The Ogilvies are in an awful state of doubt, talking of Naples, of Paris, & of Florence by turns. I think it likely that they will decide on Paris, after all. We shall miss them. They are excellent persons, & very cultivated. The little baby is very pretty—a model baby—and not much more fault is to be found with the maturer members of the family. Quick sympathies, fine tastes, & a great deal of kindness, make them agreeable friends & neighbours. I am not drawn into love with Mrs. David Ogilvy . . with all her prettiness, liveliness, intelligence, & feeling . . there is wanting somehow the last touch of softness & exterior sensibility—I like her much . . like her society, respect her good qualities, feel an interest in her actions & sentiments . . yet I dont love her, & I dont feel that she loves me. You meet with delightful, unloveable people, you know, sometimes, & then you blame yourself for finding them unloveable when you undeniably find them delightful. Observe— she has sentiment, goodness, kindness—brightness: masculine, no one could call her! there is just a want of softness in the character . . a want of tenderness, somehow. I would'nt say such a thing to any but you. She & her husband are our friends, & have shown us every sort of attention, and we shall be most sorry to lose them.

It is most important to emphasize in commenting upon this statement that the Brownings did not "lose them," nor did the Ogilvys lose the Brownings: in fact Elizabeth makes these observations within a relatively short time after having established the friendship which was to continue for more than ten years. During that period the extant correspondence in this volume attests to the growing respect and affection between the two women. Elizabeth's delineation of Mrs. Ogilvy's character in this letter is better understood by recognizing Mrs. Ogilvy's Scottish origin: her connections among old, reserved, traditionally cultivated, but somewhat stern Scottish families were a sealed book to the Brownings. In spite of such differences of personality between the two women, they were friends.

Even when Elizabeth writes to Arabel in May of the following year describing the time they spent with the Ogilvys in Venice (see Appendix C), she quickly retracts whatever criticisms she has:

> Most agreeable fellow-travellers they have been to us—full of intelligence & good humour . . really clever in their knowledge & apprehension of pictures & churches . . and yet, and yet, . . Robert & I agree sometimes that being alone is a good thing. The whole day, for instance, he was outside & I inside, travelling . . and I had to talk . . talk— Now I like to receive impressions quietly & deeply, without so much talk of this & that. Still, it seems ungrateful to write down any drawback to a delightful journey, & to really delightful persons.

And in June of 1852, the following year, after the Ogilvys left the Brownings behind in Paris (having spent a month's time together there), Elizabeth writes to Mrs. Ogilvy with the sincere and genuine affection that marks the correspondence generally:

> We shall not be there [in London] until the beginning of July, & our chances of finding you must be small. Which vexes me to think of. Yet I dont at all feel as if I should'nt see you soon—indeed I do feel as if I should: and Robert has the same sort of presentiment, happily for both of us. So, we agreed as we passed your house the other day, consoling one another for having to pass it.
>
> (Letter 15, p. 78.)

Mrs. Ogilvy's published remembrances of Elizabeth likewise indicate that such respect and affection were reciprocated.

IV

It is quite understandable why Elizabeth was attracted to Mrs. Ogilvy, for she was a cultivated and delightful person. Eliza Anne Harris Dick was born on January 6, 1822 in Perth, Scotland, in the family of Abercromby Dick. It is known that she left for India with her sister Charlotte in 1838, presumably staying with their grandfather, Dr. William Dick (who was the chief surgeon to the Hon. East India Corporation in Calcutta), until their return to Perthshire, Scotland in 1841.

On July 6, 1843, she married David Ogilvy who, though

nearly nine years her senior, was a similarly cultivated and distinguished member of the old Scottish families of Napier and Ogilvy. On March 19, 1844 she took up the business of motherhood with the birth of the first of her seven children, Rose Theresa Charlotte. The joy which Rose's birth brought to the proud parents is evidenced in a curious letter containing Mrs. Ogilvy's whimsical verses on the happy event (this is published for the first time in this volume as Appendix A). When Rose died in infancy fifteen months later, Mrs. Ogilvy was moved to express grief in *Rose Leaves*, a thin volume of poems on Rose's short life and sudden death, privately printed in 1845. (More than forty years later the death of her son Alexander, Pen Browning's contemporary, forced her into comparable poetic creativity; her "Allan Water, August 27th, 1887" appears in Appendix B, p. 204.)

Mrs. Ogilvy was undoubtedly engaged a great deal in writing during this period, for in 1846 G. W. Nickisson produced in London her first commercially published collection of poems, *A Book of Highland Minstrelsy*. This volume, which went through two subsequent editions in 1848 and 1860, was considered a success in the *Athenaeum* when it first appeared; "it contains," the *Athenaeum* review states, "the evidence of a poetic and accomplished mind, and discourses pleasantly, as well as feelingly, of the characteristics and superstitions of the Highlanders." It was this book which most influentially recommended her to her contemporaries.

Throughout the period covered by the present correspondence, Mrs. Ogilvy continued to write poetry, recording therein her reactions to events in her private life, thoughts and feeling evoked in the course of her travels, political observations, religious convictions, recreations of past historical events in narrative forms—in short using her poetry in much the same way the Brownings used their writing during the period (Elizabeth producing *Casa Guidi Windows*,

Aurora Leigh, *Poems Before Congress*, as well as various collected editions; Robert producing *Christmas-Eve and Easter-Day*, *Men and Women*, as well as his *Introductory Essay* to the spurious Shelley letters).

Mrs. Ogilvy's *Poems of Ten Years, 1846-1855* appeared in London and Edinburgh in 1856 under the Thomas Bosworth and John Menzies imprints respectively. Its subjects, as the *Athenaeum* reviewer pointed out, "range through a wide variety of themes: Italian scenes, Highland remembrances, and the last year's deeds in the Crimea all finding a place in the volume." (The metaphorical framework of one poem in the collection, "Despondency," may suggest just how wearying Mrs. Ogilvy found the frequent traveling which became a part of their way of life on the Continent; see Appendix B, pp. 189-190). Undoubtedly many of the poems she forwarded to Elizabeth in manuscript form during their correspondence were later published in this volume (see Letters 18 and 25).

Traditions of Tuscany, in Verse, published by Thomas Bosworth, appeared early in 1851, about five years after the date of the first poems included in the *Poems of Ten Years* volume. It follows the format of the earlier *Highland Minstrelsy*, though the scene has changed to reflect the Ogilvys' living in Italy for the previous four years (it is to the anticipated publication of this volume Elizabeth refers in Letter 6). In this connection, one interesting criticism the book received was that "Mrs. Ogilvy is among those who have listened too long and too submissively to Tennyson and the Brownings." Although such a criticism tends too strongly to minimize Mrs. Ogilvy's achievement in this collection, it is fair to say that the book reflects the common interest in Italian history, art, and politics which many of the Anglo-Florentines shared, and accordingly allows us another measure for appreciating the magnitude of the Brownings' achievement. When the families travelled and stayed together in Venice (in May of 1851) or Paris (in May of 1852), it is clear that their common interests in experiencing the novelty of life and art in these cities far outweighed any estimation of their relative literary successes.

In *Landmarks of a Literary Life, 1820-1892*, Mrs. Newton Crosland introduces a letter from Elizabeth, written to her in September, 1852, enquiring if Mrs. Crosland might forward to Elizabeth the periodical numbers (of *Chambers's Edinburgh Journal*, presumably) in which a story by Mrs. Ogilvy had appeared. Mrs. Crosland then identifies Mrs. Ogilvy for her own readers as

> a lady better known by her initials E. A. H. O. than by her full name, and recognized as a writer of clever stories and able criticisms, as well as of spirited poems. Her volume entitled "A Book of Highland Minstrelsy," though differing in subjects treated, deserves to be compared for vigour and national enthusiasm with Professor Aytoun's "Lays of the Scottish Cavaliers."[1]

The difficulty of piercing through the anonymous authorship of stories appearing in *Chambers's* makes identification of Mrs. Ogilvy's work in this genre impossible.

After returning in 1852 from the four years spent on the Continent, Mrs. Ogilvy continued her writing career: in addition to these periodical contributions and the already mentioned *Poems of Ten Years*, she published in 1867 a popular book which nonetheless attests to both her verbal facility and religious interests, *Sunday Acrostics, Selected from names or words in the Bible*. This was published in London by Frederick Warne and Company, the same publishers who for their 1893 edition of Elizabeth's *Poems* asked Mrs. Ogilvy to contribute the Memoir of Elizabeth, printed in the present volume from the original manuscript.

In 1852 her fifth child, Walter Tulliedeph, was born, to be followed by Angus in 1855 and her last child, Violet Isabel, in 1857. Until the time of Elizabeth's death in 1861, the Ogilvys lived at different times in Perth, Edinburgh,

1. Camilla Dufour (Toulmin) Crosland, *Landmarks of a Literary Life, 1820-1892* (London: Sampson Low, Marston and Company, 1893), pp. 234-35.

Peckham Rye, Lower Sydenham and Forfarshire. From various entry titles in Mrs. Ogilvy's commonplace book we know she had become friends with a number of people associated with the community surrounding the Crystal Palace at Sydenham: Sir David Brewster, Henry Chorley, Anna and Susan Cushman, Helen Faucit, the actress, and Sir Arthur Sullivan, the composer of operettas. After her husband David Ogilvy died in 1879, she went to live near her father's home at Bridge of Allan; she lived there until 1900 when she came South to live with her daughter Marcia Bell and her husband (who died in 1903) until her own death at Ealing on January 3, 1912. On an earlier visit from his mother-in-law in 1881, Horace Bell described her as a woman "of remarkably vigorous intellect and wide range of sympathy in everything."

Indeed manuscript collections of her poetry written during these years attest to her wide-ranging interests over subjects as diverse as "The Rookery on the Hill," "Grannie's Birthday" (see Appendix B, pp. 203-204), "The Lord Hungerford" (a description of the ship in which she sailed to India in 1838), "Work for Work's sake," the marriage of her son Angus to his cousin Rose Serena Dick in 1886, "A Ditty in Praise of Good Wine," "Allan Water, August 27th, 1887" (see Appendix B, p. 204), "Sleep the Sleep that Knows Not Waking," "Victoria and Her People," "The Ant and the Bee," etc. Toward the end of her life, as her failing eyesight deteriorated into complete blindness, her skewed writing on these pages attests in another way to the insistent creative impulse which continued to influence her until her death.

V

During the period of their correspondence, Elizabeth clearly appreciated many of the virtues, interests, abilities and experiences Mrs. Ogilvy brought to the friendship. In fact, it is not mistaken to say that the circumstance originally bringing them together as friends was also that in large measure responsible for sustaining and deepening it. In Elizabeth's words, many of the Anglo-Florentines were drawn together "from a communion of babies"; children were born to the Ogilvys, the Brownings, Count and Sophia Cottrell, the James Montgomery Stuarts, the Horatio Greenoughs, the Rev. and Mrs. Wolley, and the Coxes in the several months preceding and following the first letter in this correspondence. Because Elizabeth had had three miscarriages, when she concluded she was pregnant with Pen around September of 1848 she was particularly receptive to the attentiveness of Mrs. Ogilvy, who had just had her third child, Alexander William. We know from unpublished letters to her sisters that Elizabeth was much in contact with Mrs. Ogilvy in the late months of 1848 and early months in 1849 before Pen's birth in March: "A visit from Mrs. Ogilvy's nurses & pretty children interrupts me," she writes to Arabel on December 16, 1848, "& she has sent me four crowns for little caps . . gifts to herself she says in a note, but which in the case of her own baby she did not put to use, having enough and to spare. They are beautifully worked . . Indian and French . . & will complete everything I shall want in the same way." (Mrs. Ogilvy's previously unpublished memoir recounts in considerable detail some of the confusion surrounding the hiring of a nurse for Elizabeth, her being the first person to hold Pen after his birth, and so forth; see pages xxvii ff.)

And throughout the correspondence, even though it appears there were differences of opinion between the two friends as to how their children were to be weaned (see Letters 3 and 6), to be dressed (see Letter 29), to be treated when they were no longer babies (see Letters 28 and 37), to be disciplined (see Letters 5 and 20) and even how their hair was to be kept (see Letters 7 and 28), their children's activities nearly always are given prominent treatment in Elizabeth's letters, most often appearing as the last item mentioned before her closing. In this connection it is important to add that throughout the correspondence Elizabeth is "filled up to the brim with covetousness"—to use her own words—when she hears of others having baby girls. Even as late as 1858 and 1859, Elizabeth writes to Mrs. Ogilvy: "Always, always! I shall hanker after little girls to my dying hour" (see Letters 29 and 31).

Although children are important to both the origin and continuation of the friendship—indeed the correspondence is unique in that it evidences one of the two friendships the Brownings as a family had with another family (the other being that with the Storys; see Letter 24)—children are not the exclusive subject. In fact, the correspondence displays Elizabeth in a number of ways: her private life (her deep love for Robert despite her glimpses into his sometimes impetuous temperament [see Letter 4], her extreme sensitivity, her poetic plans, her earlier shock over her brother's death at Torquay, her relationship with her family in England, her reactions to her miscarriages, her distress in hearing of Margaret Fuller's death, her love of their Casa Guidi home in Florence, her confidence in the integrity of the spiritualists' sessions she attended, etc.); her reactions to contemporary artistic and literary accomplishments (mentioning, among others, Wordsworth, the Tennysons, Carlyle, Arnold, Thackeray, Miss Mitford, Kingsley, George Sand, Hiram Powers, William W. Story, William Page and Harriet Beecher Stowe); and her concern over political events in France, Austria, Prussia, Italy and England.[1] Because of the diversity of its topics, the correspondence accordingly provides a reliable and direct introduction to the personality of Elizabeth Barrett Browning. Unlike the voluminous correspondence with her sisters, or the perfunctory social note to one person or another, the correspondence with Mrs. Ogilvy is both rich in revelations about

1. See in this connection, Giuliana Artom Treves, *The Golden Ring* (New York: Longmans, Green and Company, 1956).

herself (owing to their trusting intimacy) and manageable because it is self-contained and relatively brief.

One dimension in the correspondence which a reader in the last third of the twentieth century will find unusual, perhaps, is Elizabeth's emphasis on the recognition women rightfully deserve in the mid-nineteenth-century literary world. To a fellow-poetess she is able to concede "the usual difficulties & sadnesses which await a woman in literary life" (see Letter 6), but can therefore speak with pride when they overcome the greater challenge (see Letter 23). Aurora Leigh makes an apposite observation in Book Five of Elizabeth's poem (which was in composition during this period):

> We women are too apt to look to one [man],
> Which proves a certain impotence in art.
> We strain our natures at doing something great,
> Far less because it's something great to do,
> Than haply that we, so, commend ourselves
> As being not small, and more appreciable
> To some one friend.
>   . . . . .
>   This vile woman's way
> Of trailing garments, shall not trip me up:
> I'll have no traffic with the personal thought
> In art's pure temple.
>
>   (V, 43-62)

Although both women express love for their husbands and a respect for the institution of marriage, and despite the differences of opinion the two women had about the way poetry should be written, it is apparent from the present correspondence that they were both enthusiastic exponents of the intellectual and literary accomplishments of their sex. Although Elizabeth can at times be whimsical about literary achievement—"We are all poets in Florence. Not to rhyme would be a distinction" (Letter 27)—she is especially careful and serious when recounting the accomplishments of women authors.

VI

The letters are reproduced in full and as faithfully to the originals as possible (including misspellings) except for two minor departures: slight punctuation changes have been made for clarity, and superior letters have been aligned unless to do so would give rise to confusion. Following current practice, single underscoring is denoted by the use of italics, and double underscoring by the use of capitals.

Square brackets are used for editorial interpolations in a few instances within the text. Angle brackets indicate torn or missing parts of the manuscript; where possible, conjectured readings are offered, lacking which elipses are used within the angle brackets. The use of consecutive periods within the text of a letter is characteristic of Elizabeth's epistolary style and does not indicate an omission. Conjectural dates have been supplied in square brackets for letters not dated by Elizabeth and derive either from postmarks, internal references, or references made in other correspondence.

Editorial comments have been confined to a minimum and placed in headnotes to the letters. Most headnotes amplify a reference to the movements of the Brownings and Ogilvys or provide biographical or historical information necessitated by an obscure internal reference. A reader wishing more complete background information on the Brownings during this period will turn to the standard biographies by Griffin and Minchin of Robert, by Hewlett or Taplin of Elizabeth. The most informative documents relating to the Ogilvys during this period are Mrs. Ogilvy's written recollections of Elizabeth which immediately follow.

P.N.H.

Recollections of Mrs. Browning
by Mrs. David Ogilvy

On two separate occasions, Mrs. Ogilvy wrote recollections of her friend. The first, hitherto unpublished, she recorded in a commonplace book containing her personal reminiscences of interesting people she had met during the 1850's and 1860's as well as manuscripts of her own poems written during the 1890's. This memoir is undated, but from internal references it had to be written after 1857.

The second memoir, drawing on material contained in the first, was written for inclusion in the 1893 Frederick Warne and Company edition of Elizabeth's *Poems*. Passages which their house editor deleted have been retained. It is a tribute to Mrs. Ogilvy's powers of observation that she recalls the facts almost perfectly; the few discrepancies are noted. The Browning Institute is grateful to Mrs. Ella Ogilvy Tomes, Mrs. Ogilvy's granddaughter, for the gift of this manuscript to its library.

I

We were driving through the Piazza Navona in Rome with Mr. and Mrs. Martin Lindsay whom we had met in France, when suddenly Mrs. Lindsay exclaimed: "How you would like Ba!" "Who is Ba?" we asked. "My cousin, Mrs. Browning the Poet. Ba is the name she gave herself in infancy, and by it she is known to all her relatives." We caught at the idea, and the Lindsays, as good as their word, wrote to the Brownings to say we would call on reaching Florence.

My first acquaintance with Mrs. Browning's writings was owing to the enthusiasm they inspired in my husband's friend James Adamson who was always quoting them and who lent us his copy of her works. Her husband's *Bells and Pomegranates* were made known to me by Camilla

Toulmin's, now Mrs. Newton Crosland, admiration; and, the marriage of the two poets was announced to me by Professor Aytoun thus: "Have you heard that Miss Barrett who was said to be in a decline has jumped up out of bed and run off with Robert Browning?" Altogether I was prepared to be interested in these new acquaintances.

I shall never forget our entrance into the large room at Casa Guidi, then only half furnished, with a big grand piano as chief feature, at which Robert Browning was at that moment trying over some melody by ear. He strode quickly across the floor on hearing our names, shook hands most heartily and led us up to the sofa where his wife sat or lay curled up in an attitude peculiarly her own. She was just like a King Charles Spaniel, the same large soft brown eyes, the full silky curls falling round her face like a spaniel's ears, the same pathetic wistfulness of expression. Her mouth was too large for beauty, but full of eloquent curves and movements. Her voice was very expressive, her manner gentle but full of energy. At times she became intense in tone and gesture, but it was so spontaneous, that nobody could ever have thought it assumed as is the fashion with later poets and poetesses.

We did not stay long in Florence that month, as my health required change. It was in autumn when we again met frequently. We had returned in July but the Brownings spent some time at the Baths near Pisa.[1]

My eldest son was born in September and Mrs. Browning took a great interest in him. Her boy was born in March, six months later. She was often very low spirited about the event and afraid of not having a living child as she had already had several miscarriages.

In those days young infants wore lace caps with cockades of satin ribbon—a round cockade for a boy, an oval

1. In the summer of 1848 the Brownings were away from Florence for three weeks. They travelled to Arezzo, Fano (3 days), Ancona (1 week), Loreto (1 day), Sinigaglia, Fano, Pesaro, Rimini, Ravenna, Forli, before returning to Florence.

one for a girl. I used to make up these dainty caps, and decorate them with boys' cockades and take them to the despondent mother-expectant and holding them up before her I said "There! does not that make you feel as if the little son were close at hand," and she would smile and own it cheered her to see them.

I had liked a very decent English woman who had served me as monthly nurse and I recommended her to Mrs. Browning who conditionally engaged her for her own confinement. Sir Henry Harding the doctor, who was to attend Mrs. Browning, did not think this Mrs. Eagles[1] sufficiently experienced for what he considered a very critical case, and he insisted on a particular nurse of his own recommending being engaged. The Brownings behaved very liberally in compensating Mrs. Eagles in her disappointment, but to my intense disgust, her husband who was a courier tried to impose on them, and made himself very annoying indeed by threats of legal proceedings. I was thankful that Dr. Harding had been so peremptory as Mrs. Browning was by no means an ordinary patient. The old Italian nurse said to me after the birth "E un miraculo quello bambino e venuto da quel corpo." Mr. Browning came to tell us of his son's birth the same day, and I was the first person after the nurse who took the little "Wiedeman" in my arms.

We often went to tea at the Brownings. "Lisa" their maid had a talent for baking a particular kind of north country scone, which were always forthcoming, and if it was in summer, a water melon that had been let down into the well to cool was another feature of the meal. We had many tastes in common, in Literature and in Art and Religion too, though as they were keen Dissenters and we were Church of England folk, we had many discussions. Baden Powell just then brought out his *Christianity without*

1. The name of the nurse appears as Madame Pietri in Elizabeth's correspondence and in contemporary copies of Murray's *Hand-Book*. Unless Eagles was her maiden name, Mrs. Ogilvy's memory seems to be in error.

Judaism. Mrs. Browning said on hearing the title "Christianity without Judaism is Hamlet without Hamlet." She was theoretically a keen Calvinist, but her breadth of nature and of training perpetually rebelled against its restrictions and nothing could be less Democratic than they both were in Poetry. Their idea of Poetry was to be written for the Higher Intellect, the Lords of Mind, and they were to interpret it to the common herd. As for being "understanded of the people," they as little thought Poetry should be so, than did the Peers and Bishops of the middle ages think the Bible should be comprehensible to the masses. My husband, who looked on poetry as much the life [and] breath of the commonalty as is the air around us, used to battle boldly with them, and urge the duty of every poet uttering as clear and pellucid thoughts as running water. Another subject in which we differed was rhyming. My husband depreciating their favourite assonance, and insisting on the more complete consonance of accurately responsive rhymes. In politics too we had many arguments. From the beginning Mrs. Browning's imagination was dazzled when mine was alarmed by the significance of Louis Napoleon's re-admission to the Legislative Assembly of France, and his mode of return and speedy grasp at the Presidentship. She saw in him the Saviour of European peoples, where I and my husband saw the selfish snatcher at personal power.

In June 1849 we all went to the Bagni di Lucca. We lived in the lower village not far from the river but rather elevated above the road to Bargo westward. We had a beautiful view over southward where the valley opened and showed a fine mountain at some distance. The Brownings lived in the Bagni Caldi up the hill in a narrow ravine where the houses clung to the sides of the rock—and where, as Mrs. Browning said, one felt like a squirrel in a wheel cage that could not move without going up or down.

As Mrs. Browning could not suckle her baby, she had a balia or Italian wetnurse. The child throve very well while

my boy six months older was cutting teeth and in alarm-
ingly delicate heath. Well do I recall the round full face
of little Wiedeman enclosed in a red knitted hood with a
full border of red knitted frilling—while my poor little
man under a round straw hat showed one of those pallid
sunken countenances with preternaturally large wistful eyes
which are the anguish of mothers and nurses. Mrs. Browning did not expect my boy to live and often expressed her
deep sympathy to friends, but never said anything to increase my own fears for him.

II

In the early spring of 1848 my husband and I were driving
in Rome with a Mr. and Mrs. Martin Lindsay. Mrs. Lindsay
was talking of her cousin, Mrs. Browning. Suddenly she
said, "You are just the people to suit 'Ba'—would you like
an introduction?" We jumped at the offer.

"Ba" was Mrs. Browning's pet name. Her husband called
her so, her sister Arabel called her so, and so did the large
family of Gloucestershire cousins who came to Florence in
1851-52.

On reaching Florence from Rome, June 1848, we at
once called at Casa Guidi. Robert Browning was playing
with all his heart and soul on a grand piano. He sprang
up, striding forward with outstretched hand. His wife was
curled up in a corner of a sofa in the middle of the large
dim sala, hung with old brown tapestry and ancient pictures. With her profuse feathery curls half hiding her small
face, and her large, soft, pleading eyes, she always reminded
me of a King Charles spaniel. Something unutterably pathetic looked out of those soft dog like eyes, and I could
fancy that when her beloved dog "Flush" was young and

handsome there might have been a likeness. But by the time I knew Flush he was an old mangy creature, an uncomfortable fellow-passenger in a vettura. Light was not in favour with Mrs. Browning. She habitually sat in dark rooms, and was so little out of doors that her accuracy of observation was all the more remarkable. Her son was born on March 9, 1849, and as my son was born not long before, we were much drawn together by motherhood as by intellectual sympathy. We were four eager enthusiasts, and quite in accord about painting and sculpture. But in poetry we had different canons, and the Brownings were too original-minded themselves to wish for servile assent in our opinions. Mrs. Browning read largely of French novels. I once saw a huge pile beside her; "They will soon melt down!" she remarked. She greatly admired George Sand's writings, and, on meeting her in Paris in 1852, wrote to me, elated that George Sand had kissed her. She was scandalized by my reply, that such a kiss reminded me of Becky kissing Amelia when they met in later life. In truth, Mrs. Browning with all her genius had the simple purity of Thackeray's heroine.

We spent the autumn of 1849 near each other at the Bagni di Lucca, and in October we Ogilvys rented the upper floor of Casa Guidi, where the Brownings occupied the first floor or Piano Nobile. Of course we met daily, and had many common acquaintances—the Trollopes, Montgomery Stuart, Powers and Greenhough, the American sculptors, Kirkup, the friend of Trelawny, Mrs. Jameson, the authoress, etc. In 1850, after some months spent at Naples, Capri, and Sorrento, we again wintered in Florence, and in May 1851 my husband and I joined the Brownings in a vetturino journey by Bologna, Parma, Modena, and Mantua, to Venice, where we had rooms on the Grand Canal, the Brownings on the first floor, and we Ogilvys on the floor above. We generally went together for dinner to the Piazza di San Marco, and if Mrs. Browning and

I came back alone, she invariably lost her way, unless I did the piloting. I think those were the longest walks I ever knew her attempt. She very much depended for strength on a daily dose of ether in some peculiar mixture prescribed for her. One day the child got hold of the medicine after the maid had measured and poured it out. He drank it off, and great was the alarm, but it did not hurt him.

Both she and her husband ate little. I remember a quail once sufficed for dinner to them both; but he was very eloquent in food, and found out the special dainty of every place we visited and insisted on its being included on the bill of fare. He and his wife were a contrast in temperament. He so vehement, talkative, and hasty, full of gesticulation, and fond of argument. She quiet, half-proud, half-humorous in her expression, as he expatiated, coming in now and then with a little deprecatory "Oh, Robert!" as a gentle drag on his impetuosity. She could fire up on occasion but in general, she was intense rather than excitable, and she took life too seriously for her own happiness. She could so little bear to pain any one she loved, that I had to administer the baby's medicine, to save her the trial. It was well for her that she went before husband and child. She could not have survived them.

Mr. Barrett, her father, was a stern unforgiving man. He never forgave her marriage. When another sister, Henrietta, married Mrs. Browning wrote to me: "Henrietta has followed my example in marrying against his will. It is the only way possible in our family." Still, she hoped that her father might be softened by his grandson, and when they left us at Venice and went to London her sister, Arabel, one day took the child and carried him to his grandfather's house, and set him on the table in the study. When the old man saw the child he said abruptly, "Whose child is that?" "It is Ba's boy," was the timid reply. The implacable grandsire rose up and left the room without word or glance back.

Mrs. Browning's tender heart was deeply hurt.[1]

After a fortnight or three weeks together of delightful wanderings about Venice, and long talks on the balcony of an evening, overlooking the canal, the Brownings went to London, via Paris, and my husband and I crossed the Brenner to Munich, and through Bavaria to England. We met again in the Great Exhibition, which was too gaudy, too noisy, and too fatiguing to please Mrs. Browning.

In the autumn we were all back in Florence, Mrs. Browning's Gloucestershire cousins, the Peytons, having the first floor of the Villino Lustrine, opposite the Pitti Gardens, and we had the ground floor.[2] The Peytons told me much of their cousin's early life, and of her brother's sad death at Torquay. In May 1852 we left Italy finally stopping a month at Paris, to be with the Brownings, who had found us rooms near theirs. It was during the short Presidency of Louis Napoleon, who did not then seem popular with the Parisians. I think Mr. Browning mistrusted Louis Napoleon, as my husband and I did; and as yet Mrs. Browning had not discovered his merits. We had much good talk in their Paris salotto, Mrs. Jameson and "Orion" Horne being often present. One evening we all told ghost stories, till Mrs. Browning cried "Basta!" Madame Doche was then playing in "La Dame aux Camelias," and Mrs. Browning was very enthusiastic about her.

We saw the Brownings again in London once or twice, and they came to London in 1855 for a short time, when

1. Mrs. Ogilvy is probably thinking of the episode of 1855 when Arabel and her brother George took Pen to Wimpole Street. Elizabeth wrote to Henrietta: "George was playing in the hall with him and he was in fits of laughter. Papa came out of the dining-room and stood *looking* for two or three minutes. Then he called George and went back, 'Whose child is that, George?'—'Ba's child,' said George.—'And what is he doing here, pray?' Then, without waiting for an answer he changed the subject."

2. By "all back in Florence" Mrs. Ogilvy does not include the Brownings because they wintered in Paris. When Elizabeth lived at Hope End, in Herefordshire, the Peytons lived on the adjoining estate, Barton Court. There is no evidence to substantiate their being cousins of the Barretts, although they did own property in Gloucestershire.

we were living in the suburbs; but after 1852 our intercourse was chiefly by letter. She made me promise to keep
her letters private, and I have respected her wish. In 1860
her sister Henrietta died; my mother-in-law, whom the
Brownings had known well in Florence, died at the same
time, or a little later. After her sister's death, Mrs. Browning
was for two months quite prostrated; then she wrote me a
touching letter, quivering with pain, and, speaking of her
motherless niece, she said, "I see my own child's face
through a mist of tears." Not long after she wrote con-
doling with us on my mother-in-law's death, and her own
sorrow was still bleeding. Very soon after she was herself
laid in the grave.

Her letters were written in minute scratches no thicker
than the hairs on a daisy stalk, on tiny note sheets, folded
sometimes into tiny envelopes, the whole forming apparently a doll's epistle. But if the writing was thin, the
thoughts and feelings were stout and strong. Nearly half
of every letter is made up of anecdotes of "Penini," as her
boy called himself. How he longed for a little brother;
how he wished to be either the Pope or Louis Napoleon;
how he went to the Carnival in a rose domino and a mask,
and resented the holding of his hand by his nurse; how he
read Grimm's fairy tale of the Twelve Brothers, and sighed
for a dozen of the same, and how his mother too sighed for
a little daughter that never came. A daughter was born to
me while I lived in Casa Guidi, and I can see vividly in my
mind the figure of Mrs. Browning pacing up and down with
the baby girl in her arms, her long curls dropping over the
tiny face, her eyes full of love and yearning. As Penini
grew older, the letters told how his mother taught him
English, French, and Italian; how he kept a journal, and
read Dumas in his bed, by the light of a candle in his
wash-basin, and recited the patriotic songs of Dall' Ongaro
to the Sienese peasant boys. His father gave him two hours'

daily musical instruction, and one letter tells proudly that
he could play a sonata of Beethoven at eight or nine years
old. Penini had one rival only in his mother's heart, and
that was Italy. All her letters are full of Italian politics.
Her doubts of Mazzini, her rapturous admiration for Louis
Napoleon as Italy's deliverer, her wrath at British apathy,
her dread of priestly machinations; the letters are seething
from end to end with passionate emotion. It irked her that,
with almost equal desire for Italian freedom, I could not
believe in Louis Napoleon's disinterested greatness and magnanimity. She had condoned the coup d'état of December
1851; I could not. It was strange that, with such boundless
sympathy for Italy's troubles, she expressed scant feeling
for either the Crimean or the Indian Mutiny troubles of
her own countrymen. The little she does say of them
refers chiefly to my anxiety over relatives engaged in both
of those terrible wars.

She professed an abstract horror of all things military.
She had little of the clinging to ancestral traditions which
has so large a place in my Scottish temperament. Her
cousins, the Peytons, abounded in family traditions, but
one might know Mrs. Browning for years, and never hear
of one of her "forbears." I attributed this greatly to old
Mr. Barrett's sturdy Nonconformity; but I have since met
well-born Dissenters with plenty of family legend.

Mrs. Browning was reared in Nonconformity, and Mr.
Browning was brought up in Calvinism. Both to a certain
degree shook off their trammels, but both lived and died
Puritans at heart. Mrs. Browning added to her religious
faith a keen hankering after mesmeric spiritualism, more
than, I fancy, her husband thought safe for her impres-
sionable nature. In the summer of 1855, when they were
in London, she was telling me her recent experiences at
séances. He was impatiently pacing up and down the room;
suddenly he wheeled round and broke out, "And what does
it all end in? In your finding yourself in a locked room,

and the keeper putting in his head, and asking what you will be pleased to have for dinner!" "Oh, Robert!" was all his wife's rejoinder. Looking back over thirty years since her death, I can see that her high and noble mind had many limitations; that she was a powerful torrent foaming against the rocks, and not a wide sea spreading over a hemisphere. But her perfect sincerity and purity of motive, her freedom from jealousy or pettiness of feeling, her warm heart and sweet temper, would have made a stupid woman lovable, and made her, with her intellectual power, adorable then when she lived in the flesh, and now when she lives in the memory.

A picture of Casa Guidi when I knew it would hardly be complete without a sketch of its servants. The Brownings treated their servants as friends, and made few changes. Wilson, the North-country maid, was devoted to her mistress, and became the boy's nurse on the departure of the "balia." Later on, she married Ferdinando, her fellow-servant. She was not a typical lady's maid, being gentle and unassuming; after her marriage Mrs. Browning often lamented her lack of strong-mindedness, she was so easily victimised. The cook in 1848 was a fantastic old fellow, Alessandro, of whom his master had always new anecdotes. His wife died at Christmas. The disconsolate widower could not stop crying to concoct the "Gran Budino" (plum-pudding). The next week he presented it with all due honours, apologising elaborately for his wife having committed the "inconvenience" of dying at the date she did.

Elizabeth Barrett Browning's
Letters to
Mrs. David Ogilvy

Letter 1

The first letter in this series was written a year after Mrs. Martin Lindsay (*née* Clara Bayford) had given the Ogilvys a letter of introduction to her cousin, Elizabeth Barrett Browning. Shortly after the Ogilvys had settled in Florence in July 1848, Alexander William, their first son, was born on September 9; six months later to the day, the Browning's son, Robert Wiedeman Barrett was born on March 9, 1849.

The Brownings' elation over their son's birth was soon shattered when Robert's mother, who resided in New Cross, suddenly died without knowing of her new grandchild. Robert's grief was so deep and long-lasting that by summer Elizabeth was greatly alarmed at his appearance, loss of appetite and sleep. She insisted that they leave the baby with servants and find a place where they could spend the summer months away from the heat of the city. In search of such a place, they travelled for five days to Pisa, Carrara, Spezia, Seravezza and Bagni di Lucca, then a fashionable mountain resort for the English-speaking communities of Italy. At Bagni di Lucca they found the Ogilvys who recommended that they take an adjoining house to their own. The Brownings considered this suggestion as well as other villas, and obtained a quotation for rooms in one of the three hotels owned by Pagnini. This letter asks Mr. Ogilvy to make a counter-offer to Pagnini. Ultimately, however, an earlier offer made to the proprietor of Casa Valeri was accepted. The Brownings left Florence for Bagni di Lucca on June 30, taking with them Pen, Wilson, Alessandro, Flush, and Pen's wet nurse.

Many aspects of the political scene were in turmoil when this letter was written. Ledru Rollin had just failed in an attempt to overthrow Louis Napoleon's government; Rome had earlier been proclaimed a republic; and the Pope, Piux IX, was in exile at Gaeta where Leopold II, Grand Duke of Tuscany, had joined him. Leopold returned to the Pitti Palace in Florence at the end of the following month under Austrian protection. At the same time, Rome was let "out of her pain" when Louis Napoleon destroyed the Roman republic. He restored the Pope to power, hoping that he would be a mild and progressive ruler under French protection. The Anglo-Florentines did not consider the Austrian presence a salutary one as Mrs. Ogilvy's poem, "The Austrian Night Patrol, Florence" (see Appendix B, pages 191-193) indicates.

[1]

San Giovanni Battista is the patron saint of Florence, so each year June 24 is traditionally celebrated with games, a cortège in Renaissance costume, fireworks and illuminations. Elizabeth writes to Mrs. Ogilvy on the 25th with a report that the traditional celebration was held to a minimum—just a band concert in the Cascine, a large public park on the right bank of the Arno.

Florence, June 25. [1849]

My dear Mrs. Ogilvy,

As you are so kind as to offer to help us at your Baths, we will venture to ask Mr. Ogilvy to make a proposition to Pagnani. Would he take us in at sixty francesconi the month, (two a day) us two, & our two maids; & letting us have the apartment which he showed us that morning? We agree to take the table d'hôte for ourselves & our servants, only we must of course have breakfast & tea in our private rooms:— and if he accepts our terms, we will engage to stay with him certainly two months & perhaps three. Six pauls each a day, & four for the servants:—our expenses in Florence do not exceed this;—making the right allowance for the rooms apart from the board: and, being of the little-eaters of the earth, we are quite sure that he would not lose by us if the arrangement were made. I should however tell you that in consequence of a letter from Casa Valeri, Bagni Caldi, we have made an offer for the second floor, of sixty francesconi for the season—*thirty* less than were asked, & therefore it is not likely that we should get in there. Still it will be well to ascertain, before an engagement is concluded (should it prove concludeable) with Pagnani. Are we trying Mr. Ogilvy's kindness too severely? Almost I am afraid.

You will wonder at our new born courage for the tavola rotonda—but I dont think we shall dislike it. We shant have to talk to anybody, you know—it will be much like looking out of a window at the world. The objection to the small rooms & the closeness, is serious,—and I have fears of the same kind about your little house, notwithstanding its most excellent neighbourhood possible. Altogether, and as we have resolved on dismissing our man-servant, there will be more comfort & less fuss in the hotel arrangement, if it could be managed.

Dear Mrs. Ogilvy, we have been expecting you from evening to evening:—but you are right. Florence begins to be scarcely habitable through the excessive heat. The nearer we approached Florence, the hotter we grew . . just as if were drawn in to the "central fire" of the universe. And what made me still hotter was a sudden anxiety about the baby—"If we should find anything gone wrong," . . Robert by no means giving me encouragement, for which I was reasonable enough to reproach him. It was great joy when the porter said "Tutto va bene," and when our door opened upon baby at the threshold, looking fatter & rosier than ever and rounding his blue eyes with a sort of wild wonder at the sudden storm of kisses. I, for my part, came in for a most cordial kiss from the scarlet-cheeked balia, who thought it right perhaps, to make up for the passiveness of her charge. Oh—of course he did not know me: that would be too much to expect. But, being in the best humour possible, he condescends to allow himself to be "lugged" about, as I can manage it—(so heavy the child is)—keeping a secret opinion, I dare say, of the superior agreeableness of Robert & Wilson who can dance him, and of the balia who provides other entertainment. I do hope your boy will prosper with his teeth, after the first *sprouting* begins. It seems to my ignorance that afterward he may be expected to suffer less.

Poor Rome! so you wish her out of her pain! And I wish France out of the dishonor of the imputations cast upon her. We shall see whether she will back Austria or face Austria. It is bad enough as it is. Did I tell you that Mr. Powers had a new little girl, & that I saw it when it was ten days old & unspeakably large & ugly? Since then, Robert says it is growing into more sculpturesque form.

But this is a break in my French politics. Ledru Rollin is certainly better out of the way, I agree with Mr. Ogilvy.

I am just beginning to grow out of my fatigue, but the fatigue seems to have done me no harm, in the way of illness—I am as well as people can hope to be when embeddied in hot embers. The thermometer rises as rapidly as Jack's beanstalk. It was at eighty yesterday in my bedroom. As to San Giovanni, he was very dull: only the Florentines comforted themselves by going to the Cascine to hear the Austrian band play. I begin to be sceptical of the return of Leopold the second, altogether. The last Austrian ordinance is against the dogs. All dogs found in the street to be killed straightway, lest they shd. interfere with the movements of the Austrian horse! So I am enraged in the interests of Flush.

Now, as I hope to see you so soon, I wont write any more this morning, and indeed I wish you to receive by the earliest post what I have written. May we ask you to write? My husband is rather better than otherwise, I hope, for our excursion,—but it was not enough to do the much which is needful for him.

Do give our regards to Mrs. Ogilvy, and to Mr. Ogilvy and your brother. I know him only as *Mrs. David Ogilvy's brother*, and he was kind enough to me the other evening to leave me ashamed of this ignorance of his name. How kind you all were!—how we thank you again & again!

Most truly yours I am, believe me,

Elizabeth Barrett Browning.

Letter 2

The Brownings arrived back in Florence from Bagni di Lucca on October 17, 1849. The Ogilvys returned at about the same time to settle in rooms at Casa Guidi, on the floor above the Brownings.

On January 12, 1850 a daughter, Marcia Napier, was born to the Ogilvys. (See Mrs. Ogilvy's poem "Newly Dead and Newly Born" which relates to Marcia's birth, reprinted in this volume in Appendix B, pages 190-191.) In late March the family proceeded to Naples, and as travellers were subjected to different customs regulations and censorship as they progressed from one Italian State to another. Books, particularly certain versions of the Bible (see Letter 33), periodicals and newspapers were vulnerable to confiscation. Elizabeth is accordingly puzzled by their being allowed the *Examiner.*

During the past winter, both Brownings had been hard at work with their poetry: Elizabeth was preparing a new edition by revising her 1838 and 1844 volumes; Robert was writing *Christmas-Eve and Easter-Day*, published April 1, 1850. Elizabeth refers to the harsh review it received in the *Athenaeum* and suggests that their friend and sub-editor of the journal, H. F. Chorley, was powerless in suppressing this criticism. (It was Chorley who recommended a month later in the *Athenaeum* that Elizabeth should be appointed to the post of Poet Laureate, made vacant by Wordsworth's death on April 23.)

The Brownings had lived at Casa Guidi since May 1848. In this letter Elizabeth describes their last major acquisition of furnishings, a collection of paintings that were hung eventually in the salon after existing tapestries were moved to the dining-room. The salon then took on its final form as painted by George Mignaty in July 1861 (see frontispiece).

The paintings were authenticated by Seymour Kirkup. Mrs. Ogilvy refers to Mr. Kirkup as "that learned and courteous antiquary, the discoverer of Giotto's fresco portrait of Dante" (see Appendix B, page 184).

Elizabeth's sister, Henrietta, had married her cousin Capt. William Surtees Cook on April 6 and settled at Taunton. Her father never acknowledged the marriage and disowned his daughter just as he had when Elizabeth married.

[Florence] May 3– [1850]

Indeed, my dear friend, I did not think of writing to you,— I was too busy in expecting the promised letter from you, which quite relieved me as far as the health of all of you is concerned. Robert had fallen into the dream of a possibility, through the delay, that you had found no rest for the sole of your feet at Naples & were coming back to us directly. But even the plague of mosquitoes wont do us a good turn, I see:—mosquitos at this time of year! High prices dont frighten me half as much. Poor little Alexander, and the dear pretty little baby! Such gods as send gadflies & the like are very terrible. If you go to Sorrento, I advise you to go to the heights,—it must be cooler there & freer from insects, and we have just heard from persons who spent last summer in a "delightful villa" below, close to the sea, that their thermometer frequently stood at eighty six, & that they had no walking room: they had to climb in order to walk, for even the coast is broken up so that you have no liberty along it. I am delighted that the dear children should be well & happy. The noise and gaiety must be excellent for them. What makes one's head ache, is the precise thing they want! . . An *idèe fixe* of mine, which sets me on sending my own child to all the fairs & festas, as you know. When Robert and I were discussing villa-plans once, one of the objections was, that it would be too much retirement for the baby!—and I assure you *that* seemed nearly conclusive to both of us. Let me not forget to tell you that a day or two after you left Florence, he began to take steps alone, and now, he patters across the floor without the help of a finger, . . staggering sometimes like a drunken fairy . . drunk with dew . . for the dew is strong these May nights. Why, yes, indeed it is May! Nobody would think it, however, with a fire, a real, live fire, actually blazing, for use & not for ornament. Italy has disgraced herself this time. The weather has been atrocious—a drizzle, drizzle, drizzle, producing a shiver, shiver, shiver, to correspond. England never did anything much worse; and if you at Naples have anything much better, why you may consider yourselves happy and compound for the mosquitoes. Today there is sunshine, but for my part I dont believe in it . . it's sham, painted sunshine, and does'nt warm even the flies, poor things.

So glad I am that you liked the extracts in the Examiner.

The sub-editor of the Athenæum is an intimate friend of
my husband's and a great admirer of the poem which he
considers his masterpiece (so he told us in a letter the other
day) and yet he had not the least power to prevent the
appearance of that article, the *animus* of which was so bad.
It is a curious instance of the impotency of private friendship in such matters. He is more vexed than we are, I am
certain, and indeed I heard yesterday that he talks of it as
one of the misfortunes of his literary life. The poem is
said to have made much sensation in London, and to be
"much accused of irreligion," which is the consequence, as
I observed philosophically, of writing a religious work. If
one ignores the subject altogether, the world does not cry
out upon one's irreverence, blasphemy, and the rest, lascia
passare . . there's nothing contraband . . they dont spill
critical oil upon one's books. By the way, how glad I am
that we have your Leopardi &c, and how I condole with
you on the piece of custom-house tragedy you did not
escape. What puzzles me is, your having the Examiner.
Perhaps your learned censors take it to mean Instructions
for the confessional. I was thoroughly pleased by the article
in question, as you may well believe.

Let me consider what news of Florence can interest you.
Mrs. Wolley does not go to England as soon as was intended,
through being ill again, & unable to move, according to
medical judgement, for at least ten days. Mr. Wolley seems
to be still hoping to keep her here altogether, Dr. Trotman's
opinion of the probable effect of the English climate being
so unfavorable. I fear she is very unwell. The baby is doing
well in spite of the weaning. Mr. Stuart goes to England on
Monday & means to stay a month. He escorts Miss Costigan,
whose name I dont pretend to spell. There's the amount of
what I know of Florence! We, ourselves, have not been to
Bologna—oh no. I have been coughing, for one thing . .
but have finished; and Robert has been buying pictures
and covering himself with glory, at the expense of some

scudi. Do you remember our angels from Arezzo, those, Mr. Ogilvy admired & dear Mrs. Ogilvy proposed taking from us, & Robert did not like parting with on account of his having written for the Madonna who was said to have formed the centre of the group when the picture was entire? Just before you went away, the answer came . . . the priest had gone to Rome & nothing could be done till his return.— Well—the other day, an accident took Robert into a corn-shop, a mile beyond the gates, and there he fell on a deposit of pictures which had been left by a collecting Jew who had fallen into difficulties & was unable to carry them to France as he intended. They had lain there for years, & were to be sold, if any one cared to pay the custom house dues, with the other expenses. Robert made his way up stairs; & in a bedroom & behind a bed, were other pictures . . a great deal of trash, but some very strik-ing things. He bought five pictures in all; and when he had placed them in a good light, he went to fetch Mr. Kirkup, & we were encouraged to name names which you will scarcely believe in perhaps— 1. Giottino, 2. Ghirlandaio, 3. Cimabue, 4, a very curious crucifixion, supposed to be too unequal to be a Giotto, but of his time, & unique or nearly so, through being painted on linen, . . 5, a virgin & child of a Byzantine master. All are in beautiful preserva-tion. The Cimabue (so called) is a Christ with an open Greek gospel . . very fine & moving. But the most curious circumstance I have yet to tell you. The Ghirlandaio, the subject of which is the "Eterno Padre," is proved to be the centre our angels belong to! There can be no doubt. The surrounding rainbow & the mystical garment of the centre figure, join on line for line with the *bits* of fragmentary colour in the angel-pictures. The centre figure is very grand, . . one hand upraised in blessing,—the other clasping a book. Two seraphs flying have darted down the tips of their scarlet wings into the angel-pictures, to make the evidence complete.

While you have been thinking of your sister, I have been absorbed in mine, . . my sister Henrietta, who has just married Capt. Surtees Cook, an upright and amiable man to whom she had been engaged for five years,—not without some of the painfulness, inseparable in our family from such events. They will not be rich—but a marriage of affection & esteem always seems to me to imply the highest kind of prudence, and I have no fears for her happiness. The fear is stronger for my poor, dearest Arabel, my youngest sister, who is now without companionship & longing for me, I know—in spite of which, it's impossible for us to decide yet upon going to England. I have been very anxious. —— So Wordsworth is gone!—the firmament is darkened of that star! They should give the Laureateship to Leigh Hunt, it seems to us, if they dont abolish the office, . . which very likely they will do in these times, when 'bays' have grown to mean nothing else but chesnut horses. Write soon—you wont write too soon, I protest to you,—& the sooner, the better, indeed! The cot looked as pretty & melancholy as possible when put up in Wiedeman's room, & no recollections of friendship prevented his being charmed with it. Kiss the dear children for me, & bear us both in your kind remembrance, all of you! May God bless you. Ever affectionately yours,

Elizabeth Barrett Browning.

We miss you more than you can miss us of course. Ma^{dme} Biondi tells me that a great safeguard against internal derangements in Italian summers, with young children, is to keep their *flannels* on day & night. We are to continue doing so even this year with Wiedeman. He has taken to writing, & holds his pen just as you wd.—better than I do.

Address: Alla Signora | Signora D. Ogilvy, | Poste restante, | Napoli.
Postmark: FIRENZE 6 MAG 1850.

Letter 3

When the Brownings first arrived in Florence in 1847, they had intended to stay only a few months and then proceed to Rome. Economic pressures prevented their going, and it was not until the autumn of 1853 that they were able to journey farther south than Siena. Their income came from three sources: the return of approximately one hundred and seventy-five pounds a year from Elizabeth's £6,000 deposited in the Bank of England; her share of profits from the ship *David Lyon*; and royalties from the sale of their works. The expressed uncertainty about travelling to England stemmed from a delayed report of the ship's income.

The Brownings were considering spending the summer at an Italian resort should they be unable to go to England. They were determined not to return to Bagni di Lucca because of its great popularity, and Elizabeth abhorred being forced into society; one person she wished to avoid was the "queen" of the area, Mrs. Clotilda Stisted of Villa Broderick, who had recently settled there and had a reputation for collecting celebrities. Mrs. Stisted was a friend of Jane Hedley, Elizabeth's maternal aunt, and had met Elizabeth some twenty years earlier. Somewhat reluctantly, Elizabeth renewed the acquaintance in 1853 (see Letter 23).

James Montgomery Stuart and his wife were friendly with the Ogilvys and the Brownings when all were at Bagni di Lucca the previous summer. There, during a series of his lectures, he referred to the Shakespearean criticism of Mrs. Anna Jameson, a long-time friend of the poets. They perhaps gave him letters of introduction to Mrs. Jameson and another friend, John Forster, historian and biographer, both of whom he saw in London during the spring of 1850.

In July 1846, Seymour Kirkup, Bezzi and Hamilton Wilde had located a portrait of Dante (attributed to Giotto) under some plaster in the Bargello during restorations. The way the work was discovered caused a controversy to which Elizabeth refers in this letter.

Shortly after the time this letter was written, the poet Samuel Rogers had an accident which curtailed his "more difficult kinds of agility." For visits the Brownings paid Rogers, see Letters 11 and 18.

Cuckoo was Alexander Ogilvy's baby-name.

Florence May 26. [1850]

I did not think I had delayed writing above a day or two but the days intertwine themselves so, day into day, that

two or three or four are apt to pass for one with me. Forgive me, dear Mrs. Ogilvy, if ever I seem slack in correspondence, (it is a besetting sin of mine, people say) and do you
heap coals of fire on my head by heaping letters. We had
just been talking of you at breakfast & wishing to hear from
you when your letter came. Really I was surprised to find
that Mrs. Ogilvy had actually torn herself away, and with
the intention of settling in Scotland too! Another set of
grand children, however highly cultivated & 'botanical,'
scarcely accounts for the miracle, do you know, and I
still expect to hear of some secret intention of returning
to you in Paris or elsewhere, being suddenly developped, and
effacing the other. Meantime we shall be very glad to see
her & Mr. Ogilvy in their way through Florence. No
Bologna for us yet. And we have not been able to fix about
England & which is'nt our fault. Perhaps all the grand
schemes may end by our spending the summer near Leghorn, but I hope not, for Robert's sake as well as my own.
At any rate the Baths of Lucca will be scrupulously avoided
. . though, by the way, I had a kind note from the queen
of the place (did I tell you?) offering to take a house
close to her own, and to overwhelm us with royal attentions. Your impressions of Sorrento dont appear to be
quite favorable, in spite of the magnificent prospect of
living in Tasso's rooms. Is the situation high or low? I
mean in relation to the mountains, for you talk of a precipice towards the sea, which implies a certain height.
Does it ever strike you that, after all, your cheapest plan
might be to take ship back to Leghorn, now you have
seen Naples & can carry the vision in your soul? Dr.
Harding recommends the neighbourhood of Leghorn to
us, for its dryness & healthfulness, besides the cheapness.
Rocks into the sea, and a possibility of spending the whole
day out of doors under tents which are provided—then, a
better access to books & more nearness to civilization.
Still Leghorn is not Sorrento, & your sister would rather

find you where you are of course—and we ourselves shall not go to Leghorn unless driven there by the absolute winds. I hope your boy is cutting his teeth victoriously, and I am quite incredulous as to his 'looking ugly' in the process. Wiedeman keeps to his eight teeth, but he has eight more coming, which teaze him occasionally but dont affect his health in the least. Still, a truthful & fanciful friend of ours gave us what is called "a turn" the other day, by advising us to get another balia whose milk might harmonize better & help his flesh & blood, as the child had evidently "too much soul," & was too like a baby in a picture. A mere fancy of course, when we came to consider. His frocks show how he grows, and he is round & dimpled all over his body, and of an untiring vivacity—an excess of it indeed. I am beginning to repent his knowing how to walk. He is on his feet now from morning till night—refusing to take a finger's assistance out of doors, running, running, running, the whole day through, setting off across the piazzas, and plunging into the crowd to get to the band at the Cascine. It is far too much for so young a child: if he were five years old, it would be almost too much. And then he is such a little creature to be seen running in that way, that his littleness looks strange. He is slightly made, you know, . . delicately, . . & certainly does look rather too like a water-colour drawing of a baby. I wish for him, more robustness & richer tones . . but we must have what we can get, & be thankful. Just now he has been amusing himself with shutting both the windows, & all the shutters, while we have him here at the balia's dinner-time. A good opportunity for my writing! We have been forced to have the two terraces roped in, lest he should squeeze himself out between the railings into the street: keeping him in the rooms is impossible. With all which, he is not weaned, nor thinks of being weaned for the present. Nor does he talk any of the received languages—shaking his head for 'no,' and giving you a kiss for '*si*' . . that's his

way of expressing his opinions; in addition to which, he
can sing various songs, and write, and sew after a peculiar
fashion, and "far il Napoleone" by folding his arms. We
have left off the cap, & the hair begins to curl now. What
a history! But my vanity is centered in Wiedeman— Robert
has to give me a hint now & then, not to be offensively
maternal. I have even been braiding two silk polkas &
two white frocks for him—having had the elaborate pat-
terns drawn for me by a man of the trade. How I should
like to see your baby. If I were a prophetess (which it is
proved that I am not) I should predict her to be the pret-
tiest of your pretty children. I heard the other day that
goat's milk & water was peculiarly good for babies. Oh,
dont let me forget to tell you that Sophia Cottrell has a
little boy. So thankful I am for her! The child is small,
smaller than ours was, but it is quite healthy, and she
suffered little in bringing him into the world. Think of
my walking to see her—there & back! In the highest
spirits she was, poor thing, yet not forgetting to speak
of her "dearest little Lily" who has turned to a radiant
memory now. Also Mrs. Greenhough (Horace) has an 'ex-
pectancy' for September. They have not heard yet from
the Henry Greenhoughs. We have a letter today from Mr.
Stuart full of the great Bezzi and Kirkup controversy on
the Dante question, and really whoever may be right as to
priority, Mr. Bezzi seems to me to be scant in magnanimity
towards that poor old man who is an antiquarian by passion
& catches at these old tapestries with the last strength of
life. A man able to achieve for himself any sort of noble
distinction would not hesitate to sacrifice so paltry a one
to an antagonist aged & weak in health through repeated
attacks of paralysis. "Who found Dante's picture?" "I,"
said the sparrow!—or "I" said the crow!—What matter? The
question of "who," is'nt worth a sparrow's feather—and
yet Mr. Bezzi is preparing a letter or pamphlet, something
like Jove's thunder, to fulminate over Florence & London!—

Mrs. Wolley has gone at last. Mr. Wolley thought it would be "providential if she were too ill to go," but she was'nt ill at all when it came to the point, and insisted on going. If they have a steady, tolerably warm summer in England this year, she will not suffer, I dare say—but to try a winter there wd. be a dangerous experiment. She is under the impression of being unthreatened as to the lungs. Now if Dr. Trotman conceals the fact from her, is he right, do you think? It struck me, from our slight intercourse, that she is a woman of firm mind & conscientious, and that any clear statement of such a fact & argument following it, would influence her more strongly than unreasoning persuasions ever could. Her life is very precious, if only to her children, and she feels that; but also she feels, as we all do, that an asthmatic patient may be as well in England as in Italy. We have heard with pleasure that Tennyson was "much struck" with 'Christmas Eve.' It was pleasant to hear. Mr. Forster read the ms. to him—so, he (Forster) wrote to us. Mr. Stuart has been dining with Mrs. Jameson, & breakfasting with Mr. Forster, & Mrs. Jameson promises to come to Italy when she has completed her third volume. They seem to me to be very dull in England in spite of everything, and if it were not for two or three people, I would gladly keep away. Oh, as it is, I shall have more pain than pleasure in going . . supposing we do go, . . and the supposition is growing very imaginary, considering how deep we are in May. Extraordinary weather it is for Italy—most enjoyably cool, when it does'nt rain, but the drizzling days are by no means done with. I begin to have a respectful opinion of the comet which is to come so near us in June. Surely it must have something serious in its tail for us, to be so efficient at a distance. I dont wonder, as you do, at the energies of your friend, because I have known many of those young old people. What is seventy five? Just, youth. Why, Rogers who is ten years older, practises more difficult kinds of agility than any driving about in carriages.

I have a deep respect for the youth of age. It proves a strong soul—does'nt it? Cuckoo speaks like a sage in choosing not to be a dunce nor learned, & I admire the epigram. A child two years old, undergoing the science of botany, must be in desperate case .. not likely to mature even into . . . a botanist! April rain for April flowers—what better? I am uneasy when Wiedeman seems to understand too much—which really he does, sometimes. Tell me always of your children, & take our love for them & yourself. Yours affect^{ely}, my dear friend!

E B Browning.

Address: À Madame | Mad^e Ogilvy, | 124 Riviera di Chiaja | Napoli.
Postmarks: FIRENZE 30 MAG 1850; NAPOLI 3. GIU.

Letter 4

The new Cottrell baby mentioned in the previous letter suddenly died. Elizabeth identifies the "nervous prostrations" Sophia Cottrell felt at this tragedy with her own condition after the death of her brother Edward.

Since the Brownings' budget did not allow for subscriptions to literary periodicals, Elizabeth had either to borrow copies or rely on her husband's access to papers in a local reading-room. Occasionally private correspondence provided her with such news, and she was delighted to pass on to Mrs. Ogilvy the latest from Miss Mitford, that Alfred Tennyson had married Emily Sellwood on June 13, 1850.

Elizabeth does not clarify her reference in the last sentence of this letter to "the enemy," since Mrs. Ogilvy would surely have recalled the events surrounding the arrival of Mrs. Gordon at Bagni di Lucca the previous summer.

Mrs. John Gordon, born Carolina Augusta Tulk, was the sister of Sophia Cottrell. She married Mr. Gordon in 1834, a year after his sister, Ann Eliza Gordon, had married Samuel Barrett Moulton-Barrett, Elizabeth's paternal uncle. This family connection prompted Sophia Cottrell to call on the Brownings immediately upon their settling in Florence.

In the mid-1840's Mr. Gordon took his family to Sydney to promote a business venture which he had financed on borrowed funds.

The scheme failed and he took employment in Calcutta; there, in 1848, his two-month-old child died. This tragedy was followed by a quick succession of deaths: Mrs. Gordon's sister (Louisa Ley) and her baby, Mr. Gordon's mother, who lived with the family in Calcutta, and Mr. Gordon himself within twenty-four hours of her burial. Mrs. Gordon wrote to her father, bidding him to expect her in England, and left India before she learned that he too had died. Accordingly, Count Cottrell went to London to bring Mrs. Gordon and her family to Italy so she could reside near her one surviving sister. When Mrs. Gordon arrived at Bagni di Lucca in August 1849, it was amidst a controversy which gave Elizabeth much agitation.

Mr. Gordon had been a barrister and among his clients was Maria Tripsack ("Trippy"), long-time companion to Elizabeth's grandmother, Elizabeth Moulton. Under the impression it was intended for Mr. Gordon's father-in-law (Mr. Tulk), "Trippy" lent him £4000 which he lost in his business venture. Elizabeth felt that Mrs. Gordon should accept responsibility for this and clear her husband's name by paying back the debt, or some annual sum: "I would rather be ruined to the last penny, than see my husband's honour left in suspicion *so!*" It was a complicated issue, with many people, mostly Elizabeth's friends, pressing for the return of some of their investment. As far as is known, Miss Tripsack received no settlement, and was consequently to a great extent dependent financially on Elizabeth's father.

In this letter we see Elizabeth's determination not to go to the same summer resort as Mrs. Gordon, who eventually settled on Viareggio. When both families returned to Florence in the autumn, the social tensions became intolerable for Elizabeth: Mrs. Gordon moved into the same house as the Cottrells, and this resulted in the Brownings not calling on their friends. By December Mrs. Gordon stopped calling on the Brownings, having felt the slight. While the friendship between the Brownings and Cottrells survived, Elizabeth and Robert never accepted Mrs. Gordon.

One of Elizabeth's final comments on Mrs. Gordon (when she married her brother-in-law James Ley in 1856) still displayed bitterness: "a second marriage after such love!— . . . and she a Swedenborgian, . . believing in the eternal validity of marriage! . . . it is monstrous. It crowns her conduct to Trippy with a triple tiara!"

Florence. July 13—[1850]

Thank you, thank you, both our dear friends, for your kindness in letting us have your experience at Capri & else-

where. And, dear Mrs. Ogilvy, you were not well enough, I
grieve to think, to have written this kind letter without
some effort, for which I ought to thank you doubly. It is
right & wise that you should have made over little Marcia
to a balia; and as really you have done duty by her most
nobly for ˉsix months, there is no surrender of maternal
office, . . you have *nursed* her, to all intents & purposes, . .
and it is much the same whether a balia or a cow does the
mere finishing stroke.—is'nt it? Now I hope you are beginning or rather have begun to recover your strength & to
lose all trace of nervous headaches & other disorders. Oh,
I wish we could enjoy Capri with you, it must be so enjoyable from what you say of it, and I should like so to be
with you there & to look at the darling children & see
Alexander old enough & noisy enough to be 'scolded'!
Wiedeman would be delighted to swear eternal friendship
to anybody with a genius for mischief. But the truth is that
we cant go to Capri—no, it is an impossibility! With a hundred pounds to take us on to the end of the year, we are
really forced to stay in Tuscany, and even Leghorn escapes us
through being too expensive. We have been full of schemes
ever since Mr. Ogilvy was here. A villa four miles from
Vallombrosa . . Siena, . . Leghorn, Viareggio, . . not a
scheme was without objection. Robert went to Siena by
himself to see if one could find any sort of nest there, . .
went at seven by the train, intending to return at seven . .
and I let him go in a resigned state of mind enough, not
feeling quite up to going with him & thinking it necessary
for Baby that we shd. get out of the heat somehow. It was
the first time for these four years he had been away from
me longer than three hours at longest, and I felt all day as
if I had lost my heart or some more vital part, & kept ex-
alting myself at intervals upon my heroic virtue in making
no more fuss about it than I did. But heroic virtue never is
properly recompensed in this world—and the crafty people
at Siena had suspended the trains, the return trains, in

honor of their *corso* & in order to keep their visitors through the night. I went to bed in despair at twelve oclock, not understanding that the trains were stopped, imagining rather that he had been too late for the last . . "and yet that was so unlike Robert!" At three in the morning his voice was under the window—he had come back in a *baroccino*, dreadfully tired, & could'nt make the porter hear with ever so much thumping at the gates, though *I* heard at the first word said softly, & made everybody else hear, as you may suppose, in a moment more. As to Siena, whether he saw things as they are or a little disfigured (which is possible) by his wrath against the trains, he declared that it struck him as the most detestable town in Italy & the least to be inhabited:—even the cathedral was talked down to the ground. Then we quite fixed upon 'Gombo' the seaside fortress in the Pisan forest, where there are two or three houses and coolness & beautiful wood-walks, & good sands & bathing, . . & just as we were about to set off, the Gordon children met Robert & told him that "Mama had found out such a delightful place . . Gombo . . & thought of going there." Which changed our plan of necessity, & now we are looking wildly on all sides for a place of refuge. I cared more about it a few days ago than I do now . . for now we have wonderfully cool days, & Wiedeman who was beginning to make me quite unhappy with the sight of a pale little face, has recovered his colour, & sleeps at night instead of tossing about in the heat. He did not cry, he kept his inexhaustible spirits, but certainly, though Robert declared that I imagined half of it, he looked as delicate as possible, & his arms had lost much of their firmness & roundness. Oh no, dearest Mrs. Ogilvy! he is not "splendid" by any means. Mr. Ogilvy relieved & delighted me by appearing so struck with his growth, and indeed he is much grown, and a sweet little engaging child, we think him, with the funniest fancies & tricks, & a spirit of joy always at overflow. I never saw such an ecstatical

little creature. When he hears music, he clasps his hands, &
beats his face & head with his fists, breaking out into
laughter at intervals, as if it was too strong for him & he
was losing his senses in the gladness of it. Robert says to
me sometimes . . 'Ba, I do hope that child is not going
mad.' Think of his making his way into the Austrian
band the other evening at the Cascine, & wanting to sieze
on the drum, . . to play on it himself! There's shyness for
you! He is the "vergognoso di Pisa"! Still what people
remark generally of him is, "What a *little* thing, to be running about,"—and I am sure he is not half the size of Alexander at his age. He looks like a small Puck in a mushroom,
with his round hat on . . and to see him dancing & singing,
is as amusing at least as the corso at Siena was to poor
Robert—the dance consisting of a series of curtsies accompanied by most curious gesticulation & performed in an
absolute "faith in Art"—Taglioni could'nt have had more.
Oh yes, I was certain that you wd. feel for poor Sophia
Cottrell. She bore up dauntlessly at first & then sank
suddenly into such a state of nervous prostration . . lying
with shut eyes & not bearing a sound . . that her husband
was in alarm & carried her away to Leghorn where she
soon revived & is now in Florence much better. He could'nt
make out why the change of place became so necessary, or
why she had caught up a nervous hatred against the house
where she had suffered—"he never could understand how
external impressions should overpower one so." My wonder
is how she can live on, sleep & eat, in that house, at all. I
lived a year, in a house, after the greatest affliction of my
life, because my family naturally listened to the medical
man who "thought I might die in the act of being carried
down stairs" . . — and I cannot look back to any month
or week of that year without horror, & a feeling of the
wandering of the senses. Places are ideas, and ideas can
madden or kill. The poor little Cottrell baby was born
with diseased lungs, in consequence, it is supposed, of a

cold taken by the mother during her journey—yes indeed—
she had better have stayed in Florence. Ma^{dme} Biondi
doubts whether she is strong enough at present to give
birth to a healthy child, & hopes that there may be a long
pause. Very sad it is, altogether!— I had a letter a few
days since from Miss Mitford who announces that ten days
previously, Tennyson had married a clergyman's daughter.
She had not seen this piece of news in the papers, but had
heard it, she said, on good authority & through Moxon.
She is not acquainted herself with Mr. Moxon, so it may'nt
be true, though I hope with all my heart it is—for no one
would gain more from a happy marriage than Tennyson
would, as far as I can understand his nature & his habits.
She speaks very coldly of his new book—which however is
no argument to me against its excellence. She is a woman
of high general cultivation, & full of poetical sensibility &
enthusiasm, and yet I never *count* upon her in poetry, of
which, in my mind, she does not apprehend the essential
qualities. She sees secondary & incidental qualities . . forms
& colours . . but the pure essence escapes her. To which she
would answer, that I was full of crotchets & sectarianisms &
given to trample down all the rose-gardens of the world in a
search for essences—and more was the pity for my own verses! I have not had sight of the Athenæum extracts—(the
Athenæum went from me with *you*!) but Robert, too, spoke
much to me of the beauty & pathos of thought expressed
in them. I dare say it is an exquisite book, for he is a
divine poet if ever there was such divinity. Has Mrs. Ogilvy
told you of her kindness (will you thank her for me & give
her our love?) in writing to me from Spezzia, under the
impression of its enchanting scenery & with the evident
wish that you all as well as ourselves wd. go there. Only
her account (aiding our recollections) of the extravagant
terms, put such a scheme out of the question. In the impulse of the moment I began to write to you & copied out
half her letter . . & then suddenly remembered that I was

quite ignorant of your address till you shd. send it. Yes—
'little Browning' had dear Cuckoo's message & so had Wilson—& both send back their love! How pretty Alexander
must look with his curls! Wiedeman too has curls, I assure
you. Now do write to me & *dont mind Mr. Ogilvy!*—though
I sympathize so deeply in your joy at having him back! And
dont call it a contradiction if I was very glad to see him
here notwithstanding. God bless you all! With Robert's
love, let me remain your ever affectionate E B Browning.

The enemy seems to withdraw, & perhaps after all we
may go to Gombo. But direct as usual.

Address: À Madame | M^{de} Ogilvy, | Hôtel Rispoli, | Sorrento, |
Napoli. *Postmarks:* FIRENZE 15 LUG 1850; NAPOLI 20. LUG.

Letter 5

After a few days' illness, on Sunday morning, July 28, 1850, Elizabeth (two months pregnant) had her fourth and most severe mis-
carriage. It was not until August 5 that she was able to leave her
bed, and even then she could only lie on her sofa for half an hour.

During this illness Wilson was unable to go out with Pen. The
wet-nurse went alone, declaring "that she should avoid the sunshine . . . but Italians naturally are less apprehensive of the evils of
their climate." Around the end of the first week of August, Pen had
a mild sunstroke which agitated Elizabeth as much as her own condition. She remarks to her sister that the attack left him with a bad
cough and a temper: in particular his "insisting on having the whole
world to do what he likes with . . . half a world wont serve. . . .
there's a fury because the great picture over the chimney-piece is not
taken down for him to play with."

To add to the state of Elizabeth's nervousness, she learned on
August 13 that Madame Ossoli (Margaret Fuller), her husband and
their child were drowned off Fire Island within sight of the American shore. Elizabeth was personally affected not only because the
Ossolis were personal acquaintances but also because she greatly
admired Margaret Fuller's work as an important American femi-
nist. Early in July the Brownings had received a letter from her,

written off Gibraltar, saying how they had been frightened en route by the Captain's contraction of smallpox, and by the quarantine imposed on the ship with no medical aid. Mr. Ogilvy saw Madame Ossoli's letter to the Brownings when he was in Florence in July, escorting his mother to Scotland (see following letter).

Elizabeth associated the Ossoli tragedy, moreover, with her brother Edward's death by drowning. It was with some reluctance therefore that she later contributed her recollections for the *Memoirs of Margaret Fuller Ossoli* (1852) edited by Emerson, Channing, and Clarke.

At this time, England was in mourning for one of her national figures, Sir Robert Peel, who was thrown from his horse on Constitution Hill, June 29, 1850, and died from his injuries on July 2.

Florence August 28 [1850]

I was much concerned, my dear Mrs. Ogilvy, to hear of your bronchitis, (what business had it with you in the heat, I wonder) & then I was glad again that you had exchanged Capri, rocks & moonlight inclusive, for Sorrento & fresh meat for the little darlings, . . yes, & for yourselves, . . the truth being, alas, that moonlight, when taken in place of beef, wont do for the least sublunary of us. It is humbling to confess, but we are all akin to the old giant, and our celestials (the life of the soul as well as of the body) depend considerably on our terrestrials—we must touch the earth . . the beef . . to have any strength worth using. So I hope you are eating beef & drinking porter & getting very strong at Sorrento. Did you catch cold in that romantic 'salone' which was only tenable when it did not rain, I wonder? Write & tell me in any case, that you are no longer suffering, & that the rest of you are as well as ever. You delight me with your account of Alexander. What joy it must be to you to see him so joyous & vivacious after the long delicacy which caused you such anxiety! I hold him full in my fancy with his rosy cheeks & curling hair— & 'how very pretty he must be!,' I keep saying to myself: because he always was pretty, & only wanted the animation & infantine '*verve*' which have come with health, it seems.

Only, what can you mean by thinking of giving him the 'toga,' the blouse,—oh, I shall be careful not to turn my baby into a boy so soon! I grudge even the reign of the frocks. I like him better in a white petticoat than in any-thing else, and our balia is quite 'vergognosa' she says, about the nudities I insist on. Why you would'nt certainly cover up the dimpled arms & shoulders? For my part, the more the little white vestment curdles up to the knees, & drops down to the waist, the more I am pleased.

And now let me tell you of ourselves, which will be be-ginning a tale of disasters. Indeed even if you should have secretly thought that nothing except our having all been at the point of death could excuse my silence to you, I shall still have some claim on pardon,—for I have been very ill, & Wiedeman has been ill too, and although through God's mercy he is quite well now, I am so far from strong, as not to be able to rise from this chair without somebody's help, & poor Robert has to carry me to the carriage like an infant,—& when I look in the glass (while everybody is crying aloud how much better I am looking) I see nothing but a perfectly white & black face, the eyes being obliter-ated by large blots of blackness, which produce an effective contrast. Wiedeman's illness came from a sort of sun-stroke & frightened us much! Think of the grief of seeing him return from his walk one day with glassy, staring eyes, hot head, & cheeks of scarlet! He lay in a half stupor, & took no notice of anybody except by kicking out his foot when he was spoken to; as much as to say 'Dont speak to me—I cant attend to it." We thought at first it was an attack from the teeth, or a milliary fever perhaps,—but Dr. Hard-ing wd. not lance the gums, being decided in his impression that it was altogether from exposure to the sun; & the result justified him fully & freed us from anxiety at the end of four & twenty hours, after the administration of grey pow-der, castor oil, & other drugs, which deprive me of my priveledge of boasting that "Wiedeman has never wanted

medicine." Poor, little angel!—when the heat & stupor were
gone he had a bad cough & cold . . the development, said
Dr. H, of the previous attack—& we wont speak much of a
most demoniacal fit of ill temper which was also, I suppose,
symtomatical. Now he is entirely well. Thank God for it.
In respect to myself, you will guess what has been the matter—but I never had so severe an accident . . not even at
Pisa. It took place more than a month ago, & Dr. Harding
has only just taken leave 'professionally' of me, with the
injunction to change the air instantly, though I feel very
little equal to such an exertion. He told my husband that
not one in five thousand women wd. be affected as I have
been (to such an extreme) & that in his own practice he
had not seen another instance. For two days & two nights
I was packed in ice, . . & Robert was with me the whole
night without going to bed,—& I could not say once 'Go
to bed,' I felt so uncertain in my own mind how it was to
end. Every previous precaution had been taken—I had not
stirred out of the house for weeks, determining not to hurt
myself by long walks this time. But the vexation is over
now, & there's no use talking of it: and, even at the time,
the sense of danger was the stronger with me, just as thank-
fulness to God should absorb me now. I dont want to leave
the world, you see, while Robert & Wiedeman are in it. Dr.
Harding says that in a week or two or three I shall be
stronger than ever, and I feel, myself, that this is like the
fag-end of debility & that soon I shall be past it. What
has affected me very much, & Robert too, has been the
dreadful event you must have seen in the papers . . the
loss, by shipwreck, of our poor friend Md^{me} Ossoli with
her husband & child. Robert wanted to keep it from me
till I was stronger—but that was impossible: I saw in his
eyes that something was the matter, &, if I had not, the
first letter, or visit, wd. have told me. She was much
drawn to both of us in affection, & we to her—& a part of
her last evening in Italy was spent here. She said with her

peculiar smile that "the ship was called the Elizabeth, & she accepted it as a good omen—though a prediction had been made to her husband that the sea wd. be fatal to him." In sight of shore, of the home, American shore! O great God, how terrible are Thy judgements! The whole associations have been the more poignant to me that by a like tragedy I lost once the happiness of my life . . the life of my life . . the colour & fragrance of my soul. But why write of these things?

They buried the poor darling baby in the sand. He was two years old. I keep foolishly thinking of his little velvet shoes which were made to be like Wiedeman's. She was very averse to going—but I dare say it is all better so,—for the child was not a healthy child, & she was not a happy woman . . & mortification & care of all kinds seemed opening before her. It is better so, God knows. I can understand Mr. Ogilvy's feelings in the sudden loss you speak of. On such occasions the skeleton of life is bared suddenly to us, & we are thrilled to the heart. In respect to Sir Robert Peel, I do not feel quite as you do—though overpraise in the burst of sympathy across a newly opened grave, is but a part of justice. Still, strictly speaking, he was not a giant, nor akin to the giants—only one of those practical men who work out the thoughts & catch the crowns of ideal men . . "verily have their reward." Did he ever see a truth before it was forced on him by circumstances rather than reasonings? Never, perhaps. It is however a noble enough commendation that he did not sacrifice the good of his country (when once seen clearly) even to the preservation of his personal consistency, and for this thing, if not for another, we should all bless his memory. Meantime, dont let us confound glories—there will be a thousand Peels before there is a second Wordsworth. In a hundred years, who will speak of Peel?—

Gombo turned out expensive & uncomfortable, & we were on the verge of engaging a villa near Vallombrosa when I was taken ill. If I had been there without medical help, nothing but a miracle could have saved me—though Baby might have escaped the sun-stroke. Now, it is delightfully cool, & we were inclined to stay in Florence from motives of œconomy, when Dr. H insisted on the necessity for me of change of air. So, our villa being taken from us, we go to Siena on Saturday. We are more than ever satisfied with Dr. H's skill & decision—& I must tell you that one morning he poured out to Robert the whole story, about his son, which set the matter in a very different light. I will tell you in another letter. No room here. Tennyson married a woman "not pretty, nor particularly young nor *likely to have influence over him*" . . Not *my* phrase, observe! He was attached to her twelve years ago, then the engagement was broken off. God bless you both & all. I lose hope of seeing your sister, as she does not come till September & we go on the first.

Your ever affectionate
Elizabeth Barrett Browning.

Robert's love goes with mine to Mr. Ogilvy & yourself. Wiedeman has another double tooth. Now he has eleven teeth. He is most imperious—he stamps with his little foot on the floor!

Write to Siena. Poste Restante.

Address: À Madame | Ma^{dme} Ogilvy | Hotel Respoli | Sorrento | Napoli. *Postmarks:* P.D. 29 AGO. 1850 FIRENZE; NAPOLI 2. SET.

Letter 6

The Brownings left Florence for Siena at seven on the morning of August 31, 1850, where they rented a small villa on a hill two miles from the city. The change of air, coolness of the breezes, and magnificent views worked wonders for Elizabeth's health. While she rested, Robert explored the district, often going to see the churches

and pictures in Siena. His delight in the work of the artist Sodoma
was shared by Elizabeth when, at the end of a month in the villa,
they moved into the city for a week before returning to Casa Guidi.

Throughout this period the friends had been working at their
poetry and both had volumes ready for publication. Elizabeth's
new edition was soon to be released, including her revised "Prometheus Bound" and the first publication of "Sonnets from the
Portuguese." Mrs. Ogilvy's book, *Traditions of Tuscany, In Verse*
was published early in 1851. (See Appendix B, pages 184-189
for selections from this volume.)

Siena. September 22. [1850]
Thank you many times my dear friend, for your kind &
sympath<etic letter> which it was most pleasant to both of
us to receive. I shall begin <by> telling you that I am wonderfully resuscitated by our residence here. <It was> a miserable exertion to have to come. I had to be carried in &
out of the railroad carriage, & from one room to another
when we arrived—and now at the end of three weeks I can
walk a mile without being tired, & I get stronger still, day
by day. As to Wiedeman, "*he* did'nt want change of air,"
said Dr. Harding, being "quite well," and certainly about
ten days before we left Florence he had begun to eat
chicken, which he never could be persuaded into before,
& that unwillingness of the appetite had been one of my
reasons for looking forward fearfully towards the weaning.
But though "quite well" at Florence, & with spirits &
activity & brightness of countenance enough to warrant
the opinion, his little face & arms & legs were far too pale—
he looked like a wax doll with the rouge left out. Now all
that delicacy of appearance is abolished—his two cheeks
are brightly rose-colored, and the dear legs (a great deal
depends on a baby's legs, you know) are properly mottled,
where the complexion of them can be seen for scratches
from the stubble of the Indian corn. Also, within these
few days, *we have weaned him*—there's glory! So frightened
I was! But it has been achieved most victoriously & with-

out an excess of vexation to him, thank God; though of course the difficulty was greater, through the habit he had had, all his life, of sucking whenever he chose & as much at last as at first, the balia's milk being quite as abundant as ever to the last day. After diminishing for ten days, we put aloes on the breast—did'nt it seem cruel? . . and so, after trying in vain in different ways, & falling into one or two desperate furies, he gave it up, poor child, and turned his attention to grapes & "presciutto," his other <natura>l but less hopeless passions. We are very pleasantly situated here <in a s>mall villa about a mile & a half from Siena, on a hill called <"Poggio a>l vento," because the wind sweeps all round us, . . in the midst <"our o>wn grounds" of vineyard & olive garden, not to speak of a pretty <rose> flower-garden which Wiedeman does the honors of to us everyday. The whole of the house is ours . . four bedrooms, a sittingroom, a sort of hall or passage-room with two windows (serviceable as another sittingroom) a kitchen, and a "specola" at the top of the house, which is Robert's delight . . and we pay ten dollars the month for it. Oh—not at all 'cheap' for Siena, I assure you! For instance we heard of another villa with twenty rooms, at six dollars the month: only that was four miles from the town, & besides we could not have taken it on into October if we had pleased. In other respects, the cheapness here does not exceed that of Florence—is much the same, perhaps; and really the good fresh air, English for freshness, Italian for elasticity, & perfectly dry . . (unlike that of the Baths of Lucca . .) would be worth paying for, were there no cheapness at all. Then the country is beautiful—not romantic, . . but verdant & various, & exquisitely undulated, intersected with green lanes as in England . . not a wall anywhere. Robert sees everything with his imagination (which is happy for his wife) & that accounts for his bringing back such a deteriorating story about all these things when he came here alone on his exploring expedition: now, he is charmed, just as I am—then he was not in a mood to be charmed by a charmer. Magnificent sweeps of view we have from all our windows which all look out different ways,—on this side, towards the fantastic profile of the city, seen in silence against the sky . . on that side, across the vast Maremma bounded by the Roman mountains. So there's our account of ourselves!—better, you see, than the last one! But I have not been to Siena yet— it was necessary to wait till I could walk & stand a little. Meantime I listen to Robert's rapturous witnessing to the glory of Sodoma whom he has never done praising!

Two pages written, without saying how I feel for your anxieties, & am grieved at your own health being less strong than usual!—and yet I think so much about both that I do hope you will write directly to let me know how you all are now. Are Alexander's eye-teeth through? If so, he must be at an end of his troubles. But the precious little Marcia is only beginning hers, & scarcely I can hold myself back from the impertinence of urging you not to wean her by any means. The *risk* of these early weanings in Italy is certainly a verified thing . . one cant doubt whether there is risk or no risk, & even if we were sure of escaping worse evils than temporary suffering on the part of the child, . . why, infancy is a part of life, and it is well not to embitter it. As to balias, there will be difficulties sometimes, & we ourselves who lighted so happily at last, . . remember how we were driven about at first from balia to balia!—one balia lost her milk just as your's did, & Ma^{dme} Biondi told me that it was not uncommon, from a sudden improvement in diet, though that sounds strange. Also she said that a change of balia was not hurtful to the child . . she "changed a balia," she said poetically, "as she changed her *camicia*" . . with as little hesitation & care. If I had been you I would have sent away your Neapolitan the same day & employed a medical man to choose you another. It is the law of balias that they should be liable to be sent away when the cause arises—they are not like other servants. Then I must tell you that Ma^{dme} Biondi would never hear of our giving milk to Wiedeman while he was sucking, the mixture of milks being, in her mind, highly injurious to the stomach. I dont make an oracle of her, but she must assuredly have a full *Italian* experience, she is famous for her good fortune with children, and, as far as Wiedeman goes, he has justified our attention to her advice by his peculiar freedom from the usual stomach-affections. Dearest Mrs. Ogilvy, I throw myself on your goodnature for pardon, if I have seemed to say all this intrusively. Of course you are the judge in your own case—but I was pricked on to my impertinences by the thought of a Roman climate, (more trying for children than our Florentine one, even in winter, perhaps) & by other thoughts warmed through by my true affection for you all.

Happy fortunes be with the book which is to come out at Christmas! What will be about the number of pages, & who is the publisher?—and does it consist of more matter than the "traditions"? I need not say what pleasure the success will be to us. My new edition is out of the press but waiting to the end of October to be published, because Mr. Chapman wishes to inaugurate it from his new house in Piccadilly. Robert's book has not reached us yet—think of that! It was trusted to somebody, who took it into his head to send it by sea & travel by land himself. I should like to send you both my book & Robert's—because mine contains *all* my poems worth a straw, though many which I should like to burn as stubble & cant. It is difficult to recover one's misdeeds from the press—a practical repentance is in every other part of life, easier. Also I want to send you (when I can get it myself & look it through) Professor Blackie's Æschylus, a copy of which he has had the goodness, I hear, to leave in London for me. Mr. Ogilvy was interested in him & reminded me how I had had some correspondence with him—& I shall like to give you an opportunity of comparing together what we two have done with the poor 'Prometheus.' Tell Mr. Ogilvy that, from me. I know he is learned in Greek *dramatists.* Tell him too, because he will remember our poor friend's note from Gibraltar which spoke of the Captain of the ship's death from smallpox, that her child caught the infection, his life being despaired of for many days. Think—without medical help . . in the midst of the seas, what she must have suffered! Then, when that grief was past, came the last agony! Yet indeed it was better, as you say, that all should have gone together! Also, she was a melancholy human being. The usual difficulties & sadnesses which await a woman in literary life, were embittered into enmity on all sides, by an unfortunate line of opinion and a most uncompromising courage. Her face & soul were full of furrows, through continual wrestling with the world. For my part, I honored her for her truth & boldness, & affectionately admired the native tenderness of character which were contrasted with both. She was chiefly known in America by her vivâ voce lectures, in which great power of analysis is said to have been displayed, & by her connection with the newspaper press. *Dont read her writings*, because they are quite below & unworthy of her. The only work to which she had given time & labour, she told me herself, was the unfinished one on Italy, lost with her. In conversation she much excelled, & one could not but be struck by the vividness & dignity (equally remarkable) of her mind. Now, may God have received her into rest. Rest, she wanted—& never found it here.

Mr. Ogilvy was wrong & you right about Gombo. Robert went to explore & came back disgusted. I do *wish* I could even *hope* for Rome this year, but I dont see how it is to be done.

May God bless & keep you all. Robert's love goes to both of you with <that of your ever affectionate
Elizabeth Barrett Browning>

It is said that some of the ms. work on Italy was rescued, but nothing could have been finished— My impression is that it must have been rather a sketch for a work than the work itself. She spoke to me of it the last evening, as if she had need of much mental concentration & labour, in order to make it a worthy book. Whatever else she had written, was thrown off rapidly—mere newspaper writing, &, that, quite inferior to what might have been expected from so masculine an intellect.

Address: Alla Signora | Signora Ogilvy, | Villa Falcon, | Sorrento, | Napoli. *Postmarks:* SIENA 24 SET. 1850; [NAPOLI] 28. SET.

Letter 7

At this time, only letters could be sent by international mail: books and parcels had to be sent by couriers or carried by friends. Robert's *Christmas-Eve and Easter-Day* had been released in April 1850, but copies did not reach him until late October. He inscribed one to "Mrs. David Ogilvy with R.B.'s kindest regards, Florence, Oct. 28, '50" and forwarded it by Mrs. Tomkyns.

This letter did not reach the Ogilvys at Sorrento but caught up with them at Florence. On December 18, Elizabeth wrote to her sister: "Mr. & Mrs. Ogilvy have returned suddenly to Florence from Naples which about ruined & quite wearied them."

The Brownings' enthusiasm for Siena may have prompted the Ogilvys to visit the area. Preserved with this correspondence is a short note from Robert to Mr. Ogilvy, probably written in February 1851. It reads:

Monday Night.

My dear Ogilvy,

The address of Sig. Nencini is "Piazza Tolomei, No. 16": if you show him my name at the bottom of this, & remind him that I lodged six months ago at *Poggio al Vento*,—I am sure he will be of any service to you in his power—for which,—tell him,—I thank him just as if it were done to myself.

Ever yours faithfully,
Robert Browning.

Florence. Nov.ᵣ 3. [1850]

It grieved me, dearest Mrs. Ogilvy, to hear of your anxieties about your little Marcia. May they all be passed by this time, & your own health strengthened in consequence, for I can understand how you were not likely to be very well yourself while you had to stand by & see her suffer. The remedy of the balia, you know my faith in,—and, if she is a sufficient balia, I hope you will witness no more illness from the teeth . . none of consequence . . for this budding of the almond tree must be supposed to draw the sap a little hardly through the tree. Wiedeman has cut one of his eye teeth, and another is just at hand—he has thirteen teeth,—& is none the worse for any of them—feeling some pain of course occasionally & giving us a supererogatory passion as the result, but with no morbid symptoms whatever . . oh, I do wish you could see him. He is small still, but round & rosy, and I assure you I can scarcely carry him through the rooms now. A most curious child he is: he wont talk a bit: when he wants to call any one, he does it as he called the pigeons at our villa, by making a little kissing sound with his mouth. That's for Flush, and that's for the horse on the tapestry, and that too is for Papa when he does'nt come fast enough to the piano. You know the child's old passion for music & the churches. Well—it has grown lately to a sort of phrenzy. First thing is, when he comes in to us, to have the piano played: upon which he goes off to the end of the room, kneels down before a chair, folding his hands, turning up his eyes, & muttering with his lips, . . kneeling so, as if rapt, for five minutes together. Then, he gets up, goes to another chair, & does the same thing, . . interspersing various gesticulations meant clearly for crossing himself & telling beads, . . bowing or making a curtsey to the chair, . . all with the gravest of faces—I doubt whether he means it for play at all: it seems rather that he is possessed with an imagination. If the piano stops for a moment, he shouts out impatiently &

stamps imperiously . . he must have music:—but, for the
rest, he takes no notice of anybody in the room . . he wants
nobody's sympathy. Is'nt it curious? I overheard the balia
the other day saying to Girolama the dress maker, that
"that child quite *martyrized* her by forcing her into the
churches, & that now he had taken to saying Ave Marias
for himself." We keep on the balia for a few months, because Wilson cant carry him out of doors, and he must'nt
at his age be encouraged in too much walking. Afterwards,
Wilson will take him. His hair curls all over his head like
a small golden fleece . . a lamb's . . as he is, dear darling—
and I am obstinate in not cutting it, though you cut Alexander's with such good effect. How he must talk, . . your
Alexander! How I should like to hear him!— But I shant.
Because, instead of coming back to us in the manner of
reasonable people, . . you who confess to have not gained
so very much by going away, . . you persist, like your balia,
in keeping to the Kingdom of Naples . . unless indeed you
go to Rome, which will be as bad. I shall not see even
your sister (. . I say *even* your sister, because I never saw
her)—for she must have passed us somehow by sea or air—
we have lost her. Therefore Robert took advantage of
another opportunity, of some friends of ours (Mrs. Tomkyns
& her sisters) going to Rome & Naples, to send his book, the
only book we have received from England. Mine, I suppose,
is not yet out, and Professor Blackie's has not reached us.
I hope you will receive Robert's in safety & unsteeped in
oil.

Shall I tell you now about Siena? We left our villa at the
end of a month & went into the town for a week that I
might see the churches & pictures properly. The cathedral
is very fine, it seems to me, with its peculiar effects of warm
marbles—so warm to my imagination, that I had a sort of
feeling of suffocation there, in spite of the chilly weather.
Perhaps the syrens under the blue weights of the sea may
feel so—it was a singular feeling. Then Sodoma is great—

though the pathetic Christ by the column wants deity, &
though the beautiful visitation of the Magi strikes me as
much inferior to the exquisite picture of Gentile on the
same subject in the Belle Arti at Florence. Still, the power
is great, the pathos true: and the anguish of the virgin
mother in Sodoma's crucifixion, it is almost anguish to
look at—it seems death & the bitterness of death together—
you remember that fainting figure. So the painter is rightly
to be admired. But what of Beccafumi? What of Pacchierotto? Did you see the divine virgin & child of Pacchierotto
in the church of San Christofero? I believe I would rather
have that picture than any other in Siena, if I had leave to
carry away any I pleased. After getting the whole town by
heart . . for I even climbed down to Fonte Branda & up
again, found out the 'pozzo di Diana' & fumbled among
the ashes of Santa Catarina's kitchen, . . we were under a
strong temptation to go on to Volterra. But the funds and
Robert's superhuman prudence (for a human poet) forbade,
and back we came to Florence, thankful for & contented
with all the good & pleasure we had been able to obtain
without ruining ourselves. Since then, I have been embroi-
dering frocks for Wiedeman, . . three merino frocks for the
winter . . and catching cold, & walking up to San Miniato,
& giving deep offence to people by not going to call on
them,—I, who really mean to be kind to everybody, on
the whole, & am always getting into these scrapes. Then one
writes & reads a little at intervals . . and so, life goes on.

I must not forget, this time, to tell you of Dr. Harding—
how with tears in his eyes, he told Robert of his son's
abilities & want of will. On his leaving the army, the father
said 'Choose' . . he was ready to advance him in any other
profession he wished. On choosing art, the father said, "For
every picture you paint I will give you fifty pounds" . .
and the young man's uncle had said the same. Besides, the
father paid for studio & models, & offered to pay the expenses of sending pictures to the exhibition in London.

'Oh,' he exclaimed warmly, "the boy might have been an academician by this time—he might have been anything." But not a picture was finished—or, as it was finished, the artist destroyed it— "A mere mania," said Dr. Harding. "The truth is, his fancy was for twenty thousand a year and no work for it." In this fancy he could not & ought not be sustained. An idle life in the caffès was what could not be tolerated. And so, after having exhausted all forms of persusaion, his father had been forced to try severity & had forbidden his house to him. Dr. Harding told all this to Robert with great emotion, & observed at last that the picture 'finished for Mr. Ogilvy' was the only one he had heard of as finished to any purpose. It was a case of pure madness, in his opinion. It seems right to tell you this, your impressions having been received from the other side of the medal hitherto. Both Robert & I incline to a full confidence in Dr. Harding's kindheartedness & consequent innocence from the implied charge. The Henry Greenhoughs, the sculptor says, are comfortably established in 'Cambridge'—but "*she* prefers Florence in some respects, and *he,* in all." Mrs. Horatio Greenhough has a little girl, by help of æther, which, however, the medical man had not courage to give her enough of, so that the pains were only mitigated. Mr. Hanna preaches at the Swiss Church, & we go to hear him. I wish I knew more Florentine news to send you. Mr. Stuart will tell you of his own arrival:—he is learning Hebrew, he says. Dont let me forget to set down that Mrs. Tennyson "has the sweetest voice in the world," and "is in many respects an uncommon woman." So, another friend writes to me.

Write soon, dear friend, & give me full details of the dear children & yourself too. I long to hear that you are well. Of course they are admired & you are proud of them. Perchè no!— The Princesse de la Tremouille occupies your rooms above us, & her people assure ours that *everything is cheaper in Paris,* whence they have just come. With our united cordial regards to both of you, I remain your affectionate

Elizabeth Barrett Browning

You will like to hear that Mrs. Cox has a fine baby, a girl.

Address: A Madame | Ma^{dme} Ogilvy, | Villa Falcon, | Sorrento, | Napoli. *Redirected:* Poste Restante | Firenze. *Postmarks:* FIRENZE 4 NOV. 1850; NAPOLI [?] NOV.; FIRENZE 25 NOV. 1850.

Letter 8

At 6 o'clock on the morning of May 3, the Brownings and Ogilvys left Florence for Venice, using John Murray's popular *Hand-Book* and Samuel Rogers' long travel poem *Italy* as guides. With them were Wilson and Pen. The Ogilvys' children remained with her sister at Bagni di Lucca, ultimately to be reunited in London with their parents. Mrs. Ogilvy indicates her recollections of the trip in the second of the memoirs published at the beginning of this volume. Elizabeth chronicled the events in a letter to her sister, Arabel, published for the first time as Appendix C, page 205.

The Ogilvys had left Venice by June 5, but the Brownings lingered until Friday, June 13, and arrived at Paris at the end of the month.

Earlier in the spring Elizabeth had sent the manuscript of a new poem, *Casa Guidi Windows*, to Sarianna Browning, who took the responsibility of seeing it through proof-reading and production. Chapman and Hall released the poem on the last day of May.

The "Mr. Reade" whom Elizabeth saw two days before leaving Venice was probably the American poet-painter Thomas Buchanan Read, who was to paint the Brownings' portraits in 1853. M. de Goethe, a grandson of the poet and dramatist, was also a great friend of the Brownings and probably knew the Ogilvys as well.

Barry Cornwall's "A Familiar Epistle to Robert Browning" appeared in his *English Songs, and Other Small Poems*, issued by Chapman and Hall, 1851.

Elizabeth had apparently run out of red sealing wax and was forced to use black wax normally reserved for mourning.

Paris. July 2. [1851]

My dear friend, if indignation at my silence has not turned away your kind thoughts from me altogether, you, yet, will not have been thinking certainly that I should write (at last) to you from Paris. Listen to the explanation of the silence, & understand how it was not an ungrateful or unfeeling one. Both your letters were most welcome, of course, . . (& we made use of your information & carried the ms.s. in a pocket of Murray, side by side with the map) but I did not answer the first, intending to be in time with a letter to meet you in London, . . and when the second came, we were in such a confusion of plan, that I could not tell you where to write back to me, & waited & waited till I could. Dear bewitching Venice, which charmed me to the last, agreed very ill with Robert & worse with Wilson. He lay awake night after night, suffering nervous pains in the face & head,—and she could eat nothing without agonies of indigestion, & grew so thin & looked so ill & haggard that it would have been homicide to have kept her there. She says now that if she had stayed a month longer she should have died. Venice is as bilious as it is beautiful. Also our rooms proved, as I feared they would, very oppressive when the heat set in—not tenable by any manner of means. Yet I was savage enough to grow fatter & fatter while we remained & others were perishing—the place agreed with me in body & soul. More's the pity—for I had to lean down an immense height in order to sympathize with Robert, & be glad when we went away. And, do you know, the first day at Padua restored everybody—Robert began to sleep again, & Wilson to eat, . . while Wiedeman & I continued to sleep & eat . . and so there was nothing more to be complained of . . . *except leaving Venice.*

After you went away, we found out that Murray was right about the gondolas & that the universal charge (apart from imposition) is, a swanziger the first hour, & half a swanziger for every hour after. So we "swam in gondolas" to our heart's content—yes, and we went to the Lido, and we went to Chioggia (and we were kept out till two in the morning & frightened Wilson) and we went a second time to the opera, & twice to the play, and twice, besides, to the Malibran day-theatre—and, once, I teazed Robert into taking Wiedeman, (as we paid eight pence for our whole box, & the performance was over at eight oclock) and we repented it afterwards, both of us. The play turned out to be an heroic melodrama, in verse, in five acts, tremendously tedious to us all—but I assure you it was only in the fifth that Wiedeman gave signs of being a little tired, by putting up his small heels on the edge of the box & singing his favorite song about 'Papa & Mama' a thought too loud. What pleased him most was the music, the drawing up & down of the curtain, & the clapping of hands— He shouted out "Heigh" to the audience, & clapped his own hands to show how they were to do it again. But he did'nt much like the putting into chains of Odolinda's father, . . (was on the point of a roaring cry after some excruciating sensibility on the part of the prisoner—) and Robert said rightly that it was quite wrong to expose a young child to the shows of grief, before he could possibly discern the meaning of the imitation of Art. So, I wont take him to see Mad<u>lle</u> Rachel —you need not apprehend it.

Well—we left Venice, . . Wilson & the gods crying out . . on a friday; the natural consequence of which was a series of misfortunes. In the first place, we were too late for the train by five minutes & had to wait some three hours in the cafè before we could get on—secondly, we arrived at Padua just as St Anthony's feast had raised all the prices, & paid, for two poor bedrooms, *fourteen swanzigers*, after being asked sixteen! Had it been only for Giotto (noble as Giotto is at Padua) we should have proceeded to Vicenza, so scared were we by these prices, but we had both set our hearts on doing pilgrimage to Arquà & seeing Petrarch's house, & I tenaciously clung to this purpose. So, leaving Wilson & Wiedeman at the inn, we set off in a caleche, . . and misfortune the third was, that our driver turned out a 'birbone' & set us down a mile from Arquà in the burning sun, protesting the inability of his horses to drag us up the hill. As ignorant victims we groaned & resigned ourselves .. when lo, & behold, the road proved excellent, the mountain not more than a gentle slope, & the villagers lifted up their hands & eyes in astonishment at the iniquity of the Paduan. To reach the carriage again, I had to be set on a donkey, and, even so, I arrived as exhausted as a pilgrim might. But oh, how worth everything was the sight of Arqua!—and Petrarch's tomb & his house .. & the little, little room, out of which the great soul issued into its spiritual sphere. We were both moved to tears .. even Robert was .. by the homely look of that little room. There are depths which a small pebble dropping down, gives notice of. It was very affecting— but then, you know, we have great organs of reverence & a taste for old slippers & such gear. Yet we never saw Titian's house at Venice. Titian is not Petrarch! And then you beat us to pieces in the ordinary energies of sight seeing, &, do you know, after you left us disconsolate at Venice, we fell into a sort of enchanted somnolence & went to see scarcely anything more.

To continue this confession, Juliet's tomb was not once enquired after .. it was through infidelity, that want of curiosity. But I am really afraid of your scorn, when I add that we passed through Brescia at night, & so tired that I was scarcely alive enough to enjoy the vision of the town glorified in the brightest moonlight possible, beautiful as the vision was. We took the diligence in sixteen hours from Verona to Milan, arriving there at nine I think, in the morning, & stopping at Brescia one hour at midnight .. Wiedeman in the highest spirits & the most soup-devouring mood. Think of that child! He has adapted himself to every circumstance, & satisfied even Robert's exeginces with his perfection of goodness. Again, we were four & twenty hours in diligence from Strasbourg to Paris, the railroad intermissions being nought, (as the carriage was only placed on the rail) and he slept at night & laughed in

the day while we were all groaning round. I was very afraid
for him & rather for myself—but, without sacrificing the
coupè, & indeed the security of places altogether, there
was no way of escaping that last four & twenty hours of
continuous fatigue. And now, though charmed with the
Paris shops, he is apt to talk longingly of the 'cavalli' and
the 'vapore'—he does'nt like to be done with travelling.
How I wander. My story has broken its own back. We
stayed two days at Milan, & I climbed to the topmost pin-
nacle of the cathedral. That cathedral is almost worthy
of standing face to face, as it does, with the snow Alps: it
impressed me deeply. Milan, indeed, delighted us altogether—the pictures, exquisite—and the famous Leonardo
keeping its promises to the full. At Como, I was suffering
rather from the cathedral, & was not fit the morning after
our arrival, to go to Colico as we meant . . so we slept at
Cadenabbia, opposite Bellaggio, & took a caleche from
Menaggio to Porlezza, & a boat across that beautiful lake
to Lugano. Slept at Lugano, & went by vettura next morning to Bellinzona. Slept there, &, leaving Wilson & Wiedeman to take care of themselves, spent the next day on
the Lago maggiore. So we did a good deal, you see, in
spite of some omissions,—and you will agree that we
could'nt have done much more when I add that Robert
had an overplus of exactly ten francs on his arrival at
Lucerne. As to the passage of St Goathard I say nothing
of it. Only I thank God for having seen such a sight. It
thrills me to the soul even now, to look back & think.
There was more snow than usual, we heard, & the cold
was intense, but I wrapt a double shawl over my head
& only let out my eyes, & so escaped any injury. Lucerne
is surpassingly lovely, certainly surpassing the lovely Italian
lakes, & the air seemed like wine, & Wiedeman's cheeks
flushed in two days as if they were drinking it deep. Oh,
I should have liked to stay in Switzerland for him . . and also
for me . . I enjoyed it so!—but we found dreadful financial

news at the post about the ship-money, and Robert fell into a despondence about the bread we should get to eat for the next six months,—and there was nothing for it but to give up lakes & mountains & come straight to Paris. So here I am at the end of my story & journey. We went to Mr. Stuart's hotel, but really such rooms as were vacant, were so miserably black & small, that Robert (not *I*, mind! I only agreed) proposed trying our fortunes elsewhere at once. I dare say it is a very cheap hotel. We came off to our own old Hôtel de la ville de Paris near the Madeleine, and by a strange mistake, were brought to another at the other end of the same boulevard, & did not find out the difference till we had taken our rooms for a week. I am sorry. Still, we are excellently off here, in a centrical situation & a quiet, comfortable, clean house, *au premier* . . a salon (very good indeed) a small dining room & anti-chamber, a bedroom for Wilson & the babe, with two dressing rooms attached, and a bedroom for ourselves, . . all for six francs the four & twenty hours. Nothing so cheap (observe) is to be had in Italy—not in an hotel, I mean—and the prices at hotels must be a fair guage of the expensiveness of a place. We dined (Robert & I did) at our old restaurant's the first day, and were magnificently served upon gilt silver plate . . only we paid seven francs for our dinner which was *de trop*. Yesterday we went a step lower in the scale, & paid five francs . . the dinner being immensely too large—but by degrees we shall understand. The worst is that it rained during our first two days here,—which, with other causes, depressed Robert, & he was "sure that he should hate Paris," & all that sort of thing . . but here is the sun, on this third day, and I hope & trust we shall be in better spirits & take heart to look round us & count our advantages.

Now, if you can forgive & understand, do write, & let us hear of you both & how you like England & the Exhibition, & dont forget to tell me of the dear children. Also, if there is anything we can do for you, by letter or otherwise, in France or England, speak. This one thing you can do for *me* . . Alter with a pen, the word "rail" in *the last line of my* new poem (which I hope you received duly, as the publishers were instructed to send you a copy at Mr. Bosworth's) the word "rail" to the word "*Vail*" . . the allusion being of course to the vail of the Jewish temple, but 'railed' out pitilessly. There's no meaning left at all. It's the only error of any consequence in the book,—a few wrong stops & the substitution of 'heart & train' for 'heart & brain,' being evident enough to the reader. Sarianna Browning has done her part admirably & most kindly indeed. We have caught sight of the book since we came here by an accident, or should know nothing of these things. I hear that the Literary Gazette in giving extracts, peppered them with misprints, . . in high good humour however,—which I never expected from the Literary Gazette, both Robert & I having fancied ourselves in disgrace there.

Everything we have known yet of Paris, I have told you. Today we shall get out & see a little clearer by sunlight. It is warm, but not too warm.

Oh—let me remember to tell you that we saw Mr. Reade two days before we left Venice. He asked after you earnestly. I never saw anybody looking so ill, or more ill, than when he took coffee with us in the piazza of St Mark the last evening. Venice had evidently siezed him by the throat. He was on his way to the German water cure. Also, in the course of those last days, we met in the street M. de Goethe, & spent a good deal of time together in gondola & out of gondola. Few persons have interested me as much as he does.

And so, here's the end of my gossip! I hope you *felt* how sorry we were to part from you, & how we appreciated your delightful companionship while it was enjoyed. It is better to feel these things than to hear them.

God bless you both! Are you well? is Mr. Ogilvy well? did you find Mrs. Ogilvy quite well & in a glow of happiness at seeing you? and your sister? & your little niece? Give my love (yes, & Robert's) to dear Mrs. Ogilvy . . & do you both of you believe its sincerity towards yourselves.

Your affectionate E B Browning

Barry Cornwall is printing or has just printed a letter in verse to Robert—we have news of it here.

no red! [written next to black wax seal]

Address: Mrs. David Ogilvy | Care of Mr. Bosworth - *Publisher* | Regent's Street | London. *Postmarks:* PARIS 3 JUIL. 51; LIGNE-DE-CALAIS 3 JUIL. 51; JY 4 1851

Letter 9

The Brownings remained in Paris for nearly a month before proceeding to London, where they arrived on July 23.

Among the many friends and family members who were delighted to see the Brownings was John Kenyon. A distant cousin of Elizabeth and a school-mate of Browning's father, he had given unqualified approval to their marriage and handled Elizabeth's financial affairs after her father disowned her. After Pen Browning was born, Kenyon settled £100 annually upon the parents, giving them more freedom of movement. Kenyon quite frequently forgot to transfer this annuity (given every six months in £50 amounts) to the Brownings' account, which resulted in some embarrassing situations. In 1856 Elizabeth dedicated *Aurora Leigh* to Kenyon who died the same year, leaving her £4000 and Robert £6500. Their perennial financial worries thereby ended.

The governess referred to is Mrs. Orme, who had been employed at Hope End, the Herefordshire home of the Barretts.

London. Devonshire Street. 26. Regent's Park.

From friday to friday. [July 25-August 1, 1851]

Can you believe, my dear friend, that we are here? For my part I scarcely can. I feel hanging on the sharp edge of some strange whirling planet—& how it cuts!

Your letter was most welcome as every quick kindness of yours must always be. I did'nt answer it because we were in a state of 'doubtful doubt' as to England, when it came,—ready to go, ready to stay, & uneasy either way. Indeed I was perfectly unhappy about Robert, who lost his spirits from the moment of crossing the Alps & grew so unwell in Paris, fell into such a state of morbid nervousness, that at last I resolved on persuading him against going to England at all. The idea of taking his wife & child to New Cross & putting them into the place of his mother, was haunting him day & night, & I was afraid to think how it might end. As soon as we had decided not to go, the imagination became quieted & he was better at once. Then, came the reaction. A letter from my sister Arabel full of the hope of seeing us, touched him (you know how quickly he can be touched) and suddenly "he could'nt bear to disappoint Arabel," and "he would go to a lodging in London near her, &, so, visit his own home by himself & get it over." Which was done. We came here a few days ago—& he has been to New Cross—thank God it is not to be looked forward to any more. He is himself again,—& I, too, am happier, for I have seen my dear darling Arabel, & such of my brothers who were in town—they came to us instantly. Yet it is a position on a thickset hedge. I cant make a movement to right or left without pain. My first step on English ground was into a puddle, with a fog all round,—& the moral influences are almost more gloomy to me.

Yet *that's* ungrateful. It is great joy to see those whom I love, & to see them so well. I see nobody changed for the worse after all these years, except one friend . . my poor old governess, who is dying, I fear, of dropsy, & shocked me much by her altered appearance. Really everybody else is rather better than worse for these five long years. Even my dear aged friend, Miss Tripsack, walked as agilely as ever to our door, with what I tell her is the bloom of youth on both cheeks. My youngest brother indeed, is changed past all recollection—but *that* comes from a pair of whiskers, & a matured latitude across the shoulders.

Also, we have all sorts of kind attentions,—& visitors enough to keep unpleasant thoughts (or any thoughts whatever) out of stronger heads than mine. Robert & I have not eaten an uninterrupted meal since we came, & we must take to living by absorption of fog, if we stay long. I had only half a cup of tea for breakfast this morning, because Barry Cornwall came,—and only half a cup of tea tonight, because Miss Mitford came. Wiedeman says he wants to go back to Paris to see the 'balloon'— He is a little impatient of the dark rooms & the flood of new faces, poor darling!

In Paris we saw, yes, & had tea with Tennyson & his wife, on their way to Florence! Nothing could be more warmly kind than he was to us, insisting that we should take possession of his house at Twickenham, servants & all, & stay there as long as we liked to remain in England. We accepted the note—it is a precious autograph, representing the princeliness of poets: For, observe, there had been no previous friendship— Robert had only met him in general society two or three times, & I had never looked in his face before. We were both very much touched. Mrs. Tennyson is a winning gentle creature, in delicate health. She lost her baby, after a bad confinement, it appears. He leaves England to escape from the dirty hands of his worshippers, and wishes to be "quite private" in Italy, if that is possible. I told his wife that there was not zeal enough for literature among the English of Florence to persecute anybody by over-worship. His nervous susceptibility amounts to malady & produces real suffering. Dont understand that we are going to Twickenham, by the way. We only accepted the note for the pleasure of the autograph of the kindness's sake.

Oh—and I think they go first to the Baths of Lucca.

Robert recommended it rather than Como, which was in
their plan. He is very natural & simple, & rather abrupt in
his manner from a constitutional shyness; a man to revolt
against any effort to make him "shine". He does'nt shine—
but you do not feel it difficult to believe him to be a
great man whether he speaks or is silent. I assure you he
smoked his pipe (a real clay pipe) after tea,—with just a
word of mere form to ascertain if it would throw me into
fits or not.

My dear friend, this letter has been lying here for a
week & more— Like my cups of tea, it is interrupted half
way, & quarter way. How can one write in such a confusion? People are overkind "knowing that the time is short."
Mr. Kenyon has forced me to break a vow against going
out to dinner—but otherwise I don't & wont go— Robert
does, instead, to represent the house. At Mr. Kenyon's
I saw for the first time, Mr. Carlyle & his wife. Mr. Forster
of the Examiner, Mr. Chorley of the Athenæum, Mr. Procter (Barry Cornwall) Miss Geraldine Jewsbury, with Mrs.
Jameson &c, & the evening was delightful, certainly—only,
a dozen more such pleasures would go too near to killing
one downright. What struck me the most in all these
people is, that they are younger than I expected—especially
Carlyle, with his slim active figure & thick bushy hair. I
heard him growl a little about the Exposition . . "a dreadful
sight," he called it: "There was confusion enough in the
universe, without building a chrystal palace to represent
it." How like Carlyle!

I write & write, & do not tell you what interest we
felt in your prompt, kind, welcome letter. The dear children, dear little Alexander, with his prayer . . may God teach
Himself to them all. Wiedeman says prayers, too, with
hands lifted up, for "Papa, mamma, Lilla, e *Tush*" repeating those names of his own accord. He has taken to call
Wilson, Lilla, I must tell you. He gets on slowly with his
talking, but can say a great many more Italian words since

you saw him, and a very few English,—such as "no more" & "come."

You amused me by the offence given to your relations by the 'Traditions.' What a proper world it is, to have so many improprieties going on in it, day & night!—*that* strikes one. But Italy is said to be not a popular subject in England just now—more's the pity. 'Casa Guidi' for instance is considered to have more power in it than other writings of mine, & it sells—only I am assured that it would gain in popularity if the subject were different. I dont pretend to understand (much less to excuse) this alleged indifference of the English people towards the Italian. And who can? I am very glad that you found anything to like in "Casa Guidi." Tell me if you would like to have the other two volumes, which are yours, you know, whenever you claim them. I only dont press them on you, because duplicate volumes to travellers, are something worse than "impedimenta."

I will tell you about Paris another time—observe how my hands shake. I have been, for the first visit, today at the Chrystal Palace, . . Robert & I, with Mrs. Jameson—I am dreadfully tired. Afterwards we went to hear Fanny Kemble read Hamlet, with that face & voice of hers so various, deep & touching in vibrations. The reading struck & charmed me, & I could not criticize, as Robert does who is more learned. She had the goodness to call on us this morning & leave us cards of free admission (which we missed through going to the Chrystal palace) but of course we shall call upon her & thank her &, so, not miss making her acquaintance.

When we go away I cant tell you. Wilson must go to see her mother first, and we are pondering seriously whether it wont be better & more reasonable to send Wiedeman with her, than to rend him away from her & consign him to half a stranger. It's horrible to think of, but we are forcing ourselves to think of it a little. Ah— I dont know.

Apartments in Paris are *very cheap*—furnished apartments, cheaper than in Florence. No city so full of gardens & fresh air! Wiedeman's cheeks brightened there into redness, & here are growing pale again. I dont think you could do better with your children & yourselves than transplant them all into Paris. It seems to me very good garden-ground for such roses. Indeed it is.

Observe what a gasping, asthmatic letter I write to you. My hand is in a tremble, & my thoughts in a crumble. Shall I tell you that I was disappointed in the Chrystal Palace, & leave you wonder at me?

My sister Henrietta comes to London tomorrow from Taunton on purpose to see us & show her gigantic baby. Not a word more. But do write to me, (because I can read letters if I cant except distractedly write them) & tell me that you have good news from Lucca. How remote Florence seems now with its bright high Heavens!

This England, with all its life & power & kindness, is a sad place to me—even as it is very sad to feel beloved by all except the dearest.

I heard from Miss Mitford, the other day (who came to spend a week in London & heard it from somebody else) that "our friends the Ogilvys were charming people." I must tell you that.

God bless you. My love goes with Robert's to Mr. Ogilvy & yourself.

<Your ever affectionate
Elizabeth Barrett Browning>

Among a heap of reviews which we have been looking over since we came, there's one upon Robert, which says, in so many words, that the critic had had "some hopes, upon the poet's marriage with *EBB*, of his profiting by her severer taste—but alas, he was worse than ever!" & there's one upon me (in another unconscious periodical) in which a second critic observes that he had "fondly hoped, upon my marriage with RB, for some modification

of my extravagance by the influence of his austerer taste . .
but alas!—I was worse than ever."

I quote this curious opposition to you, because you are
given perhaps to some over-reverence of the critic-craft—
You may suppose how it made us laugh.

Address: Mrs. Ogilvy. | (Care of Mr. Bosworth, Publisher) | Regent's
Street. *Postmarks:* Devonshire St.; AU 2 1851.

Letter 10

This letter is fragmentary, but the extant manuscript picks up with
Elizabeth's mention of Mr. Read's reaction to the proposed water
cure (see Letter 8).

The pirated edition of *Casa Guidi Windows* was issued by C. S.
Francis of New York along with *Prometheus Bound* and other poems
from Elizabeth's 1850 edition—including "Sonnets from the Portuguese."

Robert had been asked and had agreed to write an introduction
to newly-discovered Shelley letters which were found to be spurious
before distribution (see Letter 13).

[London, August 20, 1851]
< . . . > the water cure so tragically that he took fright &
his passage to England. In the course of the water cure,
said M. de Goethe, *he* would have committed suicide several
times if he had'nt had friends by him to hold his hands; and
though the cure was complete, the risk was tremendous. A
Wertherian recommendation which failed with our friend
from America. His plans seem unfixed still. He may stay
a week, or two or three weeks in London—and he likes it,
he says, for the sake of the continual "twilight." Now he &
I always agreed about a half light being better than a whole
—but this sort of twilight (half fog, half smoke,) without
vesper star or silence, really does not charm *me*.

Think of a copy of an American edition of 'Casa Guidi'
being sent over the other day to Mr. Kenyon. The pirates

keep early hours, you see. Robert has agreed to a proposition about editing some new ms. letters of Shelley's, for
which he is to be well paid. Monkton Milnes married
lately, . . *well*, it is considered both in a worldly & un-
worldly sense,—but bride & bridegroom are of course in-
visible so far.

Such dislocated scratches I send you. Wiedeman tugs
at my gown at every sentence. Only you will know that
we dont forget you. How should we indeed? With Robert's
love & mine to both of you, & with our warm regards to
dear Mrs. Ogilvy,

      ever believe me your affectionate friend
      my dear friend—
            Elizabeth Barrett Browning.

Do write. Oh—I quite understand your finding your first
love again among the scotch mountains. That sort of local-
love does not die out—unless it is *killed* by some slow,
murderous grief. I honour the Grand Duchess for appreciating your children. You see there is apt to be some sort
of human good even in a Bourbon.

Here has this letter been lying for days! My head, my
head, my head, I have no head. Your reproach comes to
remind me, not of my ingratitude but my stupidity. I send
this off now without another word—except 'thank you,'
—& except the Paris address. The hotel we were at *last*
was, "Aux armes de la ville de Paris, Rue de la Michaudiere,
Boulevard des Italiens." The hotel "Ville de Paris, rue
Ville Eveque (I think) was more elegant & cheerful, &
scarcely more expensive . . so we found on our way to
Italy—but we shall return to the one we last left on account
of its great cheapness & quiet.

We shall be in London on the 29th & after, certainly, &
very glad indeed to see you— After all, we found < . . . >

Address: Mrs. David Ogilvy | King's Place | Perth. *Postmarks:* Devon-
shire St; AU 20 1851; PERTH AU 21 1851.

Letter 11

Having seen each other in London in mid-September, the Brownings and the Ogilvys both left shortly thereafter. The Brownings remained in Paris during the winter of 1851-52 and the Ogilvys settled for a third season in Florence.

"Poerio" is Elizabeth's short title for *Two Letters to the Earl of Aberdeen on the State Prosecutions of the Neapolitan Government* by Gladstone. The pamphlet appeared in the summer of 1851 and went through at least eleven editions before the end of the year. It contained a defense of the Italian patriot Carlo Poerio, who was consigned to life imprisonment in June 1850, after a mock trial for insurrection. In 1859 Poerio and sixty-six companions were released and sent to America, but en route they seized the vessel and went to Cork and then to London, where a subscription of £10,000 was raised to supply them with arms.

Mr. Fox is William Johnson Fox, Unitarian minister and Member of Parliament for Oldham. Miss Dick is a sister of Mrs. Ogilvy. The article in the *Revue des Deux Mondes* was written by Joseph Milsand who later became one of the Brownings' most intimate friends. He was among the first who agreed with Elizabeth in describing Robert's poetry as superior to her own.

138. Avenue des Champs Elysèes.
October 17. [1851]

My dear friend, we were very glad to have your letter from Italy & the delightful news of your darling children. I fancy I see them with their 'shining morning faces' & pretty curls, & enter deeply into your joy at being all together again. For ourselves we stayed in London more than a week after your departure, & at last there was a violent tug to break those sweet old new ties which had unconsciously knotted themselves fast again. But it was necessary. Setting aside certain bitternesses which were with me constantly, spoiling the savour of everything, the English climate really is not tenable. I coughed through the last night almost incessantly, and slept perfectly at Dieppe— perhaps simply the effect of change of air: but it cant be the effect of change alone, that, since I have been in Paris, this cough which more or less lasted through the whole of the two months we spent in England, has almost wholly vanished. The air here is very light & clear. Not a touch of fog! and the sun shines after the similitude of an Italian sun, really. We are established in a very pleasant apartment in the great avenue of the Champs Elysèes, in the full blaze of the sunshine, & have not yet had occasion to begin fires. A pretty sitting-room full of comfortable chairs & sofas . . a great luxury to such a Lollard as I! (my sisters laugh at me for caring so about spring seats & such vanities, & I declare that I scarcely ever sate down in a sympathetic chair all the time I was in England! –) & with two windows opening upon a large terrace, . . large enough to serve the purpose of a garden . . and all the brilliant life of Paris sweeping to & fro among the trees beyond. Then, there's an adjoining sitting-room for Robert to write in, and a dining-room on the other side of that. Which three doors open on the antichamber & face the doors of two excellent bed-rooms, our own, & Wiedeman's, there being a third bedroom up stairs for the femme de service. A kitchen &c of course. For all which we pay two pounds a week – more than we intended! But Paris is overflowingly full, & our situation, you see, is first rate, – and for the sake of sun & air it was well worth while to pay, on this winter of trial. Wiedeman is in full bloom. Wilson never knew him to have such an appetite, she says, as since he has been here, & his spirits which are not apt to flag anywhere, have risen to the point of ecstacy through the immense resources on all sides. Why, there's the balloon that fills & goes up within a stone's throw – and there are four Punches in the immediate neighbourhood! There's civilization for you! – To say nothing of dancing dogs, turn-about horses, and the President at the head of the troops, who with trumpet & drum passes & repasses our windows for the review outside the barrière.

Wiedeman makes progress in his talking – using Italian & English words indiscriminately, but most of the former.

He has now taken to call himself *Peninni*—by an extraordinary revolution of syllables: he means *Wiedeman* I assure you, though you may'nt think so. Peninni can do this, Peninni can do that, Peninni wants this & that, all day long. The personal pronouns are set aside, after my own fashion when I was a child. Certainly he would be puzzled to say "come sta" like Marcia; but "ti voglio bene" he articulates beautifully, translating it by "I love you" . . which sounds more like "I wash you." Every now & then he kneels down at a chair & says "Dio, Mamma, Dio!" Mama is to help him to say his prayers. But he does not make great progress after all, I fear, in theology,—for when we had talked some time the other morning about 'Dio,' (who, he told me, lived *"among the birds . ."* pointing upwards) I asked him "Chi è il piu buono di tutti?" To which which he answered, without hesitation, . . *'Peninni'*— But again, it was pretty yesterday, when he knelt & said this prayer out of his head . . "Ate (grazie) Dio. Pane Mamma, pane Papa, pane Peninni . . *dinè*, té, uova. Ate Dio." He says *"dinè"* already, unfortunate child, instead of the 'dinner' he learnt in England.

Our two last London evenings except the very packing-up last, we spent, one with Mr. Fox & the other with Mr. Rogers—& really I grudged both of them from my sister. Yet I am glad now to have seen Rogers,—for, apart from the irresistible kindness of the message that drew us, it is not likely that I should ever see him again in this world, and he is one of the links to the golden past, precious chiefly through what he touches. We passed a most interesting evening, Mr. Leslie of the Royal Academy, the only other person present. The old poet (nearly ninety) sate in the armchair from which he can no longer move—for it was found impossible to remedy the fracture of the thighbone resulting from that accident a year ago, though he miraculously survived it. His features are colourless as marble, with a certain monumental majesty too, & the serenest benignity of expression. He looks as if he well remembered standing face to face with the great Dead, & was not unworthy of having done so. His speech is very slow & measured: he does not converse: the time is past for conversation: he speaks to you his last words and you are to listen. He talked a little about Italy—oh, and I told him of our vain search at Modena, & he smiled gravely, & observed he had given as much trouble to many persons & ought to be sorry for it,—the story was an invention altogether. Then he talked about 'God's dumb creatures,' and of the duty we owed them & did not pay—his voice deepened with reprehension as he spoke of the "men who called themselves *sportsmen—sportsmen!*" The celebrated bitterness of his repartees, I heard nothing of. All was gentle & genial. He promised us a copy of his works, which we should have liked from his hands, but it went out of his head of course, and no book came. His mind is a little shaken, rather than dimmed. He sometimes loses what he is about to say, and his favorite servant (who stood by while we were at tea) prompts the word—but whatever he does say is as elevated & refined as ever it could have been. This servant told us that he was recovering the coherency of his intellect fast; the effect of the accident, which had made him old on a sudden, gradually passing away— Still, he is very old, & I cannot believe that he will last long.

We travelled with Carlyle to Paris—we are fortunate you see, in our fellow-travellers! He was coming here to pay a visit to Lord Ashburton, & put off his journey for a day in order to travel with us, which was honour & pleasure at once. He is the most interesting companion in the world— highly characteristic & *Carlylish*—and we enjoyed everything except the voyage to Dieppe which the society of the angel Gabriel could scarcely have made a pleasant thing. We crossed in the wrath of winds & waters, the stewardess telling me comfortingly (when I asked if there was danger) that "it was impossible to know how things might end in such a stormy sea." Everybody was sick, even I (oh shame!) even Wiedeman, & Flush who was ordered off deck in consequence—while poor Robert & Wilson suffered horribly. Carlyle said with feeling, "Sea sickness is the most humiliating of the casualties which afflict human nature, except a cold in the head." Wiedeman however took quite another view of it. He had resolved from the first that it was proper to be sick in a "vapore," & made a point of complaining of a pain in his stomach the moment we set foot in the vessel. Therefore it was with the utmost satisfaction that he sate up gravely to the great consummation, "like Papa Mamma & Lili." There was a decided accession of social dignity in it. I said "Ti do consiglio di stare zitto, zitto," and down he lay again, as still as a dormouse, for seven hours together,— till I told him we had arrived, upon which he sprang to his feet & laughed loudly & long, & cried out "Latte e tè!" You may suppose that the illness was not very severe—but I wondered at his not being tired or frightened—for we had the dead-lights close against the beating of the sea, & the rattling & creaking on every side was tremendous enough. He never cried once,—not he!—(he has the very genius of travelling) & was in a fervour of joy at being taken through the soldiers in the custom-house. We arrived at nine, in the dark: and (talking of the custom house) everything passed —even to the twenty-five cigars which Carlyle had the audacity to put at the top of his box. We slept at Dieppe, & went into Paris in a blaze of sunshine the next day.

Now I dont think I have much more of personal history to tell you. Yes, let me remember to tell you that all is right between us & my brother George— He came to London, as soon as Robert's letter found him out, & the last few days had a good deal of love & consolation in them. Thank God for *that*. Other things are too painful to write about.

I shall direct this letter to the Baths of Lucca, though I do hope you may have left or be at the point of leaving it.

I dont like what you say about not feeling well—& about fevers. Do let me have good news of you all. And give a kiss from me to each of the darling children & bid them not forget me.

Do you hear anything of the Tennysons? Father Prout declared to us, that they were in Paris, but we hear nought of them at their hotel.

I saw your 'Poerio' advertised . . I think in the Chronicle, with an extract from the *Despatch* praising the eloquence of the defence . . comparing it to "Curran & Grattan"— Well, I confess to you (and I *may*, since you are not Poerio) that I do not think as well of it. It seems to me weak— eminently Italian in many ways. I must end, Robert cries out, or lose the post. God bless you. Robert's love with mine to you both— Write soon & at length & believe me your ever affectionate EBB.

My regards to Miss Dick, if she shd. be within hearing.

But 'Poerio' sells, I hope— I could not hear in London. You have done your part for Italy.

We see the advertisement of an article in the Revue des deux mondes, *15th August* . . on Robert—but we have not set eyes on it yet.

Letter 12

In this and subsequent letters Elizabeth defends Louis Napoleon at great length. Nephew of Napoleon I, he had received the required vote of three-fourths of the electors in the December 1848 presidential election. The constitution did not allow the President a second term, and a vote to amend this provision failed to receive the required three-fourths majority of the Assembly. Louis Napoleon, however, convinced that he acted with the backing of the majority of the people, felt no obligation to observe the letter of the law. He called on the support of the people and in December 1851 managed a successful *coup d'état*, breaking down barricades on the streets and unwittingly killing over a thousand Parisians who resisted. His new government prescribed severe treatment for opponents and restricted the freedom of the press; Elizabeth nevertheless

saw in Louis Napoleon the leader to free Italy and maintained un-
swerving faith in him. Mrs. Ogilvy's skepticism about Napoleon's
intentions is evidenced in her poem "The End of 1851," reprinted
in this volume in Appendix B, pages 193-194. Napoleon desired
an Italy free from Austrian oppression, but he envisioned a loosely-
federated country of independent states rather than a unified power
that might threaten France's interests.

The Ogilvys, in Florence, were enjoying the company of the
Peytons, old and close friends of the Barretts. The first cousin
mentioned by Elizabeth was Charlotte ("Arlette") Reynolds. Her
mother, Charlotte Butler (*née* Graham-Clarke) was Elizabeth's maternal aunt. Arlette spent the winter in Florence with her husband
and daughter, born a few days after Pen Browning.

> 138 Avenue des Ch. Elysées.
> Dec.ʳ 30. [1851]

I am not shot dearest Mrs. Ogilvy, only deserve it: for certainly nothing can have been worse of me than not answering your letters. I do believe that the chief reason of my
not having done so before, was the having too much to say
to set about saying it—that, & the sort of languor which
always falls upon me in cold weather. Forgive, & believe
me capable of behaving better for the future, & incapable
of being careless even in the past, of you, in my real feelings. Your letters were most welcome, answered or not
answered. Thank you too for the American enclosure, for
which we owe you . . how many pauls? No, it was'nt
quite as plain inside as outside. A bookseller's friend writing for a bookseller, desiring to bring out a very particularly
complete edition of my poems & hinting particularly darkly
at the "advantage of author & publisher"—a sublime vague-
ness which considering the result of distinct propositions
from that quarter, is not promising nor worth an answer
by any means, says Robert.

Do you know that scarcely for the sight of the Alps, as I
keep repeating to myself & others, would I have missed
being at Paris during this revolution-time. It has been & is
still intensely interesting: you have the great heart-beat of

the world under your hand. Also, the dramatic effect of
that second of December cannot be exaggerated. The pour-
ing in of the troops into Paris in a real sunshine of Austerlitz,
& the immense shout of soldiers & people through which
Louis Napleon rode on horseback under our windows . .
the long living shout, sweeping from the Carrousel to the
Arc de L'Etoile, and triumphing, as a living thing should,
over the triumph of the military music . . these things are
indescribable like an electric shock, & thrilling to you much
the same. Certainly I would not have missed them for
anything,—though one could not escape afterwards from
the painful emotion of the situation. On thursday night,
for instance, after straining one's eyes & ears at the rumbl-
ing cannons, gallopped by in the dusk in answer to the
distant signals of the trumpets, and after setting one'self
down to listen dreadfully to the rounds of distinct firing,
it was impossible to go to bed as usual, as you may suppose.
I put on my dressing gown & sate up sadly with Robert who
had some writing to do, in the drawingroom till one in the
morning. But there was no sort of room for personal fear—
it never even occurred to me. Thursday was the only day
on which there was any fighting to signify, & upon that
day Wiedeman was taken out of doors as usual . . only not
far from the house: we took that degree of precaution.
One thing was clear to me from the beginning, that the
sympathy of the people of Paris went fully with the President. To judge by our own tradepeople & their retainers,
wine-merchant, water-carrier, milk-bringer, poulterer, baker,
& the rest, . . yes, our very cuisiniere & concierge were full
of sympathy & exultation. "Ah Madame—c'est le vrai neveu
de son oncle! il est admirable." A woman came from the
barricades during the fighting, to this house— "Mais vous
avez donc le diable au corps vous autres," said to her our
little vivacious cuisinière, "pour vouloir combattre ainsi le
neveu de l'empereur." "Oh" . . she answered . . "you
think that Napoleon will give you everything—but *we* dont

trust him. *We* dont want an emperor, nor a King, nor a house of assembly neither! We want to have money, & to govern ourselves." "Mais, ma chere, c'est bête, ce que vous dites là."

But now you ask for my impressions about the right & wrong of this matter,—& I will tell you, all the more sincerely, that I have been exercised to sincerity in relation to it, Robert & I having had various domestic émeutes on the subject. From the first moment, down to this last when my convictions have strengthened themselves, I have believed that nothing better could have been done for France than what has been done . . and that *a Washington might have done it*, and *would*, under the circumstances, if he had the necessary intellect. This is my opinion. At the same time, I profess no faith in Louis Napoleon as a pure patriot & political moralist—he may be pure or impure, for aught that I know on either side—he may do well or he may do ill . . he may deserve to be blessed or cursed by us all, this day three months. But that he was justified in not holding pedantically to an impossible constitution & an impracticable assembly . . that he was not bound to choke France into mortal convulsions, through keeping the husk of an oath—nor to tread upon a living people through a strained reverence for the formalism of an unrepresenting Chamber . . this I believe & maintain, & this, France itself believes & maintains, which is a matter of more consequence. Certainly he broke the letter of an oath—but so did Lamartine & the civic heroes of '48—& the world clapped its hands. So did the civic heroes of '30—and the world clapped its hands. Why are the necessary conditions of every revolution inadmissable in this case only? Then the position was altogether wheel-locked. We all knew that something was coming— Robert said, a fortnight before it happened, that "he felt it in the air." The question with everybody was, "how will this end?" Of course that it should end SO, has thrown all the extinguished parties, (all ablaze with hope a moment before) into agonies of rage, & we who live in the midst of them, can scarcely describe to those who do not, the sort of gnashing of teeth & wild-beast-roaring which we hear on all sides. From our position, we have got to know a good deal of the ex-journalists . . of the National & Presse, for instance— Good heavens!— how they roar & writhe! I heard the old Napoleon called "un scelerat atroce" in this room a few evenings since, & all his marshalls & their families "des coquins infames," & the empire itself, "le regne de Satan." Indeed there is a great deal too much foam through these black beards, for distinct articulation. I ventured to ask what could have been done, if there had been no iniquitous coup d'etat (for, observe, nobody defends the assembly, everybody of every party admitting that the assembly was out of sympathy with the people)—when a moderate suggested that Lamartine might have done something. But Lamartine, as a dear friend of his admitted an hour before, "stands quite alone," being by no means as "fort" nor as much "on a level with the times, . . as he was in 48, & the parties all recoiling from him.

It is curious to me how these democratical partymen, who have been professedly living & dying by the 'universal suffrage' flag, now delight in talking of the "intelligent minority," and of "the minority which is France." Their abuse of the "masses" keeps pace, I assure you, with their abuse of the president. The agriculturists are "des animaux," the bourgeoisie, "des hommes sans conscience," the capitalists, "des hommes sans cœur," while I hear that poor Lamennais exhales his private wrath by declaring that the "whole people is putrified at heart."

But no, no. Do not let us judge so, we who are not in the dust of the circus, but can see from a higher & quieter position. There is one tradition still dear to France,—it is the name of Napoleon. What wonder that she should roll herself in the banner of the loved colour, in this mortal con-

fusion of many banners, & when it is associated with the
possibilities of repose & material prosperity? The people
is a noble people; they are not thinking of the sale of their
birthrights, be very sure. But they love, and they fear.
They love the name "Napoleon"—a word, you will say!—
but the 'sentiment' of a people if it referred only to the
shade of a word, the rap of a fact, would still be a great
thing. They fear social chaos, & the socialistic societies—
an exaggerated fear, perhaps!—but natural, under the circumstances, to the very instincts of national life. Such a
fear has been at the roots of all the repressive policy since
48. Give security to this people, & they will take liberty
themselves. Louis Napleon is in a magnificent position
at this moment—and if he does not abuse it, he will stand.
If he should attempt despotism, he will not stand—and
my hope is (rather in his ability, you see, than in his virtue) that he will not therefore attempt it. He has the
Buonaparte blood to the end of his finger-nails. The prompt
& complete combination of the 'coup,' was a proof of
undeniable intellect . . of the sort of intellect that rules.
As to the stuff talked (chiefly by English) of 'military
despotism,' why the thing is impossible—the army is bound
heart to heart to the people in France—flesh of its flesh.
We know Orleanists & Systemists too—all in despair, of
course, & various states of frenzy. One orleanist lady is
under the delusion that the barricades were only three
inches high, & that the cannonading was purely for Louis
Napoleon's private amusement. Yet a clever woman really!
We are speaking of hallucinations. Dont let those of the
Times newspaper deceive you. The myths on the other
side of the channel seem to be of the most Titanic order
of mythology. The English never understand the French in
the first place . . that's a matter of course.

Robert & I do not agree on this subject with our usual
harmony, I must confess to you. I expect him to come
round in time, & perhaps he expects the same of me. Of

course I could only tell you (as I was writing), my own impressions & not his. He sympathizes with some of the fallen, though not, when you come to examine the assembly. He always hated the Buonapartists, & expects no good out of him, with such a "galére."

And if you enquire into Wiedeman's opinion on the revolution, he will say for himself "Buono, buono." He was in a state of ecstacy those three days when we saw so much military "grand spectacle." (Now it has all vanished, & Paris is as gay & free from the click of musketry, & as crowded on the boulevards with the fair of the "jour de l'an" as you could hope to see it.) Wiedeman has been taught by our Napoleonic *cuisiniére* to cry "Viva Peone," which she accepts for the intention of "vive Napoleon" though it doesn't sound very french, & which he shouted yesterday in at the president's carriage-window. Wiedeman told me when he came home that he had seen "Peone," but (shaking his head) Poene had'nt a "penna *vass*" . . (*rossa*). Alas for ideals! When they turn into actuals they are all apt to want the red feather—are they not?

The child speaks chiefly Italian still, as in duty bound, but his talk is very composite, & both English & french enter into it. For instance he talks of "uno apeau" (un chapeau) & says "*Lis* non buono," for 'This is not good.' The mixture of tongues combined with the extraordinary mispronunciations, together with an active vocation for talking & determination of being understood against nature, occasions amazing difficulties to us all. I puzzle my brain & make out what he means, sometimes, just as if he were Proclus instead of *Peninni*, which is the quaint name he calles himself by . . never using a pronoun. He is invited to a grand Christmas tree & party on New Year's eve, where there are to be thirty children & where Eugene Sue would have been invited (. . "only," said the lady of the house, "he *is* such a scamp . .") & Robert & I have had a wrestle about it, he taking the sensible side of course, &

maintaining that Wiedeman is far too young for Christmas
carouses, but generously yielding the point to my preeminent foolishness. So Wilson is to take the child for half
an hour . . just to please him & me . . and I have had the
extravagance to buy him a black velvet frock for the occasion at thirteen francs the yard (a yard & three quarters
make the frock) with blue ribbons at the shoulders & blue
shoes, & I charm myself with thinking how very pretty he
will look. He grows prettier, it seems to me—his hair hangs
in golden ringlets all over his head, so thickly & glossily,
that people insult us by maintaining that we *must* put it in
papers—"hair does'nt curl naturally that way." The scissors
have never touched it yet, & Robert has come over to my
theory now, seeing that it grows thick without any manner
of cutting. He is very much admired when he walks out, &
Wilson makes oath to his leading all the child-fashions in
the arrondissement. What pleases me most however (next
always to his goodness & sweetness, little angel!) is the sight
of his red cheeks & round, firm limbs. Paris agrees with him
superbly. I told him the other day that Papa thought him
"troppo picino" to go to the Xmas party. "No, no, mamma," said he . . "he was very large indeed" . . stretching out
his arms at full length & roaring like a lion . . (which is his
way of expressing *size*) . . and then suddenly pulling up his
petticoats quite round his waist, to show what enormous
legs he had. We often talk together of the dear 'tre bambini!' Your children are always forward, I think, in language. Remember how Alexander proposed "going to
school," as you wrote to me at Siena, before he was two
years old. Does Marcia mix up the two languages? As to
Louisa she must be getting on fast indeed. Give her, or
rather all three of them, kisses & loves from me & say that
I never forget them.

Robert is charmed with Paris, & I dont very much wonder,—particularly as he is popular & receives all sorts of

kindness & attention. Also, though we live here most comfortably, we spend no more .. perhaps rather less .. than in Florence. This will surprise you. Even the fuel, which is the dearest thing, is not dearer than we found it there. As to the social advantages, they are obvious & facile of access & peculiarly inexpensive in the mode. The climate sets me longing sometimes for Italy, but it is tenable, & we are in the very warmest house I ever lived in. In November we shared in the universally cold weather—then we had a very mild interregnum & I was able to go in a carriage with Robert on the 8th of December, to examine the field of battle on the boulevards & count the cannon-holes & windows dashed in. Last week came three days of a mixed frost & fog which brought back my cough with fury & took away my voice. I cant speak above my breath even now. But we very seldom have fog—it's better than England, be sure.

The Peytons are the cream of the milk of good kind people: & my cousin, whom you saw, is as amiable as she is pretty. She is my first cousin. Warmest regards from Robert & myself to dear Mr. Ogilvy. Dear friend, your ever aff^cte *EBB*

I see in an advertisement that you have been "peeping into Saving Banks!" Dont treat me as I deserve by not writing. Here are three letters in one, I think! Rumour says that the president will have offered to him the imperial dignity at the Hotel de ville next friday. A mere rumour perhaps. So sorry we are to hear of Mr. Stuart's illness. I have been wishing to write to him, to thank him for the excesses of his kindness to me in reviews .. I will write soon.

Address: A Madame | Madame Ogilvy | Poste Restante | Florence | Toscane. *Postmarks:* PARIS 30 DEC. 51; PD; 4 GEN 1852 FIRENZE.

Letter 13

On January 1, 1852, the Cathedral of Notre Dame had been magnificently decorated, and to mark Louis Napoleon's new régime the "Te Deum d'actions de grace" was performed in his presence; a similar Te Deum was chanted at the same hour in every cathedral in France. In December of this same year he proclaimed himself Emperor.

Not long after the previous letter reached Mrs. Ogilvy, Elizabeth learned of a reference to herself in her friend Miss Mitford's new book *Recollections of a Literary Life*. The passage, including a reference to Elizabeth's brother's death, was picked out and reprinted in full in numerous periodicals. Mrs. Ogilvy clipped and preserved one such reprint which appears as Appendix D, pages 209-210. Together with the Philaret Chasles lectures, this invasion of privacy was extremely painful to Elizabeth.

A phenomenal reader of novels, Elizabeth had long been familiar with contemporary French fiction and had greatly admired George Sand for years. Hearing she was in Paris, the Brownings presented a letter of introduction from Mazzini and Elizabeth risked a rare winter's outing to call upon her on February 15.

Elizabeth had enthusiastically followed the career of the poet and statesman Alphonse de Lamartine for several decades. A leader in the 1848 revolution, he became the chief spokesman for the provisional government, but lost his power when Louis Napoleon made his *coup d'état*. Elizabeth made several unsuccessful attempts to meet him.

It was about this time that they learned of the death of the traveller and novelist Eliot Warburton. He was on a mission to explore Panama aboard the *Amazon*, when it was destroyed by fire on January 4, 1852. Mrs. Ogilvy published a poem, "The Death of Eliot Warburton," in *Poems of Ten Years, 1846-1855* (London: Thomas Bosworth, 1856). This poem is reprinted in Appendix B, pages 198-201.

On March 8, 1852, Thomas Carlyle wrote Robert a long letter praising his "Essay on Shelley." This letter is printed in full in *Letters of Thomas Carlyle to John Stuart Mill, John Sterling and Robert Browning* (London: T. Fisher Unwin, Ltd., 1923), pages 291-293.

138 Avenue Ch. Elysées
March 18. [1852]

I have behaved so undeniably ill, my ever dear friend, that I am very much ashamed of myself—and it does not improve the matter extremely, that I was on the point of writing to you when your second letter arrived. Yet if you could read my inmost feelings as well as you can even this page, I should not have to say to you "forgive me." I have taken to be a great sinner lately about writing letters—everybody complaining of me the same way,—and my apparent bestial ingratitude . . to Mr. Stuart for instance . . being almost beyond sackcloth & ashes. Ah, but dont punish me . . that's all . . dont punish me with silence against silence . . an eye for an eye! *Write* daggers (if there are to be daggers) & use none otherwise. If I had been at Florence, & you here this winter, I should have behaved more decently, I think. I have not been as well as usual . . for one thing . . though, of late, I have revived again, & am looking not much the worse perhaps for the fog on the Te Deum day. We have had a sun during the present month, like a Florentine sun, almost . . a sun that burns, & necessitates parasols, & forces one to put the fire out. Nothing can be more absurd than to say that the climate of Paris does not materially excel what is found in London. It is altogether another thing. At the same time, I yearn back to my Florence—I love Florence to my heart. Paris is to Florence, a set of advantages against a set of attractions—though you must not think that I do not very much like Paris. Robert who "began with a little aversion," likes it even more than I do, I fancy, . . which is not surprising when you consider one thing with another, for he can breathe just as well in the cold as in the warm, & has gone a good deal into society, which I insisted upon. He might have stayed at Florence without loss, if he had shut himself up here, you know. That would have been absurd.

Always I have put off writing to you till I could write fully & at ease . . & little things have happened very vexatiously sometimes. For instance . . when your first letter came . . I was precisely then, wishing for a broad piece of one of Carlyle's "eternal silences" to wrap myself in . .

wishing to be in a desert somewhere, with the sands over
head. Of all the birds in the air, fish in the sea, & beasts
on dry land, I would rather, just then, have been an ostrich.
Which did not make me less glad to receive your letter,
understand . . only loth to write a word in return, or indeed
do anything in the world that I was'nt forced to do. So
vexed I was . . so completely upset I was, by my dear
friend Miss Mitford's most affectionate intentions involving lamentable indiscretions . . by that clasp of her warm
true hand which cut to the bone. Ah, you do not perhaps
completely understand . . it is difficult perhaps for any . .
for I do believe that I am morbid on some points. There's
an arrow which broke in me, & the common air makes the
wound ache. I cannot bear one sort of word even from
Robert . . & when he says "my poor little Ba, how they
teaze her!" perhaps his very tenderness does unconsciously
imply the knowledge of some weak childishness on my part.
Certainly the idea of unnameable agonies being pulled up
out of their dark hole, & classed & ticketed & held up to
the public, was horrible to me, & turned me sick, almost to
fainting. Not that I had courage to read the paragraphs in
question. It was enough to have them suggested, & to know
that such things were going the round of the English newspapers, as something very entertaining indeed. Good Heavens!—how hard it is for one's best friends to know one.
She meant very well—she meant really to *please me*!!!—
She did not say I think, that I had red hair or blue eyes,
yet she mistook the colour of the heart as completely.

Yet I had got over all this a good deal. The soreness
returns, on the use made of the materials so supplied, at
the Collége de France, by M. Philaret Chasles, who has
been lecturing about me the last two tuesdays. We heard
of it accidentally from my uncle who happened to be there,
& Robert went yesterday to hear the rest of it. M. Chasles,
not finding the Mitford story sufficiently romantic for his
ends, embroidered deeply with gold & silk, & produced a

tragedy about a fiancé, which would have done honour, Robert says, to Dumas himself. Not one word of truth from beginning to end, but the most picturesque details (en revanche) including the "waving of handkerchiefs," the consolations received "in farmhouses," & final residences in "magnificent palaces of the Medici," called Casa Guidi. One poem of mine, "The Poet's Vow" was written, do you know, to reclaim Robert from "pantheism" in which he was deeply dyed—"ce poete obscur, mystique . . du reste celebre."— M. de Tocqueville said to an acquaintance of ours that "he & the friends who were with him, were offended by the indelicacy of the whole exhibition, . . that such things were not commonly done in France, & could only be considered ungentlemanly." Lie upon lie, too—lies heaped up, pressed down, & running over. The *animus*, excessively kind, it is right to say. But lie or not lie, & whatever the animus . . to be cut up alive on the anatomical table, seems to me a hideous fate for a woman . . even though it be done with a golden knife & by her particular friend—even though it be done in the Collége de France & by a kindly inclined lecturer. Cut up my poems & welcome . . cut them up heart & brain . . probe & burn . . I never yet complained of what was done to any work of mine. But my *me* should be safe till I am dead. These nerves, this live flesh, should be forborne, while they can yet quiver & shrink. I should be let alone (I who never did much harm to anybody) to build wooden houses on the floor with my child, a short time longer. Surely one may love Art, yet keep the door shut.

All which vexation is nothing of course, beside the fear I had about my darling. Robert says I exaggerate . . & the panic I had *one night* was *not* justified by the occasion— still, it was natural to be frightened, for he rolled his eyes & did not recognize us for a quarter of a minute . . that was plain. Robert was out then—I sent out for him & bade him bring the physician of the embassy . . but by the time they came, the child was in a deep sleep, & Dr. Macarthy assured us that much could not certainly be wrong while a sleep so tranquil was possible. He came again the next day & examined the little creature carefully—eyes, skin, expression, stomach, head . . "The child was in perfect health it seemed to him quite clear, & he could not conscientiously tear him to pieces with medecines." He ordered quiet, & the sixth part of half a grain of 'Bella donna' every night, & so took leave as a professional visitor. Two double teeth are coming, the twenty first & second, but the gums, though swollen, are not inflamed, & there has been no pretext for using the lancet. I think myself we were too slow about giving medecine. Dr. Macarthy said it was a tendency to hysterical convulsion through some over excitement of the system . . the teeth probably abetting. Since then, he has had no attack to frighten one, though nearly always after waking in the morning, there has been something of the sort, . . only more & more slight— You would observe nothing, if you were not watching. If you watched, you would see a catching of the breath, for half a minute at a time, just as if he were plunged into cold water, . . accompanied generally with a slight quiver through the legs . . then he laughs, . . & immediately (without transition) begins singing quietly to himself, & beating time to the music with his hands. It's the most curious affliction you ever saw, I am confident. When it's at all bad, he fixes his eyes for a moment looking upward with a seraphical look—the cheeks being redder than usual. When I have said, "Dont laugh, darling; why do you laugh," the answer came sadly, "Peninni no bene, Mamma." There seems to be a sort of discomfort, which he expresses by kissing us all passionately, as if we were to help him. As to fretfulness or anything like it, it seems impossible to the child. His disposition is angelical to a degree which makes my blood run cold sometimes. When I have been wrapping his feet in a warm flannel, he has caught hold of my sleeve

& kissed it, saying "Mamma è buona." Well, but at last, I may thank God & admit that the evil seems gradually wearing itself out—indeed I may almost call it gone within the last few days. The curious thing is, that since the child has been an "invalid," he has seemed to everybody to particularly grow & flourish. Appetite good, sleep sound, spirits unquencheable. When the teeth are *through*, we shall be all right I hope & pray. Thank you gratefully my dear kind friend, for your excellent advice on guarding him from the excitement of too much amusement. I think you are right, & we have been ill advised very often. He is now banished from the face of Punch, & taken out to walk beyond the 'barrière.' He has too many ideas in his head, & is far too exciteable in every way.

So very sorry I am that you should have been anxious too about your boy. Only, . . remember (so at least Dr. Chambers says) what is commonly called *chicken pox*, is nothing but a modification of small pox—and thus, one of the dangerous possibilities of life is escaped through his illness. He must be a darling, & I long to see him—indeed I long to see all the dear children, to say nothing of hearing Marcia talk. I dare say she talks better than Wiedeman, though he is tremendously loquacious after the manner of the Sphinxes. Should *you* understand "a roasted apple" I wonder, by "uno pomme *yoicko*" (arrostito.)?

Oh yes—we shall be in Paris still I think, early in May, & very glad we shall be then to take an apartment for you near us, & very delighted to have you near us again. Take care of yourself, & dont be too tired on the road, if you can help it.

With regard to politics, . . no, I am "pleased" with nothing very much. I like compression of journals no better than the journalists do, nor confiscation of Orleans property, than the Orleanists themselves. I do not even hold fast to model constitutions. A Buonapartist, I am not indeed in any sense, although Wiedeman compromises me a good deal by his favorite cry of 'Viva Peone' (Napoleone.) which people say I teach him. But what I differ from you all in completely, is (I think modestly) some comprehension of a most difficult & exceptional situation, some effort towards guessing at the nature of motives & impelling causes, . . much hope therefore for the future, . . & a most ineffable indignation & shame for the tone taken up in England. The misrepresentation of facts, the gross falsifications & exaggerations of the English press . . from our friend the Examiner, to the Quarterly Review have profoundly disgusted me,—& the "invasion cry" the burden of all, is still more puerile & considerably more immoral, it seems to me, than the "ecclesiastical titles" cry last year, was. I feel really grateful to the Cobdens & Humes for talking a little sense, where the poet laureate failed. The whole French situation has been mistaken to a degree which would be ludicrous if it were not lamentable . . to a degree which history will scoff at, & which I (for one,) have often been inclined to shed hot tears upon, in the fear of possible consequences to that mistake. Great irritation was caused by the English journals among the French . . & I dont mean the Buonapartists. I heard one of the most loyal & noble of men, a man of the highest intellect, (much more Anglomane in general than I am) admit that it was scarcely possible for a frenchman to keep his temper in the face of such falsehood & insult. *"England means well to us, I believe . . but it is certainly shameful to the press of England, that correspondents should be employed who pick up lies in the mud & call them facts."*

The great fact is (when all has been said & sworn about military despotism & the rest) the great fact is, that Louis Napoleon stands entirely at the moment by the *democracy*, & that the apprehension should be, of his going too far with measures in the ultra-popular sense. There's the danger just now. It's the very reverse of what has been predicted by certain prophets. The bourgeoisie, which approved

of the coup d'etat, shrinks back, but the people press nearer
& nearer. The Orleanistic decree was very popular with
the people, for instance, from the first . . & the late financial measures have commended themselves much to the
masses. His tendencies are that way, most clearly. But I
do not think, myself, that he will touch socialistical ex-
tremes—he has too much ability & has considered the subject too deeply for it, I think. I hold him to be a man of
very extraordinary powers, & to have the Napoleon blood
in him, let the scandalmongers swear what they please.
Guizot says too that he is honest—so does George Sand—
so, does our noble friend M. Milsand . . all three of them
eschewing Buonapartism, & constituting together a high
testimony to my mind—& to Robert's . . though Robert
says frankly that having a "personal hatred" to the man
(& the blood, he might add) he has not patience to ana-
lyze things very closely. Sympathy with the monarchical
parties we have none,—and if the extreme Reds had carried
their alternative, France would probably have perished.
The Marrast constitution had become an impossibility! You
should examine the socialistic ideas as stated by their
writers, to judge if liberty could have been greater with
the Louis Blancs than the Louis Napoleons,—Louis Blanc's
great doctrine being political centralization,—& the suppres-
sion of all journals except one in the right sense, being,
according to Cabet, a condition of a perfectly "free state."
Also, we shall have more liberty presently—we must be
patient & wait. The decrees are not "carried out"—for
instance, you get as usual all the English journals—more
freely than under Louis Phillippe.

We made our way to George Sand with the greatest difficulty, & with all the stones of the enchanted mountain
calling us back. But she received us most cordially, &
"likes us," it appears, which pleases me extremely. My
heart beat when we met first, & in the natural emotion of
that moment, I stooped & kissed the hand she held out

to me, . . but she said quickly "non, je ne veux pas," & kissed my lips. She has radiant black eyes & a noble forehead, but the mouth is not good, & the smile of it rather flashes than shines, over the white projecting teeth. Her glossy hair, very dark, is braided back from the face. Never was a more simple woman.

Robert knows Lamartine too, but I could'nt go with him last saturday when he went. I would run the risk of my life, only to see George Sand. Yes—I went out, too, to buy toys for Wiedeman on his birthday, & Robert & I nearly ruined ourselves on that occasion, spending fifteen francs & a half!—

Robert was only an acquaintance, not a friend of poor Eliot Warburton—but the event shocked him much. Mrs. Warburton was in a state of distraction at first. She is expecting the birth of her third child, the eldest being not much older than ours. You should read Ma^{dme} Ossoli's memoirs, though it is a heartbreaking book. A noble woman, indeed! Carlyle says that Robert's essay is "the first human voice he had heard for ever so long"—but you see what a scrape we are all in about the forgery-conviction. Still, Robert is not implicated any wise. God bless you all. Our love to Mr. Ogilvy, & your sister. I have written at last I think. Your ever affectionate EBB.

When dear Mr. Ogilvy calls next on Mr. Otley, will he leave this note for M. Centopanti in the mezzonino. It takes Casa Guidi on for another year. But our plans remain uncertain.

N. B. *Blouses* are not worn here by children as young as Alessandro. I asked a high mantua-making authority about Wiedeman's & she quite smiled & said, "Not before two or three years." Love to the darlings. A Mr. Shore enquires about you, & speaks of Miss Dick as being celebrated in India for refusing everybody!! Can you read this? I have scribbled so fast that I fear for the results.

Address: Italie | À Madame | Madame Ogilvy | Poste Restante | Firenze | Toscana. *Postmarks:* PARIS 18 MARS 52; PD.; 22 MAR 1852 FIRENZE.

Letter 14

This letter announces that the Brownings had found an apartment for the Ogilvys shortly before they arrived in Paris around May 1, 1852. Mrs. Ogilvy's poem on their leaving Florence is reprinted in this volume in Appendix B, pages 196-198.

The brief mention which Mrs. Ogilvy gives in her memoir of their visit to Paris relates only the pleasant events. She failed to recall that when she arrived she found Pen with a cough, which she correctly diagnosed as the whooping cough. Her children, despite precautions, caught the ailment as well, and their departure was delayed for a week.

138 Avenue des Ch. Elysées.

April 24. [1852]

My dear friends, we have succeeded I think in the great search, and if you dont object to the price (two hundred & fifty francs) & to being on the second floor, I am almost sure you will like the rest. We had intended to settle you at a much cheaper rate, and I confess to you that your requirements might have been met at a less sum,—but as you give us licence as far as three hundred, I really do think that we are justified in giving two hundred & fifty for such a quantity of room & cleanliness & such a delightful situation. You have five bedrooms, salon & salle à manger, kitchen, antichamber &c, & carpets everywhere. Mr. Ogilvy can have his dressingroom, & you will all have air, & silence at need. To have taken you a squeezed up apartment at two hundred, involving the necessary nursery-thunders during every half hour of the day, would scarcely have been fifty francs cheaper to you, dearest Mrs. Ogilvy, now that you are ill & nervous. You have attendance in the house (for everything except cooking dinners) at twenty five francs the month. Of course you bring linen & plate, therefore I have said nothing of either. A family is in occupation of the apartment at present & will be till the twenty ninth, so that I have taken it exactly as you desired, from the first of May. You will be close to us, and your windows have a splendid view of the great 'Avenue,' & I earnestly hope that altogether you will be as contented as I am.

Yet we failed of one desire we had—that of settling you in this house. But as Mr. Byrne our Irish 'proprietaire,' insists on asking three hundred francs for very inferior accommodation, we must be just to you & not think of our own interests too much. Also, you will be very near us. It will be just the difference of putting on a bonnet.

How glad we shall be to see you—how very glad! Wiedeman is properly indoctrinated in the approaching arrival of "suo fratello," but as a "fratello" seems to remain a very mythical sort of personage to him, clearly to be classed with at least the "angiolini," I have more success in evoking the memories of the "tre bambini" of Florence who used to take tea with him. Either he remembers or pretends to remember them perfectly, . . together with the 'gondolas' of Venice!

Mrs. Jameson has taken rooms in this house, & will remain for a month or more. Our own plans are uncertain, but we shall probably be in England at the end of June for a time, reserving Italy for the winter.

"Miss Mitford's great age"!— But she is not of a great age, I am glad to say. She is as young, too, in the spirit, as you yourself are,—and as to any man or woman on the earth, venturing to put out a finger in order "to arrange her papers," it is quite out of the possibilities. So—all that can be said is, . . what's kindly meant should be accepted in a kind spirit . . if the temper can admit of it.

I direct this as you desire. You may arrive at any hour on the first of May,—only I wish it were possible to have a line from you naming the hour, for your own sakes, that there might be preparation according to it.

Dont fancy I have been taking writing lessons, though I do write so much worse than usual. Here's a pen like a poker, and a post hour too pressing! With love from us all three to all of you, believe me your ever affectionate
                    Elizabeth Barrett Browning.
Drive to *1. Rue de l'Oratoire, Champs Elysées.* It's a corner house. The coup d'etat has had the effect of raising prices & Paris is very full.

Address: Madame Ogilvy | Poste Restante | Lyons. *Postmark:* LYON 25 AVRIL 52.

Letter 15

The Ogilvys left Paris for London on June 8, with plans to remain there for two weeks before proceeding to Perth.

                    138 Avenue des Champs Elysées
                    June 18. [1852]
My dear friend, I was delighted to have your letter—quite thankful & relieved. Yes, and I sympathize deeply with your burst of patriotism, and with that admirable interpretation of the phrase, "mal de pays," for which you should be honored among interpreters. Certainly that peculiar form of the "mal" is the very one I am subject to myself. "Hence these tears," would say a classical writer. Hence this cough & all manner of evil, must *I* say, who have the misfortune of being romantic & a modern Briton.

Your letter found us in sunshine, but for the last five days we have been humiliated, I confess to you, in our weather, . . the thunder having at last succeeded in upsetting the summer. We have had a great deal of rain, in fact, with lucid intermissions of April skies,—& rather a cool April too, which has not done me much good, especially since I went out one night when I should have staid in the house. Not one of the five days was absolutely a rainy one, although yesterday it rained till *three*, & then let the sun shine. Now it shines beautifully . . but there are questionable clouds in the horizon which may be swept up by the south wind. We cant trust this sun of ours.

I am afraid of hearing that you are to leave London on such a day. We shall not be there until the beginning of July, & our chances of finding you must be small. Which vexes me to think of. Yet I dont at all feel as if I should'nt see you soon—indeed I do feel as if I should: and Robert has the same sort of presentiment, happily for both of us. So, we agreed as we passed your house the other day, consoling one another for having to pass it. Kiss the darling children for me. A "sposa" lately was proposed to Wiedeman, but he said . . "No. *Lis*" (this) "no bella— Peninni, Lilla. Lilla bella e *lanc*" (grande.) Peninni would have Louisa, Louisa being both "bella e grande." After such a proof of constancy, I am ashamed to spoil all by admitting that he finally proposed an arrangement of having two wives. He suggested that it would cut the difficulty. Tell me if Alexander's cough has teazed him again or not. Wiedeman's is perfectly gone.

We went to Ary Scheffer's again two evenings ago, to hear music in the atelier. Madame Viardot, the great 'prima donna,' was there . . but "her voice was still in bed" she told us, to quench all hope of her singing. No wonder—as she had a baby about three weeks ago. She accompanied on the piano, however, M. Léonard, the first player on the violin, from the Conservatoire—a wonderful performer indeed. And Madame Léonard sang—and altogether it was very pleasant. Madame Viardot was the original 'Consuelo' of George Sand. She is plain—a large face with irregular features, but capable of extraordinary expression of course . . although in society one does not see it much. You know she has always been absolutely pure of reputation . . which does not hinder a strong friendship between her & George Sand, of whom she spoke warmly to me as "so good" and "such a thorough woman." Another friend of Madame Sand was there also,— . . M. Martin, the ex-montagnard. He asked me if I did not find Paris "changed and saddened." I evaded the question by saying that I knew Paris only from last autumn. I really could'nt flatter him by any appearance of sensibility to the profound melancholy of the Parisians. Not even the rain (much less the president) has prevented the nightly dances at the château des Fleurs—& although I remember a tragic situation in Ford (which has been much admired) of a woman who dances on, dances on, while one misery after another is announced to her, & then suddenly drops & dies, . . I dont quite expect a like catastrophe of despair from the Parisian population in the middle of the Cancans dance. Do even *you*, who are anti-presidential?

Talking on which subject, let me record my protestation against the intended paper-tax. I hope it may never be more than a threat & a fear, but I quite disapprove of it, tell Mr. Ogilvy.

I think we shall not follow your example in taking the long passage, notwithstanding your prosperity *as it happened*. Robert talks of Dover & Calais in a 'signorile' sort of way—that is, in the way of a man who has been very sick. I dread it all . . that is, I dread the end of the journey. I shall have the nightmare all the time I am in England.

Tell me. Did Mr. Ogilvy pay more duty than a penny for every engraving . . which Mrs. Jameson says is the tariff? We should like to know. Mrs. Jameson particularly desired me to remember her to both of you, "because she liked you very much." I quote the exact words. Probably she will remain till we go, & travel back with us— it seems to me likely to end so.

God bless you both, & everyone—& give you a happy

meeting with your mother! I, who shall meet mine only in Heaven, may say it earnestly. Be well & happy, & be kind in telling me soon that you are. Robert's love with that of your ever affec<u>te</u> EBB.

My love to your sister, if she is near you now.

Letter 16

The Brownings arrived in London on July 6. Two days later Elizabeth wrote to Mrs. Jameson (who remained in Paris) of their calm channel crossing of five and a half hours. In the same letter she also reported the immediate family crisis: a Mrs. von Müller had sued Robert's father for breach of promise and defamation of character. Early in July the court ordered the father to pay a fine of £800; to avoid the payment, he and his daughter, Sarianna, decided to move abroad, and it fell upon Robert to escort them to their new home in Paris.

Another crisis came when Wilson decided not to go abroad again. Happily this ended with her reconsideration and her eventual return to Florence—but not without some anxious moments for the Brownings, who realized Pen's attachment to her. It is of interest to note that many years later, when Pen returned to live in Italy, he persuaded Wilson to live in his household until her death in 1902.

This letter indicates Elizabeth's concern about Mrs. Ogilvy's condition who was in Perth awaiting the birth of her child. The novelist and editor Mrs. Newton Crosland had supplied Elizabeth the latest news of her friend.

[London, August 5, 1852]

I am getting so anxious about you, my dear friend, that I do wish you would send me a word. I have heard of you through Mrs. Crosland,—& there is the last!—and by this time there must surely be good news to tell. Wont Mr. Ogilvy write to me, if you cant? Remember that you have made no sort of sign in reply to my last letter—not a sign!

Since we have been in London (& we have been here a month), we have been over laid, overpowered, by engagements & various sorts of unpleasant business. England is not lucky to us—we were not intended for patriots. Well—to make up for it, people have been & are really very kind, & we shall leave them all with some grateful thoughts. Then, the heat, this summer, however heavy & strangling, has been favorable rather than otherwise to my chest; so that I have not suffered as I usually do in England. In spite of which, we turn our faces towards Italy . . as far as winter-dreams go . . it being all dream-work with us still, & very indistinct. I have had the comfort of seeing both my sisters. Henrietta stayed a fortnight within a few doors of us. Wiedeman's frocks fit her Altham of seventeen months, much to my humiliation, . . but I catch up my glory in other ways, for my minute darling is universally admired for his 'gentilezza' & grace. He talks incessantly, with a considerably improved flow of language, & having put aside all shyness, is seen to more advantage.

Ah—so vexed I have been this morning! Wilson is going to leave us—she has made up her mind, she says, not to go abroad again. It vexes me far less, of course, as a matter of inconvenience than as a disappointment of . . . I may say, the affections. I thought she cared more for me & the child, than to leave us so. She had applied before to have her wages raised to twenty guineas, which we had'nt in our power to do—& I suppose she thinks that she can improve her position in respect to money. Well—I hope so—& that she may lose nothing otherwise.

We were asked to spend tomorrow with the Tennysons at Twickenham, but must choose another day on account of a provoking engagement. Mrs. Tennyson is very near her confinement. Also, Monkton Milnes has a baby a day old, which he swears is like a little red Indian & incompetent to produce a throb of love in him. Mrs. Milnes gave birth to it under the influence of chloroform, talking German fluently all the time (a language she is quite ignorant of) & unconscious of a pang. I am going to see the baby. I give Mr. Milnes a week to develop his paternal instincts, & then, according to my prediction, he is to be as foolish as the rest of us.

Do write a word. I send you a note upon babies, feeling instinctively that babyology will be more welcome to you just now than most other of the *ologies*. My love to Mrs. Ogilvy—& to Mr. Ogilvy—& kisses to the darlings. Peninni has learnt to say, "Peninni vuole" . . "Peninni non può aspettare," & various despotic phrases, which are called into constant use—but, after all, it is considered miraculous in my family, that so good a child should result from my spoiling. God bless you. I do long to hear of you. Robert's love.

Your ever affectionate
Elizabeth Barrett Browning.

58 Welbeck Street. Cavendish square.
Thursday.

Dont forget to say how you found dear Mrs. Ogilvy looking,—& how you bear Perth.

Address: Mrs. David Ogilvy | Perth | N.B. *Postmarks:* St. Marylebone St; FE AU-5 1852; PERTH AU 6 1852.

Letter 17

In response to Elizabeth's request of the previous letter Mr. Ogilvy had written to the Brownings to say that on August 9 a second son, Walter Tulliedeph, had been born. Elizabeth writes congratulations.

[London, August 12, 1852]

My dear Mr. Ogilvy,

I must send you one word of congratulation from the hearts of both of us, upon the happy event you have been so kind as to give me the news of. Thank you for having done so—and thank God above all! She is glad, . . is she not? . . to have another little son. I think she wanted a companion to Alexander—who, however, loses his exclusive glory of male dignity in the eyes of his sisters— Will you let me know in a day or two how the dear mother & child are going on? I shall be anxious to have the good account confirmed.

And just now I receive a letter from Mr. Tennyson, with a like happy tiding. You know, his first child was only born, & died directly, & he took it grievously to heart. Now, they have another . . "a fine boy," he says, . . and his letter is written in such a glow of delight, that one feels sure of the great heart of a man who could write so. I never liked him so much, though always I did like him. His wife's health is very delicate, & he had had fears of course, more than are inseparable from such occasions.

Nothing but babies among the poets just now, you see!

But we cant be present at your christening, as we are invited to be at Monkton Milnes's next week.

Thank you for wishing us nearer. I wish we were indeed. With Robert's love to you all, believe me, dear Mr. Ogilvy,

affec^{te}ly yours

Elizabeth Barrett Browning.

58 Welbeck street.

Thursday

I have still some hope that Wilson's intention of leaving us may not be final.

Letter 18

In this letter Elizabeth acknowledges receiving some of Mrs. Ogilvy's verses. It is possible that she sent a manuscript version of the poem later published as "A Family Picture" in *Poems of Ten Years* (see Appendix B, pages 195-196).

Friday. [September 3, 1852]

58 Welbeck Street. [London]

My dearest Mrs. Ogilvy you will have thought me (besides other chastising thoughts) unworthy of your verses. Yet I

was glad to have them as I ought . . & very, very glad to
see your writing again . . very thankful that all the perils
should be over for you & your friends . . of whom I am
one, surely!— You must be delighted with your new little
Walter—but he was not born upon "English ground" . .
how do you make it out?— "British" . . is the most that
can be said. If he is small, he must be unlike your other
children. Do tell me if the wetnurse is satisfactory physi-
cally . . which is the chief thing—& if the baby resembles
any of his predecessors in face. I want to be able to fancy
him.

My dear friend, we have not made up our minds yet
about Rome—that is, we HAVE made up our *minds*, but
the finances are not made up to the point of carrying out
the wish. It's a long journey, & it is'nt clear whether we
can afford it. If we cant, we go to Paris again, & there
are worse fates.

I have been rather worn out with the toils of London,
which have been multitudinous in spite of the dead season
of the year. How it would have happened to us, if "everybody had not gone out of town" as people say, I really
cannot imagine. Scarcely a day passes without engagements—but now I have done. Wilson is gone to pay a fortnight's visit to her mother, & I am bound to Wiedeman
body & soul, washing, dressing, sleeping with him, giving
him his meals . . I get me . . not to a nunnery . . but the
nursery . . which must be much the same thing. The child
is so good & precious, that I would rather wait on him than
on the grandeurs literary & otherwise of this world, & it
really wont tire me much more. Perhaps, not as much. I
am in spirits because Wilson stays with us. There was a
misunderstanding or something like it—& now she says
she never could leave the child or me—so we are all happy
again. We shall probably remain in England till the end of
the present month, or as long as the weather will let us.
My chest has been better on the whole, & a great deal

better, than last year, because of the comparative warmth—
but there has been some east wind & much strangling heavy
air.

. Last saturday & last monday (on both days) we break-
fasted with Rogers. He is subdued & gentle, & interested
me much—all the bitterness seems turned into sweetness as
he approaches the great Light. He may live years yet,
sitting in that armchair with that monumental face of his.

Tennyson's child I have not seen, but it is said to be a
nice baby. He was to have been present at Mr. Milnes's
christening luncheon, & we were disappointed when people
began to whisper that, as it was three minutes past the time,
he would'nt come certainly. He is celebrated for the royal
virtue, punctuality.

Do you really think of Dresden as a place of residence?
The climate is perilous, from what I hear of its peculiarities
—but the advantages of cheapness & artistic resourse are of
course undeniable. Tell me whether Marcia talks most English or Italian now. Wiedeman is wonderfully improved in
matters of language, and keeps steadily to Italian for the
groundwork. He has collected heaps of English words, &
struggles to use them as much as possible in 'colloquies'
with the natives, but he twines his sentences by means
of Italian—talking from morning till night—he ought to
speak plainer, my sister says, after so much exercise. Oh—
he uses verbs now, I assure you! he discourses eloquently.
And do you know, he is really a better, sweeter child than
ever, & quite as affectionate. Write soon to me, do. I
have seen Mr. Kingsley, "Christian socialist" & author of
'Alton Locke' &c—& was much struck by his originality &
intenseness. Few men have pleased me more. With every
tendency to wildness & exaggerated colouring, he never
can speak or write otherwise than according to a noble
nature, I am sure.

Our love to all of you. Thank dear Mr. Ogilvy for his
little note—& think of us sometimes both of you. My dear

friend, I am most affectionately yours EBB.

Address: Mrs. David Ogilvy | King's Place | Perth | N.B. *Postmarks:*
St. Marylebone St.; SE 3 1852; PERTH SE 4 1852.

Letter 19

The Brownings delayed their departure from England to attend the
christening of Hallam Tennyson, but because of the weather Elizabeth was unable to attend. During Robert's absence Elizabeth began
this letter telling her friend she would be able to return to Italy for
the winter, since John Kenyon had provided the necessary funds.
The Brownings left London on October 12.

15 Bentinck street [London]

5th October [1852]

My dear friend, We are still here . . that is, in London.
We have had a revolution in our house from the insolence
of the landlady, & at half an hour's notice had to remove
. . which was nearly as much trouble as going to Paris. We
remain in England till next saturday, & then we go. Here
is the scheme. We stay in Paris one, . . two, weeks . . as it
may happen; proceed to Italy by Marseilles & Nice, along
the coast, by Genoa & Spezzia,—stay at Florence (if our
house should be unlet) till the beginning of December,
then, go to Rome, & after Easter to Naples. A most delightful prospectus, I think, and one rendered possible only
at the ninth hour . . for we had quite given up Italy this
year for financial reasons, when our dear generous friend
Mr. Kenyon insisted on modifying them because of having
strongly in his head that Italy would be better for me than
Paris for a second winter. So we go—we are in spirits about
it, & are prepared to enjoy ourselves as far as God will permit. For my part, this England (after the pain of leaving
my sister Arabel passes) will be, as ever, a load thrown off,
& heart as well as lungs will be the better for crossing the

sea. We mean to be extravagant & cross at Folkestone, & have no more water-voyage afterwards. The coast-travelling by Nice will be delightful,—will it not? I forget if you ever went that way.

We intended to have left England today, but a letter came to ask us, with so much earnest kindness, to be present at the christening of the Tennyson-baby at Twickenham, that we resolved to stay till saturday. After all, today comes with a bleak, bitter wind . . & when I had my bonnet on, Robert took fright & insisted that I should not run the risk of it. So he went alone— There's to be the christening at one oclock, and the christening breakfast at three—and I am vexed, for I should have liked to have seen the baby, to say nothing of the poet. But Robert was undeniably wise. For the last ten days I have suffered much from a tearing cough, & cannot leave the house except at intervals. Such a climate! We are much too late, & have been caught in the fogs & winds. Wilson was three weeks away, & although I wished that, there was a great deal of accumulated work to do on her return. We could'nt get away earlier. Then came the Tennyson christening.

I must tell you that my sister Henrietta has a little girl . . which fills me up to the brim with covetousness. She was ill only three hours, & is now as well as possible,—thank God for it! Such joy it is to know of her safety before we set out on our journey. Her boy is beginning to walk alone.

How I should like to see your Walter. But I thought he was to be called *Napier*— How is that? I am writing while Arabel & Peninni are in full conversation & I cant help listening to what they say to the manifest deterioration of my letter-writing. Peninni has learnt heaps of English words, & discourses fluently now . . for *him*! Whether he talks Italian or English, you might take him all the same for a Chinese or Ætheopian. Always he uses the third person when speaking of himself—and he tells you, or would tell you, that "Peninni knows *plompity* poems" . . (a quantity of poems) . . He does really know . . learned, during the three weeks of Wilson's absence, . . some two hundred nursery rhymes. "Baa, baa, black sheep" & such like. The child's intelligence for such things seemed to take a sudden shoot. He insisted on all manner of such classics being repeated to him, & after one or two times of hearing, he could repeat them himself to the surprise of all of us, using the most dramatic intonation & gesture to make up for the imperfect articulation. He means to have his father's memory. We could just as soon teach him a "Latin verb" as anything else—but we *would not*—oh, not for the world! Nobody thinks of giving him a lesson. Robert would be furious if they did. I assure you, I rather try to keep him from drawing & writing too much . . he is absorbed in his drawings for hours together very often . . the industry being incited a good deal by a prodigious quantity of self-approbation & aspiration. Oh, he had the modesty to present one of his drawings to Mr. Ruskin & another to Mr. Millais the head of the Pre-Raffaellites!—just as I have the conceit to send one to you— The autograph accompanying the drawings is absolutely genuine, unassisted by push or pull of a finger, & I am about as vain of it as the child himself, (it must be confessed) who accomplished the various great works contained in this paper, with shouts of triumphant laughter. Oh—such a darling he is! So good & sweet! There was some regret in me after all, when Wilson came back, & I missed the clinging arms round my neck at six oclock in the morning while the darling voice said *"De—ar Ba! Mama! apro occhi."*

The account you send me of the children is delightful, but of yourself, not so good. Do take care of yourself this winter, & get away from Perth if it does decidedly disagree. And dont be sorry that Alexander has not yet begun the Latin grammar—I would as soon regret that he was'nt up to the three per cents & such like valuable knowledge . . useful enough at a mature age. Grammar & dictionaries "will come when they will come." We say the same of wrinkles.

Peninni prayed the other day that the soap-bubbles migh'nt "tomber." Did I tell you that before. He continues to use extempore prayer, & really it is pretty sometimes, to hear him. Once I heard him say (after the usual supplication for Papa, Mama, Lili & Flush) Peninni ama bene Dio. Dio ama bene Peninni. Amen." Was'nt that sweet of the child.

October 6.

The pressure of business on me just now is so great, that I am at my wits' end fairly. Forgive that I cannot write more.

Tennyson's child was christened *Hallam* Tennyson— There was a brilliant breakfast, Robert says, & the Laureate was very kind. The Tennysons talk a little of Rome for the winter & I shall be glad if they more than talk.

Much there is to say, but I cant say it. Write to me under cover to my sister, 50 Wimpole street, till I can send you a better address. God bless you. Our united love to all of you, not omitting dear Mrs. Ogilvy. Kiss the darlings for me. Remember us with a little love, & believe in the sincere affection of R & EBB—

Mind you keep Paris in thought & prospect.

Address: Mrs. David Ogilvy | King's Place | Perth. | N.B. *Postmarks:* Too Late G.P.O.; OC-6 1852; PERTH OC 8 1852.

Letter 20

Following a hard journey, the Brownings reached Casa Guidi in early November after an absence of nineteen months. They chose to settle in Florence for the winter rather than proceed to Rome.

In this letter Elizabeth speaks of her many local friends, including the elder brother of Alfred Tennyson, Frederick. Until they later moved to the Channel Islands, Frederick and his Italian wife were often in the Brownings' company. In the following letters, unless Elizabeth specifies otherwise, it is this Mr. Tennyson to whom she refers.

Florence. JanY 24. [1853]

My dear friend,

If you have not punished me by forgetting me altogether, you must be punishing me by hard thoughts—so I hope, upon the whole, you may be thinking of me very ill indeed. It seems to myself that I deserve ever so much punishment for my incredible idleness & procrastination, . . only none at all, believe me, for any want of memory & affectionateness towards you. So forgive me, because I can say that earnestly. Even now, . . so bad I am, . . perhaps I should not write if it were not that I long to hear from you. So dont deal with me according to the Law, but the gospel; & let me rather have coals of fire, than a long silence to avenge my own.

I found your letter on our arrival in Florence, & it was the next best thing to finding yourselves. I have the face to thank you for it now. A disastrous journey we had from Paris . . which perhaps made the beginning of my slowness about writing . . we were tempted at Lyons, by Bradshaw & the summer warmth, to cross the Mont Cenis— and the cold beginning at Chambéry, (together with the necessity of travelling three nights without once undressing) I was nearly extinct before we got to Turin. On the Mont Cenis itself, almost suffocation came on . . & our two days at Turin, though I got out painfully one morning to see the pictures, did not avail very much. The winds there, are chill with Alpine snow. So at Genoa, being broken down entirely, we had to remain at the hotel for ten days, I just fit to lie on the sofa by the open window, through which poured the full Italian summer . . Oh, such an exquisite climate. Every breath brought the life back to me—but I *wanted* life . . for the continued night fever & cough had worn me to the bone literally. You never saw such a spectral thinness! Poor Robert was horribly vexed of course, & so was I for his sake—only Italy soon revived me & I made a vow to him to take cod's liver oil as soon as ever we should arrive in Florence . . which (to cut short the subject) I did accordingly, and am now particularly well & strong, wonderfully well for me. We have had a nominal winter here. I dont remember such a winter in Florence at the very best of Florence, & though the Florentines object to the absence of the ordinary cold, you may suppose that I rejoice in it.

We found our house in excellent order, the carpets & furniture generally looking better than when we left them, we thought, . . and as, after all expenses were paid, we had six months use of the house for nothing (either to let or occupy as we pleased) there was no reason for lamenting our having retained it in our hands. Well—the old warm nest, still warm, was so very pleasant to us, that, instead of going to Rome, here we have lingered, . . & shall stay on till March. Then, we *must* go to Rome, then to Naples . . & then, then . . the cloud begins . . but I suppose we shall return to Paris to settle . . as far as we ever shall settle. In any case we have by no means decided on giving up this house. I *love it*—there's the truth.

And *you* . . what are your plans. We are so anxious to hear them. Yes—if we could take a house together in Paris, it would be excellent,—but when & how? I am afraid that only some sublime coincidence could bring us together, for we cant see an inch before us after Naples. My poor sister Arabel is expecting us in England this summer! We shall understand in time. Do write to say what *you* see for your parts.

We are living the old life just as if we had never known Paris. Paris is cast into a parenthesis . . and the sentence goes on. I can scarcely realize to my fancy the great whirl & thunder of Paris & London, in this silence & stilness. At first Robert felt it—dull—but we are very happy, though we have not spent one evening from home since we came. A few people, chiefly men, come for tea & talk, & that's all we see of the world. Mr. Stuart, Mr. Tennyson, the poet's brother . . a shy sensitive, refined man whom we both like much, . . Mr. Lytton (Sir Edward's only son) very young, but full of high aspiration; & somewhat visionary . . which pleases me . . he is attaché to the embassy. We miss you I cant say how much, but you may imagine it. Mr. Powers, too, comes to see us . . a great favorite of mine . . with his great spiritual eyes, and slow calculating voice . . wise for two worlds perhaps!   As to Mr. Kirkup, he is plunged into some mystery so deep that it hides him from our sight. "All his evenings are engaged," he says, "*he will tell Robert how some* day." Meanwhile . . it may be in the discovery of the true 'elixir vitæ,' for I never saw a man grown so much younger in the time.

I do wish you could see Wiedeman. His fellow citizens of Florence think him much improved, much prettier & more *grazioso*. His grace & golden ringlets draw so much attention in the Cascine that Wilson swears she is abashed by it. Seriously & earnestly there seldom has been such a darling! Do you know either I must be very happy or very vain, for there is not one thing in that child which I desire to see otherwise. The vivacity & the sweetness, the cleverness & the lovingness, the joyous nature & the tender ways . . all is complete in him as I see him . . all is rounded off harmoniously to my eye. Certainly the child has it all his own way . . he is never crossed in anything . . he has not that sort of temptation. But the most prosperous of spoilt children will have bad, violent tempers sometimes, & we used to think that he was naturally passionate. Well—there is no sign of it now. "Happily for him," . . as Wilson says— for there would be "no possibility of punishing him": we could'nt find it in our hearts. "Tiss me, Lily" he said to her one day after being a little naughty. "No—she would'nt

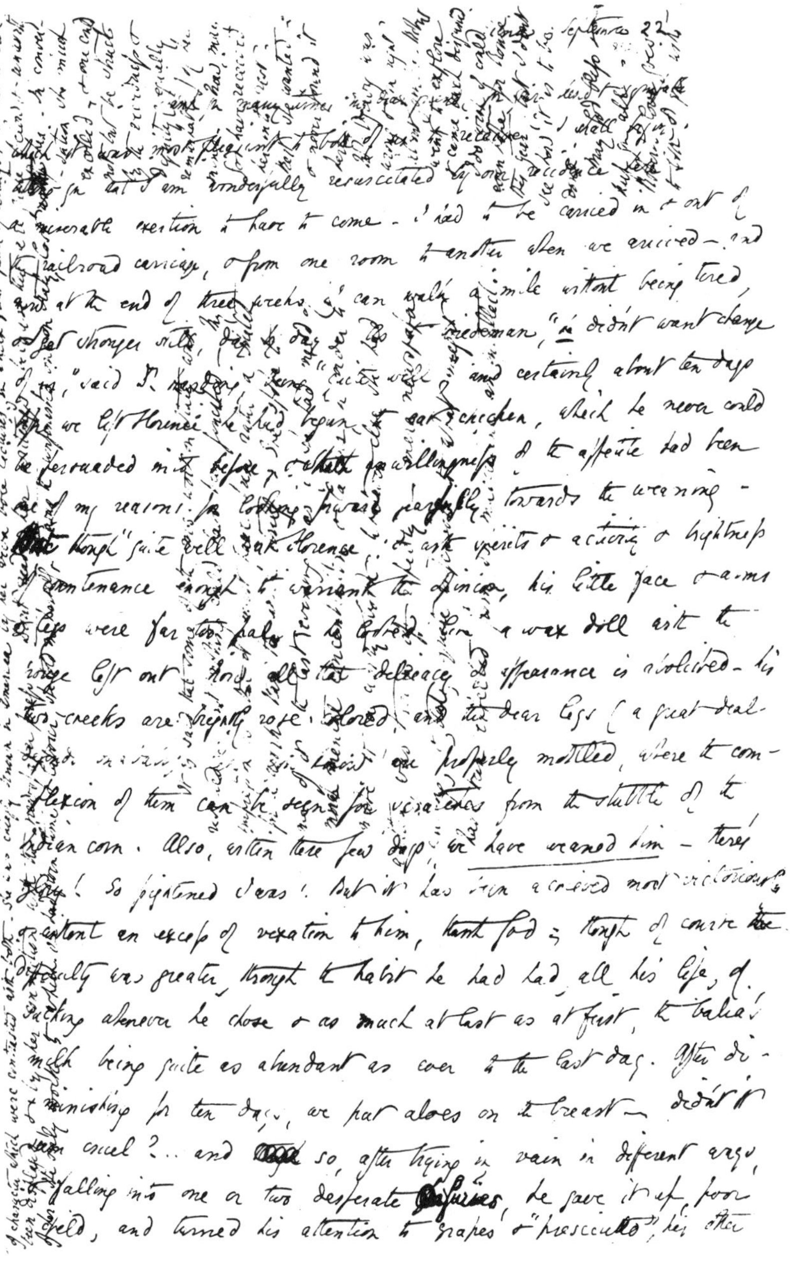

September 22

... that I am wonderfully resuscitated by our recent ...
a miserable exertion to have to come - I had to be carried in & out of the railroad carriage, & from one room to another when we arrived - and now at the end of three weeks I can walk a mile without being tired, & get stronger with day by day [illegible] Wiedeman, "He didn't want change [illegible]," said Dr. [illegible], "[illegible]" and certainly about ten days before we left Florence he had begun to eat chicken, which he never could be persuaded into before, & which unwillingness of the appetite had been one of my reasons for looking forward fearfully towards the weaning - though quite well at Florence, he wanted spirits & activity & lightness of countenance enough to warrant the [illegible], his little face & arms & legs were far too pale to look at. Now - a wax doll with the rouge left out - and all that delicacy of appearance is abolished - his two cheeks are brightly rose-coloured, and the dear legs (a great deal [illegible]) are properly mottled, where the complexion of them can be seen for scratches from the stubble of the Indian corn. Also, within these few days, we have weaned him - there's glory! So frightened I was! But it has been achieved most victoriously, & without an excess of vexation to him, thank God; though of course the difficulty was greater through the habit he had had all his life, of sucking whenever he chose & as much at last as at first, the baby's milk being quite as abundant as ever to the last day. After diminishing for ten days, we put aloes on the breast - didn't it [illegible] cruel? .. and [illegible] so, after trying in vain in different ways, falling into one or two desperate [illegible], he gave it up, poor child, and turned his attention to grapes & "prosciutto", his other

I. Letter 6: September 22, 1850, with signature excised.

II. Elizabeth with Pen, Rome, 1860.

III. Pen, Rome, 1860.

IV. Robert, Rome, 1860.

V. Elizabeth, Rome, May 27, 1861.

VI. Mrs. David Ogilvy, Dunfermline, 1864.

VII. Mr. David Ogilvy, London, c. 1865.

Both she and her husband ate little. I remember
a great mess suffered for dinner to them both
but he was very eloquent in food, and found not
the special dainty of every place we visited and
insisted on its being included in the bill of fare.

Mr Browning

He and his wife were a contrast in temperament
the one vehement talkative and hasty full of gesticulations, and fond of argument. She quiet,
half proud half humorous in her expression
as he expatiated, coming in now and then with
a little deprecating "Oh Robert" as a gentle drag
on his impetuosity — She could fire up on occasion but in general she was intense rather than
excitable, and she took life too seriously for her
own happiness. She could so little bear to pain any
one she loved, that I had to administer the baby's
medicine, to save her the trial. . . It was well for her
that she went before husband and child She could
not have survived them. Mr Barrett, her father was
a stern unforgiving man He never forgave her
marriage. When another sister dared to marry
Mrs B wrote to me "Henrietta has followed my example
in marrying against his will, it is the only way
possible in our family" Still she hoped that her
father might be softened by his grandson and
when they left us at Venice and went to London

14

VIII.   Manuscript Memoir by Mrs. David Ogilvy.

kiss a naughty boy." "Well, den! tiss *dat!*" putting his hand on her mouth with a sigh of resignation. Such a senti-mental child it is!— Yesterday Robert & I were sitting by the fire. He took a hand of each of us, and said softly . . "You two, mine flends!" (friends.) "Yes," observed Rob-ert," you know that we love you better than anybody, dont you?" "Les. I know. If you go away, nomony more (no-body more) love Penini. Only Lily. I tome in lis dwawing woom—No Papa and Mama! Den I tly (cry) velly mush. Den I die." Said in such pathetic tones that Robert had the tears in his eyes afterwards.

Robert has rather a passion than a love for the child. If I spoil, he spoils doubly—and I must tell you that I suffer pangs of jealousy just now, having been "pushed from my stool" where I used to be preeminent in the lit-tle creature's affections, somewhat too early I think. Now, Papa is everything—Mama though she draws "pretty well," is in a lower style of art altogether . . Mama can draw donkeys . . whereas Papa draws soldiers . . Papa plays on the *'plano'* superiorly . . Papa is to sing him to sleep at nights . . Papa is to walk out with him—did you ever hear of such a usurping Papa? On the other hand he means to "tate tare" (take care) of Mama . . "mine dear Ba, mine poor, dood Ba . . . , " as he calls me sometimes in a fit of love, . . so I must try to be satisfied.

Since he came to Italy he has taken to talk English en-tirely by way of contradiction. Also he has nearly left off calling himself Penini & speaking in the third person . . which was a vexation to me at the time, for I cling to the infantine ways. He is very fluent in talking, but talks by no means plainly as you may observe from my quotations,— and I like that all the better. Such a child for travelling never was. He 'bated no jot of heart or hope' in our long fatiguing journey. Three nights without being undressed— think of that for a child! But he slept through the night . . or woke at one in the morning to cry out . . "O Mama,

fine mountains!" In the day, there was a perpetual singing, & talking, & sketching of waterfalls, . . & the name of
every place was enquired into as if he kept a journal. "Are
you *never* tired, you child?" I said to him one day— "Oh
no, *nemmer!*" (never) was his answer directly. He has
gypsey blood in him somehow or other.

Note bene—we did not pay a sous for Penini *from London
to Pisa—not a sous.* On the Pisan railway we paid something, & that was the whole expense.

His drawings absorb him as much as ever, & his progress
is remarkable. I wish this letter were not too heavy to send
you one inside of it. He writes too, (prints) long letters to
his "nonno" Robert's father, & my sister—but I teach him
nothing. I believe Robert would hang me up on a tree if
I did. We shall wait till he is eight or nine years old at least
before we think of lessons. I am a little conceited of course
about his drawings & his writings, which are really curious
for a little child of his age, but I dont in my serious mind
build up any expectation on them with respect to *faculties*
& the like. Mental precocity may mean just nothing—
whereas the moral qualities, ever so early developped, may
be relied on & rejoiced over, as I rejoice over his,—dear
darling!

Now, pay me out in kind, & send me a long history of
you & your treasures. I yearn for it really. I do hope you
yourself have not suffered too much this winter, . . and that
you have had pleasure in giving so much to dear Mrs.
Ogilvy, if for no other reason. My love to her, & Robert's.
Tell me of yourself . . what you are doing, & the rest . . as
much as I may hear, I mean. Everything will come to me
with interest.

You have probably heard of poor Mr. Greenhough's end
—the sculptor, our friend. The exciting society & keen air
of America acted on the brain injuriously, &, after having
been confined in a madhouse a short time, he returned
home & died at Boston.

God bless you, dearest Mrs. Ogilvy, both of you, all of you. Our united love to dear Mr. Ogilvy & yourself. Write to me, do, . . & think of me now & always as your very affectionate friend

Elizabeth Barrett Browning

We dont doubt about Paris, observe. Pray dont be taken in by the absurd estimate of American ministers, the Times commenting. We *lived* on poultry in Paris, which scarcely we could have done if chickens had been nine francs a couple!!!— A monstrous misrepresentation. In London, if you please, poultry is dear.

Address: Angleterre viá France. | Mrs. David Ogilvy | King's Place | Perth. | N.B. *Postmarks:* 26 GEN 1853 FIRENZE; PT-DE-BEAU-VOISIN TOSC 1 FEVR. 53; FE 2 1853; PERTH FE 8 1853.

Letter 21

The name of Gigia appears in this letter for the first time. She was an Italian nurse, hired probably soon after the Ogilvys arrived in Florence in the autumn of 1852. She stayed in their service until 1860 (see Letters 33-35), and Elizabeth sometimes forwarded letters to and from Gigia's family, who remained in Florence after she journeyed to Scotland with the Ogilvys.

Alessandro was the Brownings' manservant, whom the Ogilvys knew. Before the two families left Florence in May 1851 both had had problems with their servants. The Ogilvys' maid was apprehended opening Mr. Ogilvy's desk and removing money—brandishing "a knife, as if to stab herself" when caught. Alessandro was found to be conspiring with merchants to overcharge the Brownings for provisions. Rather than make a scene, the Brownings kept him on until they left. When they returned they found him engaged with the Costigans, so they felt free to hire a new manservant, Vincenzio. Because Robert interviewed him at night he did not recognize Vincenzio's slovenly appearance, which became a constant bone of contention with Elizabeth and Wilson. He did not, however, remain long since he fell ill and requested to be let go. Since the Peytons were leaving Florence at about this time, the Brownings employed their manservant, Ferdinando Romagnoli, who proved most satisfactory. He

married Wilson in 1855 and remained in the Brownings' service until
Elizabeth's death in 1861. Pen Browning later took him into his
household, where he died in 1893. Giovanni, mentioned in close
connection with Alessandro in this letter, must have been a servant
of the Ogilvys.

It is in this letter that Elizabeth first mentions the subject of
spiritualism to Mrs. Ogilvy. This would absorb her for the rest of
her life and be a topic, like Louis Napoleon, upon which the two
friends could not agree. Séances, table-turning and rapping spirits
were a craze at this time (see Letter 23).

Their friend James Montgomery Stuart had encountered problems
in his job at the embassy, where the chargé d'affaires complained of
his not working enough—"just going about dreaming over Mrs.
Browning's poems!"

Helen Faucit had seen Robert's play *Colombe's Birthday* through
seven performances in April 1853 at the Haymarket Theatre.

Florence. June 2. [1853]

My dearest Mrs. Ogilvy you will think me worse in Italy
than anywhere else in the matter of letter-writing. One
takes as you know in Italy, to lotus-eating instead,—confin-
ing ourselves on epistolary points to expecting other people
to write to us with the 'reciprocity which is all on one side.'
I have a sort of excuse however for my omissions in having
waited for a letter from Gigia's family. Just as I begin to
feel it impossible to wait a moment longer—just as I snatch
up my pen . . while it is in my fingers literally & truly . .
the letter comes. Tanto meglio. Now I do want to hear
from you, my dear friend. Be kind & generous, & dont
pay me off "tooth for tooth" and worry me. Send a long,
large sheet, rather, full to the verge, of every sort of detail
about you all. Tell me of the darlings. Tell me of yourselves. Tell me of you personally. What are you reading,
& writing, & thinking most of? Turning tables, like the
rest of the world, & me in particular? Nobody here does
anything else. The revolutionary 'circoli' are revolutionized
into magnetic circles:—and the pope & the cardinals "serve
tables" like the laity. There's an engraving at the shop

windows of an animated four legged pine, with the inscription " . . E pur si muove." "Having one's feet under the mahogany" has attained to a spiritual significance. And the new Knights of the round table have taken ladies into their company & shamed the miraculous days of the sangrael with a modern anachronism.

Ah—one laughs. But one is laughed at besides. I am up to the throat in all manner of superstitions, so called, . . swimming in spiritualisms. There has been a continued stream of Americans through the Casa Guidi this winter—and if you could hear us talking in this room, Mr. Powers, Mr. Tennyson, Mr. Lytton, & me, . . while poor Robert overwhelmed (in his scare of courtesy at least) by the majority against him, declares with his last breath that until he sees & hears with his own eyes & ears, he will give credence to nothing . . you would set us down as mad. You know my tendency to visionariness—though alas, I never saw a vision.

Now I am ashamed of having to tell you that we have not yet been to Rome (the spirit of the sun, who prophecied to us out of Lord Stanhope's chrystal ball, was so far wrong!) and on this second of June we cant of course think of going. We have put it off till next winter:—so farewell Paris & London for a year to come. It is a vexation to us—a despair to my sister, a despondency to Robert's sister, . . but we could'nt help ourselves & cant. A small "digging" found in a flower pot, would have facilitated matters,—in absence of which, a proper degree of resignation & philosophy is exceedingly desireable. For my own part, you know how I love Florence & Italy. It's like being kept prisoner, on a diet of ambrosia, in paradise. We have been particularly happy this winter—*I* have . . to speak for myself. Plenty of books, plenty of thoughts, health enough, love enough! Plenty to thank God for . . is it not? . . without 'room for finding fault.

And you? Shall you come southwards, really? Ah, you never can live in England or Scotland after life on the continent. While you are in the cramp of orthodoxy, I am in the delirium of heresy . . but I may be even orthodox where I am, without being persecuted for it by the meek eyes of my next door neighbour, which must be counted as an advantage. I could not bear, I think, the state of things you describe. Well, but let me admit frankly . . that on the day I had your letter, one arrived from Mrs. Jameson blowing the trumpets for the state of liberty to which English society had attained . . freedom of religious opinion & expression to the last degree!— But she is peculiarly situated—in the most intellectual society in London, to which "*I believe*" or "*I disbelieve*" is, unfortunately, an indifferent formula. Either in London or Paris, you may say what you please among thinking people—but in Paris, still more than in London— Shall you return to Florence this year? I dont know what to wish. Because next year we shall be in Paris, *I think*. Then, rents are raised in Paris just now, through the abolition for the nonce of so many streets: it will be cheaper presently. But nothing is as cheap as Florence, notwithstanding that through our . . my . . want of management, *we* dont live very cheaply:—only there is an undeniable difference in the prices, taken per se. Mrs. Tennyson who is an Italian & learned in housekeeping, says we *ought* to live for a scudo a day. We have a servant, engaged in the twilight which accounts for his outside, regular & attentive, but not excellent otherwise. Alessandro is out of place, having just left the Costigans, by whom his 'amour propre' was cruelly offended, & they had better have cut his throat. The vital principle with Alessandro is in the vanity, you know. Giovanni is in a place somewhere.

Poor Mr. Stuart has been in trouble & wrath lately about the embassy which he has left, & is in great difficulty I fear. He is making application among influential friends to get some sort of occupation in England or elsewhere. I am very sorry for him. His state of debt seems to be tremendous. Then he has not been very well, though this is not serious. We have seen a good deal of him this winter, but much more of Mr. Tennyson & Mr. Lytton who have grown to be our familiar spirits,—& Mr. Powers too has often come. Robert quite loves Mr. Tennyson—he is very loveable. There's a believing man for you, by the way! Though he & I are much in sympathy, I feel myself almost a sceptic by comparison with him. He's a man to believe in a muffin's turning crumpet because of a devil on the left hand side; & to think it *nothing surprising*. He has just printed two great volumes of poems (not published, understand) in which there is much fancy & sweetness . . much elemental poetry. Young Lytton too is preparing poems. He has made me think more highly of his father from the degree of his filial reverence. A young man full of the noblest aspirations—religious, & not ashamed nor afraid. I like him very much.

Suppose you come at once & we all go into the mountains together to pass the heats? Would'nt that be delightful? We have no plans yet. At the end of June we shall have to go somewhere, I suppose . . though the weather now is wonderfully exceptional. It has rained for three days, and I can bear to wear a sort of poplin-gown. This, in June!—

Penini was found guilty of saying yesterday as he looked out of the window . . "What weazer! *Santo Dio mio!*" I suppose it was a plagiarism from some tragical Italian. He is well & a darling in every way. A few weeks ago it was agreed that he should learn to read—so he gives me about five minutes a day to that purpose, & can make his way already among little sentences of one syllable. But he does'nt like reading as much as writing—I suppose nobody likes learning to read. It's more for his pleasure than profit than [sic] I wanted to teach him, & that he might be able to amuse himself among the fairies & witches & Jack the giant killers presently, . otherwise the time for lessons is'nt come. When he does'nt attend I simply refuse to hear him any more. The other day he came back to me after half an hour, with a most insinuating smile . . . "You dood now, Mama?" Yes, I said, I was tolerably good— "Well, den, I say mine lesson aden." He talks very badly still—only he does'nt mix the languages as he used to do. Oh—you would be sure to think him improved —& what joy he would have with your children!

Robert's play succeeded as you would see by the papers. Miss Faucit acted it seven nights out of the ten of her engagement. How does Alessandro's reading get on? Among Peninis accomplishments, is dancing—& he really dances with grace, playing the tamburine & keeping accurate time to the music. There's a great deal of girl-nature in the child. Tell me that dear Mr. Ogilvy is better. Old age does'nt explain his malady as well as the British climate does, happily. In the decline of faculties (at any rate) I hope he remembers still the friends of his youth, such as Robert & I. God bless you both. Love to Mrs. Ogilvy. Write to me, do. Your ever affectionate friend,

EBB.

Mrs. Trollope has a little girl. She cant nurse.

Address: Angleterre via France. | Mrs. David Ogilvy | King's Place | Perth | N.B. *Postmarks:* 6 GIU 53 FIRENZE; PT-DE-BEAUVOISIN TOSC 11 JUIN. 53; JU 12 1853; PERTH JN 13 1853.

Letter 22

To escape Florence's summer heat, the Brownings left for Bagni di Lucca on July 15. Prior to their departure a lively discussion on spiritualism was held at Bulwer Lytton's villa. The focal point of the evening was Michael Faraday's letter on unconscious muscular action (published in the *Athenaeum* on July 2, 1853), in which he suggested that a medium's personality could account for phenomena which were given spiritualistic explanations.

In 1853, William Edmonstoune Aytoun received an honorary D.C.L. from Oxford University. Apparently Elizabeth felt that his

position on the staff of the influential *Blackwood's Magazine* had
more to do with his achieving this distinction than his poetry. In
March 1860, he printed in *Blackwood's* a slashing review of her
Poems Before Congress.

Casa Tolomei. Alla Villa. Bagni di Lucca.
July 21. [1853]

Though wishing to hear from you, my dear friend, I do wish
that your coming letter may not cross this as happened last
time. That is so uncomfortable. See where we are! At the
Baths of Lucca without you! I scarcely know how we
got here. We meant not to come indeed, but the tempta-
tions of facility & convenience conquered us. First, hearing through the Cottrells that Mrs. Sunderland wanted to
get rid of a house here for nothing we wrote to enquire.
She answered by denying the report but by speaking of
another house close by . . which brought us to the Villa
in spite of our prejudices in favour of the Bagni Caldi.
It's a large house with a second sittingroom & a spare bedroom, besides the dressingroom for Robert—a house withdrawn from the village & curtained in by a row of seven
plane trees in which the cicale sing all day. For above
thirteen weeks we pay fifty francesconi. Also it is very
cool, & our Penini is as happy as the fairy-king he looks,
in the garden, from the moment his blue eyes are open.
Mrs. Sunderland has overpowered us with kind attentions.
She has been ill, but is better & able to get on with her
paintings & make long excursions on her poney. Florence
was beginning to blaze when we left it, yet I was sorry to
go, as usual—sorry to break the thread & let the beads run
away on the floor—not to be strung again, perhaps— Who
knows? We had an agreeable sort of bachelor society . .
which made no trouble . . only required tea & coffee . . &
in which there was a great deal of sympathetical talk, &
permitted smoking!— I am gracious you know, in such
things. Now, Mr. Tennyson, our favorite friend, is on the

point of going to England for three months. The evening before our last in Florence, Mr. Lytton had a 'reception' on the terrace of his Bellosguardo villa where I made tea . . being the only tea-making animal present, . . & Mr. Villari (an accomplished Sicilian) Mr. Powers, Mr. Tennyson & our host discoursed upon Spiritualism, & concluded on the "arrogance & insolence" of Faraday's inconclusive letter. Between the fire flies & the stars, & with that purple wonder of a vision at our feet . . city & mountains dissolving gloriously together . . it was almost easier to believe in spirits than in men. Tales that would have been incredible two years ago were swallowed with our strawberries & cream like last week's easiest gossip! We stood up for our "new truths" . . side by side with Galileo, . . said somebody modestly . . looking at his villa. Seldom have I had a pleasanter evening, foolish or wise, modest or arrogant, right or wrong!

Faraday's letter does not meet the facts, but I was wrong in calling it inconclusive. It is conclusive in two respects. First . . that the simplest phenomena of the subject in question are not accountable by the *known* laws of nature. Secondly . . that the humility of our Bacons & Newtons do not mark the men of science of our age.

Among the numerous Americans whom we have seen this winter, is Mr. Kinney the minister at the court of Turin who arrived a few days before we left Florence—& he & his wife spent our last evening at Casa Guidi with us. He is an intelligent, high minded, interesting man, & made our souls burn in us by talking cheerfully of Piedmont . . of the rapid progress of the people, and the invincible honesty of the King. There is hope still for Italy, thank God. The body is not dead while the heart beats beneath the hand!—

Mrs. Kinney is not very refined for an "Excellence," but she is excessively goodnatured & rather a pretty woman. Also, she dabbles a little in literature. They promised that

we should see them here before long for at least a week,
& as I much like Mr. Kinney, I hope we shall. The bishop
of Maryland sent a message to Robert through them, that
he had read *"Christmas Eve* twice through one night."
There's an exemplary bishop for you!— If there were
more of such it would be better for the church!— Mr.
Stuart has taken his family down to Leghorn for a fortnight's bathing, after which he talked of coming here, probably alone, to see his friend Sir William Miller. How happy
I should be if any prospect were opening on him: but I
hear of nothing specific. He seems to think it probable
that he will have a situation in England,—& if influential
friends can do anything, he thinks right—only a situation of
two hundred a year there would not be worth one hundred
here—there is much to consider. By the way he desired me
to ask if you received the box of books which he duly sent?
Dont forget to tell me. Robert made immediate enquires
about the picture. Nothing to be heard of it!— Mr. Harding is at Venice, and Mr. Costigan quietly wonders at your
simplicity in expecting to get a picture from his hands,
with or without eyes. The circumstance of its being paid
for, appears to enhance the difficulty. Dr. Harding spoke
quite pathetically to Robert the other day about this son,
observing that it was as clear a case of monomania as he
had known of. He had provided him with everything &
sent him to Venice at his desire. The other day the father
had a letter from an hotel keeper, with a bill for the son's
six months expenses. "He has his room hung with his
own pictures," said the letter, "& if he would give me one
picture I would desire no money—but he refuses any sort
of compensation to me." I am afraid it is a very bad case.
Professor Aytoun has made himself talked of certainly,
& he had a friend in the Times who praised him so absurdly
as besides to make him laughed at—but *reputations* are not
made by such means, be certain. He is a clever rhymer & no
more—not the cleverest even of rhymers. It was simply as

a representative of the Blackwood interest that he "shared the triumph" and partook the political gale at Oxford—& nobody mistook motive or end. As a lecturer he may have drawn fashionable listeners for one reason or another—but, for every reason, so bad a critic must take slight hold on any reasonable public. For the rest, my dearest Mrs. Ogilvy, . . bad writers have had good & tender mothers from the beginning of time, & we ought not to mix good & bad things in the excess of our sympathy for the good?—now, ought we? And when bad writers are good sons, we may blame the writer while praising the son in all reverence. Otherwise, heaven & earth would be a blot & a confusion.

I have left no room to talk of my Wiedeman today! Make me amends by sending me full news of your darlings! He looks paler through the heat. Oh yes—he speaks Italian— and English too. He does not mix or confound as he used— but the pronunciation & grammar of each language are still very infantine. My darling!—with the most musical of voices! Let me remember to tell you that Mrs. Cox has another little girl. God bless you all! Our love to Mr. Ogilvy & to Mrs. Ogilvy . . ask her to remember us!

    Your ever affec^te friend,

      Elizabeth Barrett Browning.

We mean to work here, & print next year in England. Do tell us what you are about.

Address: Angleterre vià France | Mrs. David Ogilvy | King's Place | Perth. | N.B. *Postmarks:* BAGNI DI LUCCA 21 LUG. 1853; PT-DE-BEAUVOISIN TOSC 26 JUIL. 53; JY 27 1853; PERTH JY 23 1853.

Letter 23

The literary sensation of the season was caused by the publication of "Life Drama" and other poems by the Scottish poet Alexander Smith. Also published during this time was Mrs. Gaskell's novel

Ruth, which treated the problem of an unmarried mother. (Some modern critics feel that *Ruth* was a source for Elizabeth's *Aurora Leigh*.) Elizabeth mentions two other contemporary novels by wo- men dealing with social issues: Harriet Beecher Stowe's *Uncle Tom's Cabin* (1851) and Susan Warner's *Queechy* (1852).

Casa Tolomei. Alla Villa
Bagni di Lucca
September [9, 1853]

Having a letter for the signorina cherubina . . quella fanciulla ornatissima . . just sent to me from Florence, I dont like keeping it a post, my dearest Mrs. Ogilvy.   Otherwise I *might* have waited a day or two longer . . but no more . . in order to write to you.   Ever since you wrote last I have been going round & round you like a dog meaning to settle himself at last, in a restless wishing to know more of you, seeing that, whether you knew it or not, you wrote in bad spirits . . decidedly bad spirits . . which your friends cant be expected to put up with quietly.   Do be kind, & write again soon.   We want much . . oh, much . . to hear of you in de- tail & how you have wound up your plans for the winter . . whether you stay in Scotland or England (I hope not) or whether you go to Paris or Brussels . . we have heard of Brussels in relation to you but the "trump of fame" plays false sometimes.

You see we are still at the Baths.   We mean to stay as long as the weather will let us, the place having been extremely enjoyable hitherto.   Penini & I have had our part with the donkeys,—& there has been a great deal of mutual straw- berries & cream at friends' houses, the Storys coming & going in both generations, the children visiting Penini as the elders do ourselves. I forget whether you know them at all, but I think not.   He is a sort of universal man, sculptor, painter, lawyer, biographer, musician & poet . . & very vivid & characteristic in conversation—& she is sympathet- ical & charming.   Also, we have been twice or thrice with the Royalty of Villa Broderick—and once Mr. Green in a

fit of absence & hospitality drew us in to a regular *rout* . .
if the word were not rococo . . a soirée of some forty or
fifty persons 'in grande toilette,' at which we with poetical
simplicity appeared in foulard & alpaca somewhat abashed.
He has two children . . did you know? Mrs. Sunderland
has gone to Leghorn to look out for a winter-house, but
returns here for a while. She has been extremely unwell,
I am sorry to say, & was feeble when she went away. The
indisposition was not the chest this time. She & we talk
of you whenever we meet, & if she had not been ill you
would have heard from her some time since. Mr. Stuart
told us that we should certainly see him at Lucca, and we
expected him . . . & Shakespeare . . but he has not appeared.
I should like to ascertain what has happened since we
parted, for his situation seemed perilous & scarcely hopeful. I know too well the difficulty of getting remunera-
tive occupation in England, notwithstanding the offices
of his tribe of 'friends,' to have much confidence in his
English prospects.

Just now we have a visitor, Mr. Lytton, who is occupy-
ing our spare bedroom . . (for you are to understand that
we have the glory of a spare bedroom.) He is a great
favorite of ours, as I think I have told you, and will do
something excellent one day, even if the book of poems
which he is printing at present should fail to impress the
public. I should have wished him to wait—he is immature,—
& susceptible to influences of course, . . but nobody likes
"waiting," except in advising other people . . (I least of all)
and the poems will have signs of a true faculty, in whatever
stage of development. You ask our thoughts about Alexander Smith. Somebody told us the other day that Alfred
Tennyson said of him . . "Fancy, but no imagination"!—
which, word for word, Robert had been saying some six
weeks . . so you may accept it as a double opinion. It is
hard however to come to conclusions on so young writer.
What I see is that he has a veritable faculty,—& that it may

develop into anything . . but he has not *proved* yet that he
can think & feel, as well as make images. Petals without
a calyx . . no force of reality to hold the undeniable beau-
ties together. I must tell you that we have seen only extracts . . but even they are dislocated & without natural
relation. It is as if the gods threw him down flowers of all
the seasons, which he cant stop to sort or tie into nosegays.
Still, we have not such a multitude of poets that we can
doubt whether to call him a true poet. Much *music, I*
dont hear in him, but perhaps it is the fault of my partial
reading. His system of blank verse is one which I have
"odds against." So young a man! Not more than one &
twenty I believe, & with every disadvantage in respect to
education. Some obtuse patrons . . (we patronize poets in
England . . when we attempt it . . as men nurse babies, by
breaking their backs) propose sending him to Oxford, we
understand. Sending him to Oxford!

I have, within these few days, had a very interesting
letter from the author of 'Ruth,' Mrs. Gaskill. She appears
a simple, earnest, affectionate woman . . was married very
early & has a daughter eighteen, & another six, with something intermediate. 'Ruth' has considerable power & beauty,
& deals in a bold true christian spirit with a detestable
state of Christian society. I would rather have written
that book than two 'uncle Toms' inclusive of the flourish
of trumpets. Yet the popularity of 'uncle Tom' was really
a grand thing & meant much that was good, . . except as a
literary opinion. Oh, I know it is dangerous, & looks horribly envious or covetous or vicious somehow, to hint at
such a thing—also the words may not represent me fairly,
for I was glad & gratified in various ways at that unparalel-
led triumph in letters. 'Queechy' is another American
novel by a woman, very clever & characteristic.

My Penini grows fat & rosy . . comparatively of course . .
& is wild with joy from morning to night. Think of a
child who sings in his sleep! Literally that's what he does!

As to the arts, otherwise, they are thrown over. Not a stroke has he drawn since he came here—not a line has he written!—and I, for my part, & Robert, for his, are rejoicing in this extinct civilization, it is so good to see him quite wild & rosy! Still, I keep up his 'reading' for five minutes every morning, that we may not have to go over the sheep-paths again in the steep places—& he reads the little lessons of one syllable very nicely . . too well, sometimes I think—for I hold to the non-education theory. Does Alexander read at all? Tell me about him & the rest. Penini talks English & Italian with equal fluency & bad grammar & articulation . . but with the sweetest little murmuring voice!— Once since he came here . . that is, once in his life . . he has been punished. Robert punished him, much to my disapprobation, for I disapprove of hardhearted people . . only I had the comfort of knowing that Robert suffered for it in his soul. The punishment was . . *to have no pears all day!* The victim could'nt believe at first that anything so cruel was seriously intended, but, on becoming alive to the full horror of the situation, he burst into sobs of anguish & exclaimed with the tears raining down his cheeks . . "Oh naughty Papa! What I do, *if the peaches too sour!*" You know the peaches are apt to be sour at Lucca!— What a dreadful contingency!

I must say he is a good & darling child, & that if we had a genius for punishment it would be difficult to apply it.

We keep to our scheme about Rome. In this house we stay if we can till the fifteenth of October & then go to Florence where we shall pause for a time greater or less.

When you tell me that you are 'not interested' in the "table-turnings" & the phenomena which go with them, you make us *two*, for I can scarcely CONCEIVE of not being interested. It is *the* subject with me just now & I hear of it literally from all the ends of the world. Also I expect from it sooner or later, the solution of some of the deepest mysteries of our double nature. Do you despise me, Mr.

Ogilvy?—

How I shall like to see your little book!—and I *shall*, some day, shall I not? Robert & I are doing work in a sort of lazy way—& mean to have finished in time for England next summer. Do write soon & in detail. Our best love to Mr. Ogilvy— Now *will* you come to Paris I wonder!— Dear friend, dearest Mrs. Ogilvy, let me ever be your most affectionate EBB.

Will you give our love to Mrs. Ogilvy . . & kisses from me to the darlings. Penini & I talk of them together.

Will you be startled to know that Penini never heard the word "*hell*" in his life? Marcia is in advance of him in orthodoxy. I am schismatic in some opinions & believe little in arbitrary punishment & less still in physical brimstone as generally received. By the way, Mr. Hanna is in Ireland, stronger I am glad to hear. Now do write. Say how Marcia is. Grieved I am that you shd. have such anxieties.

Address: Angleterre viâ France. | Mrs. David Ogilvy | King's Place | Perth. | N.B. *Postmarks:* BAGNI DI LUCCA 9 SET. 1853; PT-DE-BEAUVOISIN TOSC 14 SEPT. 53; SP 15 1853.

Letter 24

The weather became so cool in Bagni di Lucca during the early part of October that the Brownings returned to Florence on the tenth of the month. They stayed only a little over a month before leaving for Rome, which they had wanted for many years to see. After "an exquisite eight days journey" they arrived at the gates of the Eternal City on November 22.

> Rome. *43. Via Bocca di Leone.* 3º piano.
> JanY 24. [1854]

My dear friend I feel as if I had belied myself in not writing long ago. I have two letters from you unanswered, and here is one arrived from Florence for your Cherubina. See how it is! First there's a good reason for delays in writing, &

then there's a bad reason, as a matter of course! I meant to send you a letter with our address immediately on our arrival at Rome—an excellent motive for not sending you one from Florence. Arriving at Rome we fell into the pit . . tumbled down headlong, & were for weeks & weeks overwhelmed with other people's miseries made our own by sympathy. Do you remember my telling you of Mr. & Mrs. Story & their two children, a boy & girl . . the boy six years old, the girl, nine . . and how they helped us to spend the happy summer at the Baths of Lucca? Well—before breakfast on the morning we opened our eyes first in Rome, Mr. Story's servant brought Edith to us, with the news that little Joe was in convulsions . . in great danger. Gastric fever tending to the brain. All that first day we spent beside that deathbed, for before evening the child was dead. Edith meantime had sickened of the same fever at our house & it was pronounced impossible to move her. She was received into the apartment below us by Mr. Page the artist, (we had no bed) & the poor father & mother left the yet unburied body of her brother to come & nurse her, the danger being extreme. A few days afterwards Emma Page the artist's youngest daughter was ill besides—and the Storys' English nurse lay on her bed delirious, apparently past help. For my part, I acknowledge to you that after the first burst of sympathy I fell into a selfish unreasoning panic in spite of the oaths of the physicians to the effect that the fever was not contagious. I "lost my head" as Robert remarked, & wished for wings like a dove . . or like any unclean bird . . so they were wings . . to fly away with my child to the ends of the earth, from this pestilent city. But I could'nt fly, or run even . . I had to stay. Thank God, he is well, & has dropped not a rose leaf from his cheeks . . not a leaf of the dear Tuscan roses. Still, nothing should induce me to remain here two winters together—and, for the rest, the feeling of *Rome* is lost to me . . the mountains & great campagna slurred over by ghastly death-fingers smelling of fresh mould . . not Cæsarean dust. Think! My first drive was with that desolated mother to the gate of the cemetery. There's the Coliseum!—that's the temple of Vesta!—and that's little Joe's grave!— Ancient gods, renowned emperors, tumbled into the new grave & forgotten!! He's buried close by the heart of Shelley & away from his mother's . . poor, good, dear, little Joe!

It was a month before Edith could be moved home from our house—for the Roman fever followed the gastric, & till within the last few days she has been ill with it, looking the ghost of herself. But now the "times" seem broken, & the settling of the weather gives promise of satisfactory & stable improvement. The other invalids too are convalescent. The light breaks through the clouds. But see why I have'nt written to you. First for a good reason, then for another good reason, (I had'nt the heart to write) and then for a bad reason, as I said before, because one falls into the habit of silence unawares. Write to me & say you understand, & are not vexed with me, dearest Mrs. Ogilvy, for indeed I have sent many thoughts after you, though not one letter!— Also, I have been hunting in vain the Athenæum columns (we see the Athenæum here sometimes) for the advertisement of your book . . the book with the "taking title" which you forgot to tell me. Remember to tell it when you write again . . for I do not see your name anywhere. Even the Ladies' companion is dumb of you—and why?

In the midst of disaster & anxiety the Roman climate has agreed with me personally. I have passed a winter like a summer—the weather having been only cold enough during one fortnight to confine me to the house—a miraculous sort of winter for me. Letters come to us sitting in the sun, full of the exasperation of the northern frost & snow, from London & even Paris. To have escaped such a tremendous winter is a wonderful gain for me of course, & I shall be the stronger for it the whole year, I dare say. Our house

at Florence we have taken on till May *1855* . . but it is
not let I am sorry to add. Our apartment here is comfortable & dear . . the Roman prices generally being tremendous,—and we shall stay in it up to the latter half of
next may & then travel northwards, . through Paris to
London, where Robert at least will have business with the
printers. For my part I believe I shall not be ready so
soon with my book, which lags from various causes, and
I shall like to make it as good as I can . . or (as good as I
cant, for that matter!) Think of my having been in Rome
all this time & never yet entered the Vatican. People have
talked so of the cold of it that I wait for the settled spring.
For the rest, I have ventured out on several evenings . . for
instance to Mrs. Kemble's, & to her sister Mrs. Sartoris's
musical parties which are open to us twice a week. By the
way, I met there the other evening that terror of poets, the
snow-man, Lockhart! He looks as if just dug out of a
snow-drift, and as if the snow-powder clave to him, . . hair,
eyes, skin, . . manners & voice!— If I made as agreeable an
impression on him as he did on me, I shall be quartered in
one of the Quarterlies certainly. I never saw so uninterest-
ing man, I think, . . for a man alive, or a man who had been
alive. Then Thackeray & his daughters are here . . he getting on with his Newcomes, & tolerating Rome chiefly, it
seems to me, through constant relays of dinners. He cant
write, he says, in the mornings, without a dinner & two
parties over night, and his Newcomes have suffered from
the still life of Rome in spite of Roman hospitalities. "Dine
out in Rome?" said Lockhart to me—"why nobody can do
it. For my part I have'nt dined since I came. There's
nothing to eat, and the wines are poison."

Tell me when you write, a great deal about the children. My Penini is much "the fashion" on the Pincio and
elsewhere, & I am complimented on all sides on his beauty
& grace. I have an especial laurel as "Penini's mama" which
gives me immense personal distinction. "Are you the mother

of that pretty child with the long curls?—" or . . "I have
seen your lovely little GIRL!!" or rather,—"I have heard
of your boy"—for we keep the compliments to the "lovely little girl" as much as possible in the background. He
has a less delicate look than he had, with a bright colour
& white round full arms & neck, & is dressed in his old way
. . only the waists still longer & the skirts shorter . . all
alive with intelligence, & fragrant with goodness & sensibility. I never saw such an habitually good child, . . joyous,
vivacious, spoilt as far as want of discipline can spoil, and
yet sweet, affectionate, moderate in his desires, uncapricious
in his moods of mind—full of natural piety. For weeks
after little Story's death which set him crying bitterly, he
used to pray at nights & mornings, . . "Take care of Joe
and put him *wiz* z angels." The other day he had the
toothache . . "oh" said Wilson, hugging him up . . "what
shall we do with this pain?"—"*Play to Dod*," said he quietly. *Within these six weeks* he has been learning to write
ms (before he used to print) and really his copybook is
extraordinary. I shall make him write a word to show
you. And he has produced various sketches of St. Peter's
which I cant send so easily!— Tell me of your plans—of
yourselves—of the children. Hold us in your kind thoughts,
both of us. Your ever affectionate EBB

[continued by Pen] Penini's best love.

[continued by EBB] Such an exquisite eight days journey we had through Perugia—oh, we fell into this gulf of
grief with heads bound in roses!

We shall winter in Paris next year—Deo volente—and
you? You are hearing the cannons from Constantinople,
& resolving on staying at home—there's my clairvoyance
concerning you!

Address: Angleterre | Mrs. David Ogilvy | King's Place | Perth | Scot-
land. *Redirected:* Ainslie Place | Edinburgh. *Postmarks:* ROMA 24
GEN 54; DI PONT. MARSEILLE 31 JANV. 54; M N.B.; LIGNE-DE-
CALAIS 31 [JANV. 54]; FE 1 1854; FEB 2 1854; PERTH FE 2 1854.

Letter 25

In answer to Elizabeth's enquiries about her work in progress, Mrs. Ogilvy sent a manuscript poem later published as "Charon's Ferry" in *Poems of Ten Years* (see Appendix B, pages 201-203.) Elizabeth's own work, *Aurora Leigh*, did not progress according to her plans and was not published until October 1856. Robert's *Men and Women* was ultimately published in November 1855.

The Crimean War, which had its beginnings the previous autumn, did not attract Elizabeth's attention to the same degree as the Italian situation. She felt greatly justified in her faith in Louis Napoleon when the alliance was struck between England and France in opposition to Russia.

Elizabeth's interesting comments to Mrs. Ogilvy on Matthew Arnold were in part prompted by his recently-revised edition of poems. The other poets whom she mentions are Philip James Bailey, whose *Festus* first appeared in 1839, and Sydney Thompson Dobell, who published under the pseudonym of Yendys.

Rome. 43 Bocca di Leone. Feb. 19 [1854]
My ever dear friend, It is strange to have a letter from you which gives no pleasure . . strange & sad. I write directly to tell you how deeply & warmly our sympathies are with you. My heart grew very mournful over the words you sent me. Dear little Marcia! May God bless & comfort you by raising her up into the sun again & placing her in your arms with all her dimples & rose-tints replaced & repainted. Children are such flowers . . as the Italians are fond of saying . . they droop & recover themselves in a day some-times—and Marcia looked such a sturdy little creature, with vitality enough for six! There's no bad tendency about her lungs, that the evil once passed should not be over. Keep up heart, dear friend, even in the face of those terrify-ing celestial aptitudes . . which have so often frightened me in my own child. I remember being thrilled through & through by something he said to Wilson before he was three years old—"*Dont tell Papa & Mama, . . but I love God more than anybody.*" That was like your Marcia, was it not? Swedenborg says that the "celestial angels" (the

highest order) minister to children very young . . & with some children the influence shines through visibly. How wonderful & beautiful, that great-hearted patience in a little child! The account you give is very touching. Dear darling! Kiss the precious pale cheeks for me. May God put back the roses there!—

What has changed your plans about the book after all, when it was apparently finished & ready for the press? Thank you much for 'Charon'. It's a pleasure to have a stroke on the head of the modern bigots from the end of his black oar. For the rest I hear with unaffected wonder of anyone's being able to write verses, with brain & heart torn to pieces as your's must have been lately, dearest Mrs. Ogilvy, & I really think you should be crowned for it. For my part, the first effect of grief upon *me* is the striking of me dumb—& it's the same with Robert. We, both of us, wait for calms before we do anything with Art. Perhaps melancholy calms—but the state of calm is necessary to most artists, I think. Even the disturbance by mere sympathy has been unfavorable to me here, & I am behind hand with my poem—thrown out of the habit of work for a whole month at the beginning, which was unfortunate; Robert swears he shall have his book ready in spite of everything for printing in June when we shall be in London for the purpose, but, as for mine, it must wait for the next spring I begin to see clearly. Also it may be better not to bring out the two works together. If mine were ready I might not say so perhaps. Mine wont be ready—what is left undone in Rome, cant be done in London where we are regularly put into a mill & ground, body & soul. I wonder if we shall meet you in London— Surely we shall brush garments with you somewhere as you come south & we go north. Next winter we are to spend in Paris at all events,—but I doubt whether, for a succession of years, any place except Italy will answer for me. Italy, Florence, is our home in thought. God keep it in the sun for us.

By the lengthening out of the negotiations, we have all got used to the idea of war—& the oppressed part of Europe open its mouth & shuts its eyes to see what the heavens will send it. Something good must come surely in the heap of evil. I triumph quietly (not too overbearingly) in the turn of men's minds about Louis Napoleon. What I saw from the beginning, liberal politicians in England are forced to see now . . and it is quite amusing to mark the change of physiognomies throughout the English newspapers. The shuffling-round of the Examiner for instance must have been attended with a great cost of mental agony to the editor,—and I am inhuman enough to find a certain pleasure in the pain of "the meanest things that feel" . . which writers of partial politics are very apt to be. The harm done by that stupid outcry of ..52 was not appreciable by the persons who made it—let that be their excuse. It almost atones to me for the calamity of war that the English & French nations should stand together as they do—for, as long as they do, the world is saved, in a political & moral sense. That is my belief, at least.

Well—perhaps I never under any circumstances should have quite thrown myself back into the past in Rome, as you did, you say, and as I might have done when I was very much younger. My chariot wheels have caught fire with running fast on the modern roads!—the present & the future are strong with me till I am all in a flame, & this old Tiber could not quench me utterly, though it rose "with its yellow waves." You cant think how eager I am about every step we take upwards though in the midst of clamour & strife. What a view there will be from that hill-top we are getting to!— It's worth while panting & losing breath for!— Ruins are only good to stand among for a moment, in looking forward to new temples, just as we only use 'Charon' against our contemporaries. Art is eternal though!— And after all, if we were in Athens instead of Rome, I might be content to forget the great present a little—who knows? Those golden Greeks were worth so much more than the iron Romans ever were. If you go to Greece I shall envy you. The Greek professor from Boston, Mr. Felton, has just brought me a paper-weight from the Athenean theatre with Greek inscriptions. Dr. Braun, the German archæologist, (secretary of the archæological society) spent the evening here a few days since, & discoursed to my satisfaction on the mesmeric & spiritual-mysticism advance of the old Greek mind. That delighted me, you may suppose. And yet, as says Emerson,

'When the half gods go
The whole gods arrive.'

and we are waiting, in these Christian ages, for the whole gods.

And yet, oh yes indeed, I do sympathize with you wholly & particularly, dearest Mrs. Ogilvy, in a detestation of the vulgar haggling & pushing & kicking, which is an under-part of the great struggle, & a condition of the progress of the masses. As to the bigotry of the churches it is hideous—I turn away my face from it. I cant help thinking that all these church-walls, English, Scottish, Roman, equally, must all be swept away, before Christ can be seen standing in the midst.

There is power & nobility of thought surrounded by a chrystalline atmosphere in Arnold's poetry. He wants vital heat, passion & imagination, & these are great wants. I too had seen & admired the merman poem long ago. He is an admirable poet in one sense—an admirable *poetical writer*. But he must break up all his ice of meditation, & consent to feel like a child & attain to seeing like a seer, before we call him a poet in the absolute sense. There's the author of Festus— Beat Bailey, swear at Bailey, call Bailey names if you like . . nobody can doubt *he's* a poet, though he should sin a hundredfold more offensively than he does sin. Now, in Arnold, the thing is not so clear. Have you seen Sidney Yendys's "Balder?" The extracts in the Athenæum had some noble imagery— We have sight always of the Athenæum which is colder & duller than ever—& of the 'Critic' too, which is a better gossipping paper, though by no means excellent for criticism.

Louisa must be quite remarkably advanced for her age, to enter into the Iliad. Does she care for poetry in general? I am sure that Wiedeman is much more a baby still than Alexander is. He's a very quick, clever child, but is a *baby*, to all intents & purposes—looks like it, talks like it, has the ways of it altogether. His speech is anything but mature though he affects hard words— Yesterday after a silence he broke out laughing suddenly—"What are you laughing at?" said I. *"I sinting of somesing velly* SLORDINALLY.'' He was thinking of something very extraordinary!— There's a way of talking for you! Do write & tell me how your darling is & how you all are, & that you yourself are less worn out. God bless you & dear Mr. Ogilvy. Our best love to him from Robert & your ever affectionate & sympathizing friend EBB.

P. S. Pr Blackie is *reactionary* in poetical criticism—is'nt he?

I forgot to tell you that Gigia's letter was sent to us *here*, & that I was not guilty of keeping it all that time. Mind you write directly—& give my love to your sister. We have had very cold weather for a fortnight, & there was sleet this morning. Thackeray has left Rome. I like his two frank intelligent girls—& I like besides his own goodnature & agreeableness. We see much of Mrs. Kemble.

Address: Angleterre | Mrs. David Ogilvy. | 3. Maitland Street | Edinburgh. *Postmark:* MAR 2 1854.

Letter 26

For many years an avid reader of the eighteenth-century mystic Emanuel Swedenborg, Elizabeth found an enthusiastic ally in the artist William Page. During the winter she read *Theological Essays* by Frederick Denison Maurice, whose position regarding eternal punishment was akin to Elizabeth's and Swedenborg's. Because of his position, Maurice was charged with heresy and dismissed from his professorship at King's College, London, shortly thereafter.

In contrast with the tragedy of Joe Story's death, Elizabeth considered her association with the Kemble sisters, Adelaide (Mrs. Sartoris), and Fanny (Mrs. Butler), one of the more pleasant aspects of the winter in Rome. It was after such an excursion as the one mentioned in this letter that Robert was inspired to write "Two in the Campagna."

Elizabeth, in a slip of the pen, refers to the *Keepsake* as the "Book of Beauty." While at Rome the Brownings contributed poems to the *Keepsake*, an annual edited by Marguerite A. Power. Elizabeth sent "My Kate" and Robert submitted "Ben Karshook's Wisdom," published respectively in the 1855 and 1856 numbers.

Shortly before returning to Florence, Elizabeth was somewhat shaken by a rumor about John Ruskin, who had married Euphemia Chalmers Gray at Perth in 1848. Because the marriage was never consummated, she obtained an annulment of the marriage under Scots law and later married their friend John Everett Millais.

[Florence] June 8. [1854]

My dear friend I begin at once to answer your letter, with a throb of selfreproach for not having answered the one before. I took for granted too much that you were all well & happy again . . dear little Marcia having escaped the danger as I seemed to understand. How grieved I am that more trial should have fallen on you. Heavy & grievous, indeed! — I pity not least, dear Mr. Ogilvy in the course of that dreadful journey from London with the weight of all that anxiety. Will it not be wise to take the children into a mild climate for next winter? I would not, if I were you, risk keeping them either in England or Scotland, while they may not yet have outgrown the tendencies to delicacy of chest. And I

too have had my anxieties . . which is the only good reason I can give you for not having written before, & which is
a reason beside for my being able to feel for you in yours.
I told you how frightened I was, without cause, all the
winter long, my Penini keeping his radiant looks through
the disastrous casualties of the season in Rome. Some
seven weeks ago, however, he had an attack . . diarhea
attended by feverishness, . . & immediately afterward, two
others . . so that we had to call in a physician three times
which was extraordinary for us. The symptoms yielded at
once to the treatment, but the child (I never saw him so unwell before) fell away in looks & strength & flesh, grew
nearly as pale as this paper, with blue marks under the
precious eyes. Oh, I was so thankful to bring him away
from that fatal Rome! He rallied as we travelled—yet it is
humiliating to hear from our Florentines . . "come é cangiato
questo bambino! Dio mio, come é divenuto secco e pal-
lido!" Too true indeed. As if a rose had shaken off its
leaves so has all his brilliancy & prettiness gone away! He
is much grown but has not shot up—there has been no irregular growth to account for the thinness & delecacy which
are traceable clearly to past illness. Now, he is perfectly
well, with a voracious appetite, (for *him*)—sleeps well &
shows his usual volatile spirits. Also, considering that he
has only been a week in Florence, it is surprising how he
has improved already . . the little arms getting firmer, &
the dreadful blue marks under the eyes vanishing fast—but
oh Rome, Rome, step-"mother of orphans" (having mur-
dered the fathers & mothers!) I shall find it difficult to
forgive THEE!

Wilson & I are meditating, only from today, the putting
my Penini into a *blouse*. I did'nt think I should bear it . .
but she tacked up a pattern & dressed him in it . . low in
the neck & with short sleeves . . and I bore it pretty well.
As for *you* . . yes you "horrified" me, just as you thought!
Alexander is six months older than Penini, & he is six years

before him in costume—I hope it will be at least six years
before Penini wears a tunic & cloth trousers . . save the
mark (on the knees!) And you a poetess! Well, I cant
make you out. If you "drew an angel down" like St
Cecilia, you would equip him directly in "pants and vest"
like an American—to say nothing of cutting the 'hyacin-
thine locks' into a 'crop.' And you have'nt even the fashion in your favour—boys are kept in high blouses now till
they are twelve or fourteen. Mrs. Sartoris's boy at Rome,
who is eleven & manly enough to ride fifteen miles and read
Latin, wears the blouse & embroidered trousers & collars.
And we used to see great boys of ten & eleven in Paris walking out in the morning with their hair in curlpapers to se-
cure the afternoon's ringlets. Not that I admire such a
process as the last. I would avoid that other extreme too.
I confine myself to hoping devoutly that by the time Penini is twelve years old, (the age for entertaining the idea of
cutting off ringlets) the fashion of the day for men may
be to wear long hair parted in the middle like Milton & the
Germans & himself.

Rome made me amends in one thing. It seems to me
that I mentioned to you Page the great American artist,
& his wonderful portraits. Well, he painted a picture of
Robert like Titian & then like a prince presented it to me.
I resisted long, & at last yielded to a generosity so earnest &
delicate that it was worthy of the nature of the man. He
told me that I should frustrate his intentions in painting
the picture if I did not accept it. It is a head the size of
life, exquisitely painted & literal in the likeness, & might
take place, as to colouring, with the work of any Venetian
master. The artist has discoveries in colour which will presently make him an acknowledged 'power' in Art. Fisher
the English artist also achieved a successful portrait of
Robert this last winter, and a cartoon of Penini, not quite
so happy. He said that the infantine character of Penini's
face made him a beautiful subject—but he never offered

me a sketch even of the finished cartoon, which I thought
rather hard but very reasonable of course. If Pages were
common (even on the point of the moral nature) the world
would be nobler & pleasanter, but commerce would'nt
flourish. By the way, Mr. Page is a Swedenborgian—and, by
the way, again, Maurice whom you admire so much &
whose last essays I have been reading with deep interest,
entertains precisely the view against the commonly received
one of the resurrection of the body which Swedenborg
teaches, & which I held unconsciously before I knew him.
Does Mr. Ogilvy remember how he called me "very heterodox" on the subject, when we discussed it once in this
room? I was struck with surprise & pleasure at Maurice's
adhesion—though from his non-reception of the Swedenborgian philosophy of the spiritual world, he does it at the
risk of certain inconsistencies & difficulties. By the way,
I dont agree with all Maurice's theology— For instance his
view of regeneration seems to me contrary to the world's
experience to say nothing of the Christian's. I hold the
necessity of the "new birth" in every individual, as much
as Methodist or Calvinist does—& I can see the fact as
clearly as the fact of sin. So it seems to me at least.

We find our beautiful Florence more attractive than ever,
green with vineyards & vocal into the very streets as we
walk along them, with nightingales. Both of us are inclined
to stay on here & not go northwards—but there appears a
duty in the case, & we should give too much pain by
changing our plans. Therefore we shall probably go in
about a fortnight, to London through Paris where we shall
remain only a few days. Robert has a book to see through
the press in London—mine is not ready. You say nothing
of the two volumes, in prose & verse, you once spoke of.
I am afraid you would find it difficult if not impossible, to
make a publisher print verse for you at his own risk. Frederick Tennyson did—but then there was the Tennyson name.
Alexander Smith was an exception every way— I dont

understand that case. My edition before the last I received about a hundred pounds for as 'half profits'—a large edition of above a thousand copies!—and if that is "all right" I cant conceive how either publisher or author can make fortunes & live in villas at Wimbledon. The present edition is out on the same terms only. Poetry makes a bad *metier*, one must confess. Have you anything in the "Book of Beauty" of this year? *We* have—both Robert & I . . Mr. Procter having written & entreated us at Rome to give a little help to the editress who has had the smallpox & is more straightened than usual in her circumstances. Tell me what you think of Frederick Tennyson's poems. He is a dear friend of ours—he has the poetical element, the melody, the richness of vocabulary—but he seems to me to see, feel, think, speak nothing distinctly. It's all haze—a golden haze certainly.

The war is lamentable, but I am considerably comforted by the fact of the Anglo-french alliance which is good for each nation, & for the general civilization of the world. Our poor Italians are in despair at the adhesion (such as it is) of Austria—and I, for my own part, am sorry at the pretext being so withdrawn for a blow over the clenched jaws of the beast that holds Lombardy.

We had some delightful days on the Roman Campagna . . one exquisite day in Villa Adriana at Tivoli, with the Kembles— That's the best part of our visit to Rome. Since our return we have spent a few pleasant evenings at friends' villas—Mr. Lytton's for one. We are going today to turn tables at Mr. Kirkup's with certain "models" who are model 'mediums' as well, it seems. I say that Robert is prepared to bear with the "spirits" for the sake of the bad earthly company (out of pure masculine curiosity) and he retorts that it's *vice versâ* with me. Mr. Kirkup is deep in the subject of tables &c just now, and so is his friend Mr. Knox the maker of rubies & elixirs. Mrs. Stuart has gone to England & Scotland with her eldest boy, and Mr. Stuart having heard of a foreign correspondent-ship in a mercantile house at Manchester, says he will go there for a hundred & fifty pounds a year if they will give it. Manchester & a hundred & fifty a year, in change for Florence! . . "AND NOTHING," you will add. No, he gets fifty from the Wises for reading three hours four times a week with the two boys, and then he has literary work & other occupation more or less certain. I think I would hesitate before accepting England & the expenses of an English life on such a pittance. But England looks well at a distance. For my part Florence seems to me preferable as a place of residence to all other places, especially now when the completed railroads bring it nearer to the north.

Do write soon & give me better news of yourself & all of you—dear Mr. Ogilvy among the rest. It must be very injurious to you to have such long trains of sadness & anxiety. May God bless & take care of you all.

As to the Ruskin mystery, if I understand at all, (and it was only an awful whisper which came to us at Rome) the woman must be . . what shall I say? . . *a beast* . . to speak mildly. This, at least, according to my own views of what human nature & bestial nature are severally.

With best love from Robert & myself to the whole round of you, believe me dearest Mrs. Ogilvy

Your ever affectionate

Elizabeth Barrett Browning.

Write at once or we may miss your letter, our movements being quite uncertain, & I long to hear of you quickly besides. I sent Gigia's letter, & will enclose back to her any answer I may receive. It will be a great loss if you have to lose her— Do the children keep up their Italian? Has Alexander begun to read yet, and to write? And Marcia? I teach Penini about half an hour a day. He reads easy books, and writes remarkably well— He is not as keen just now about his drawing. The military tasks are in ascendency, though he told me the other day that he

would'nt go into a battle till he was *seven*, which is satisfactory for the present. He is emulous of the dignities of
the earth, & confided to me when he was at Rome, that
he would like very much to be the Pope. "What," said I,
"would you rather be the Pope than Louis Napoleon?"
After a pause of consideration—"No—I would much more
lather (rather) be Napoleon. Lat's tlue." (That's true.)
Penini, too, has a certain interest about the war, & observed the other day with proper contempt that he "sought
at first lose naughty Lussians were more stlong." (thought
them stronge<r.)>

Letter 27

Although the Brownings wanted to proceed to England, they found
they could not travel even a short distance to escape the heat of Florence because of an insufficiency of funds. Fortunately the weather
remained unseasonably cool.

"We are all poets in Florence," she writes her friend, accordingly
mentioning Frederick Tennyson, Brinsley Norton, Robert Lytton,
Isa Blagden, Buchanan Read, and Elizabeth Kinney.

Florence. August. [28, 1854] Monday.
My dearest Mrs. Ogilvy I am almost ashamed of having kept
the enclosed above a week, and I do hope that it may be
none the less welcome for arriving late. We have been
first uncertain, then vexed . . quite unable at last to leave
Florence for even the Baths of Lucca on account of pecuni-
ary back-slidings—& as to Paris & England they became
early out of the question. We *must* get to London somehow next summer to print our books. Till then we remain here, & shall be more given to writing letters, now
that we are delivered from the position between the 'si' and
'no'; so do write to me & provoke me (in the good etymo-
logical sense) into answering you. I am anxious to hear
more about you, seeing that even in your last accounts

you speak of new indispositions. How much serious illness you seem to have had!—and now that a tranquil mind is so important to *you*, how doubly a trial to dear Mr. Ogilvy. As to the event which is imminent, I suppose one *should*, after the seventy seventh child, leave off congratulating the gifted mother—but in spite of everything reasonable, I cant help thinking you a happy queen-bee with such a hive buzzing round you! & wishing I had one of the supernumerary honey-makers to hum in the cell next Penini's. Last winter he expressed a humble opinion that, if he was "velly dood," "*peaps*" (perhaps) "Dod would send him a little broller" . . but now, being desperate, he confided the other day to Wilson that "leally" (really) he "tould'nt bear it any more, & that papa & mama *must buy* him a boy to play *wiz*"—. Your children scarcely can know the blessing they are born to, of companions on their own level. Penini is the most social child in the world, and it's quite painful sometimes to see the yearning with which he looks after young children, poor solitary darling! He has had a bright life of it, beset with every sort of tenderness & indulgence—but the drawback is still felt in spite of us all, & all we can do. I had hoped for him as well as for ourselves that we should have had you here in Florence—but you put the extinguisher fairly over us—we are black to the wick. Of course I comfort myself by "wondering how you could do so," and abusing Peckam Rye . . is that the name?—and all London neighbourhoods. Tell me minutely about your house & whether you like it, & if the expenses are not consuming. Mrs. Ogilvy's health is too good an excuse . . I am grieved you should be so justified . . . but for the question of education . . why people in general come abroad precisely for facilities in education. You dont think of putting your boy to a public school at six years old,—& for the rest, what can you find in England which is not here at every corner? Do set down this piece of impertinence of mine to my disappointment at not having you here. It's enough to turn my usual meekness into bitterness— I've been camomile tea ever since. For my part, in all seriousness, I hold Florence to be the most desirable place of residence in Europe, and it seems to me very probable that the result of giving another trial to Paris will be our return here to make an ultimate settlement. Oh—we shall try Paris fairly. But my misgiving is that I personally shall not be able to bear consecutive winters there on account of the climate. In other respects I like the place as you know. But I love Florence—even Robert says he loves Florence since he has been at Rome. (Before then, he used to hanker rather, you remember, after Rome.) And we have had a very pleasant summer here in spite of disappointments, want of pence, & superfluity of sun.

For the last, the season has been milder as to heat, than it usually is in Florence, and I have had the comfort of seeing my Penini grow fatter, in spite of his being, as he elegantly expresses it in pure Tuscan, "tutto bagnato" seven times a day. I steadily keep him to half an hour's application every morning, between reading & writing, & though he reads only tolerably he writes really well, beautifully . . I am very conceited about his writing. He indulges too, in compositions, which he calls his "poems" . . we have nearly a book full, in his own handwriting, of which the grammar & language altogether are something indescribable, as you may suppose. With all the faults however, (and perhaps the faults are the most precious part of the thing to me), there is a certain *verve* & intention by no means common at his age. He's so infantine in his ways too, that it makes it more striking. The drawing sometimes is suspended for a time—& then he takes it up again as he has done lately— but, dear Mrs. Ogilvy, there's a frightful constancy to gun & sword . . I am getting alarmed at it! As some of my friends may be at the state of his religious opinions—for he goes occasionally into the Catholic churches to pray, (I wd. let him go into St Sophia's) and talks & writes a consider-

able quantity of Swedenborgianism. Such a pair of black
knees he brought out of the Duomo the other day! What
have you been doing? "Saying my *players*." And what
prayers did you say? "The same sort I say at night—about
papa & mama." He has taken up a dislike to the priests . .
I cant conceive how—perhaps from Ferdinando who is a
protestant "at heart" as they say. "I leally dont lite lose
pliests! not a bit." But the "naughty priests" & the "beautiful prayer-music" in the churches, are not to be confound-
ed, he thinks.

Tell me if you have read Frederick Tennyson's poems
& what you think of them. There is another poet here
just now . . a poet in the shell . . young Norton, Mrs.
Norton's second son. He has turned Roman catholic, married a Capri girl without shoes and stockings (or beauty)
committed follies enough to win his poetical spurs before
twenty one. His verses are not quite so convincing. Even
they however are not ill-done—& he may do much better as
he lives longer, in all ways. As to faculty he is not equal to
Lytton—you will see a poem of Lytton's, by the way, in the
last Blackwood . . 'The Villa' signed *Trevor* which is an
anagram of Robert:—he's Robert Lytton. I think he will
achieve something excellent some day—I hope in him. At
present he suffers in his imagination from the strength of
his memory. We are all poets in Florence. Not to rhyme
would be a distinction. My friend Miss Blagden, who lives
in a villa & gives us tea-parties with a sunset to correspond,
is going to try to print a book in America . . (I remember
Mr. Ogilvy's hitting upon an idea of the kind & of my smiling *against* it: I doubt much still.) Then there's Mr. Buchanan Read who has just finished a pastoral epic (toned between Thomson & Cowper—will *that* do?) of some eight
thousand lines. He talks of bringing it out simultaneously
in America & England. Also, Mrs. Kinney, wife of the ex-
minister (American) at Turin, residing here now, has completed, a narrative poem, a tragedy . . I dont know what—

We have plenty of Muses you see in Florence, though the "mediums," it is pronounced at New York, are for the present deficient. Also, Mrs. Norton, her son says, is likely to come here before long. She is said to be nearly as beautiful as ever—under which brilliant circumstances it must be rather trying to be a grandmama, and Brinsley Norton need'nt have been in such haste to send her the news yesterday by telegraphic despatch.

Mrs. Gordon is gone to England . . to Devonshire . . with her family. Mrs. Stuart has returned—and Mr. Stuart's brother's daughter is now staying with them for a year. I fear they dont get on much better. He bids me give you his best regards. You received the books he sent—did'nt you?

Write soon & fully—do! Do you happen to know any lady who wants a companion & would be kind & gentle to her? Poor Haydon's daughter writes to me in a desolate state. She has fifty six pounds a year of her own, but it is not enough to keep her in any comfort of course, & she wants protection. She wd. like to go abroad she says. Under thirty she must be: father & mother gone! Will you tell me if you hear of anything? May God bless you all. With our united love to you both I am ever my dear friend most affectionately yours EBB.

I direct to Perth for fear I shd. miss you.

Address: Angleterre viâ France | Mrs. David Ogilvy | King's Place | Perth | N.B. *Redirected:* 3 Melville Street | Portobello. *Postmarks:* 28 AGO. 1854 FIRENZE; PT-DE-BEAUVOISIN TOSCA 2 SET 54; 3 SP 1854; PERTH SE 4 1854; SEP 4 1854; PORTOBELLO SE 5 1854.

Letter 28

On January 25, 1855 the Ogilvys' third son, Angus, was born.

During this time the European political scene was in turmoil. In England the Aberdeen ministry fell to the Palmerston government. In Russia Czar Nicholas died on March 2, adding even greater complexity to the already confusing Crimean War.

This war was the motivation behind the publication of various poems. Among these were *War Waits* by Gerald Massey, *Sonnets on the War* by Alexander Smith and Sydney Dobell, and "The Charge of the Light Brigade" by Alfred Tennyson. Robert Lytton's new work was entitled *Clytemnestra, the Earl's Return, the Artist and Other Poems*.

On June 20, 1855, the Brownings with Pen, Wilson, and Ferdinando left for Paris and London. They did not return to Casa Guidi until the autumn of 1856. One of the main purposes of this journey was to oversee the publication of their poetry: Elizabeth's book of between five and six thousand "blots" was *Aurora Leigh*; Robert's "rough work" resulted in *Men and Women*.

[Florence] March 6. [1855]

My dear friend, dearest Mrs. Ogilvy, I can't bear that you should be the first to write, after all. Here is my vindication— I was on the point of replying to your letter instantly, when I was taken ill with the worst attack on the chest I ever suffered from in Italy—the consequence of the conjunction of more frost & a bitterer wind than are common to us. The cough was very wearing, & the night-fever most depressing . . & by the time there was a possibility of sleep for either me or poor Robert (who passed his nights in keeping up the fire & warming the coffee) of course I had become very weak & thin, & dull at letter-writing. Then the good news reached me through the papers, of the birth of your boy, & I knew you were too happy to have time for wondering after negligent friends. Am I pardoned? Still, it vexes me that I should not have preceded you in a letter . . & after the birth of your child. I congratulate you warmly upon it—I dont feel the need of five children myself, and yet, if I had them, I should be

proud & happy. I have a decided taste for children as you
are aware. Sophia Cottrell has just produced another . . .
a boy . . which is a disappointment—small but healthy.
She submitted to chloroform & suffered nothing. They
all go to England in May for six months.

So do we. We shall linger at Paris in going,—& our plan
has always been to spend the winter there—but Robert has
taken such fright at my illness that he swears he will not
trust me as far north as Paris. We shall see. Very probably
the purse will run dry & we shall have no tide after October, for going south. Casa Guidi we have taken on for
another year . . that is, till May twelvemonth. We both
love Florence, & a house is cheaper here than elsewhere &
we must have house-room for our furniture & books. The
winter has been mild here in comparison to what it has
been in other places—and even at Rome & Pisa they have
suffered from our disadvantages. For the last six or seven
weeks, with a great deal of wet, we have had a mild temper-
ature. I am tolerably well,—only of course weakened, &
obliged to have recourse to cod's liver oil in order to
appearing in England with a decent covering on bones. It
has been an intense comfort to me to see my Penini with
cheeks of rose all this time—I wish I could be grief-bearer
for him always. You give a delightful idea of your Alexander—& all I ever wished for my child was the moral nature tenderly developped. As to genius, it is a good thing
& a great thing, but we make more of it than God & his
angels do. It does not imply happiness at any rate, to the
individual gifted so. Penini has a great deal of quick per-
ception & ready faculty—what more, remains to be seen.
I should like you to look over a book of compositions,
from five years old to five & a half or seven months, perfectly genuine & written in pencil by himself—& if you care
to do it, write a word to my sister at *50* Wimpole Street,
& she will let you have it. The book belongs to Robert's
father, & was lent to Arabel. You will know Penini by it,

it is so very characteristic. Robert & I both cried out in horror at your question about cutting off the curls. What!—break off the noses of our marble saints! We are not such roundheads. No, no— When Penini is twelve years old, it will be time enough to think of such barbarisms, unless by that time the fashion of male heads should become less barbarised. Even as it is, young England is much given, I observe, to divide the hair seraphically (& Miltonically) in the middle of the head —& Penini's costume is admired I assure you—he was called "a little Vandyke" but yesterday. He is just as you saw him, but with very short petticoats, & deep embroidered collars, when covered up to the throat as he has been this winter—(when it is warm we shall see the white shoulders again) & short embroidered trowsers. His hair has been cut several times, but only the ends to prevent splitting—& the long sweep of golden brown ringlets under the low-crowned black-velvet hat & feather, is very picturesque,—& you would'nt have the heart, if you saw him, to suggest cutting off a curl. You know I wonder at you, in the matter of Alexander! But then he had been ill—& such things give us utilitarian ideas about broadcloth. Only, you always plotted a little against his infancy. You must have dreamt of a toga before he was born. Do you remember the blouse at two years old, & how I protested? Ah well. You have a relay of babies. I have but one, & must keep him as long as I can. Six years old. Yes, it's dreadful. I grudge the six years old. He talks of the toys he is to have at "*his christmas*" (as he calls his birthday) to un-sympathizing years—(see how I have spelled '*ears*' . . I grow distracted in thinking of them!). But the child with all his cleverness is peculiarly infantine still, thank God . . which is remarkable considering that he is an only child. There's nothing old-fashioned & overshrewd about him . . & as he is open & scarcely ever shy, it's charming to hear him talk. He reads very well & with great animation . .

sometimes, when a book's amusing, twenty pages at a time. We go through heaps of books—childish books . . as high up, however, as Andersen & Grimm's fairy tales which he enjoys much. Then he writes four lines a day in running hand. Robert gets him on beautifully with his music. He plays all the scales, sharp & flat—& he plays from the book some easy airs. Robert takes the greatest pains with the child—& to hear him play & count, shaking about his small heels under the piano, is quite funny. He has a decided vocation for music. Indeed as he says of himself, . . "I *tan* do anysing when I *tly*" . . there's a want of nothing except of application—he's like a bird for keeping still . . playing at omnibus for instance on the arm of my chair while I hear him read . . but gentle & sweet. If I begin to scold . . "Oh, you darling pet Ba," says he, "be dood." What *is* one to say . . half strangled in the little hugging arms?

Dear Louisa must be very forward in all ways. She always *was* forward, that child. Tell me if the children talk Italian with Gigia, or if the English has been too strong with them. Penini always calls himself an Italian . . "io voglio essere Italiano"—also he's tremendous at Napoleonisms, which he catches up from his Tuscans rather than from me, I beg to say. Poor England. We have the most depressing statements & opinions from different quarters. Dickens, Sir Edward Lytton, & the Examiner-editor seem to have agreed that we are on the verge of a "first french revolution." The people are said to be sullen & to have lost faith not only in their governments but their parliaments. In the midst of it all, down drops the Czar, by apoplexy or other strangulation. What a *coup de theatre*! The times are turning to melodrama.—

I scarcely agree with you about Gerald Massey—reading him simply in the Athenæum. He seems to me poetical, but effeminate—somewhat feeble really. Several of the A[lexander]. S[mith]. sonnets on the other hand were intense—I thought two of them fine, in particular. A[.] Tennyson's 'Light Brigade' is ragged & unartistic for so great an artist—though, as Robert says, "with the germ in it of a great lyric." Read a new book of poems by *Owen Meredith*—meaning Robert Lytton, Sir Edward's son; & tell me how you like them. There's a good deal of unconscious sympathy rather than imitation in this young man, but, he will work his way clear & I expect excellent things from him as a true poet, . . give him time.

We shall have our books ready this summer for publication, I hope—but here are between five & six thousand lines *in blots* . . not one copied out . . & I am not nearly at an end of the composition even— Robert has at least all his rough work done. Tell me if you are doing anything . . you. Mrs. Stuart has been here with all her children. He has been well & prosperous this winter—giving lessons, & writing railroad papers. Mrs. Trollope's baby has been desperately ill with convulsions, is recovered. Mr. Costigan & his family have vanished to Leamington in a farewell dinner given to him by the English Florentines. No letter this time for Gigia! It's not my fault. We are very glad to hear of Mrs. Ogilvy's being better. I see you don't think of emigrating anymore! If I were you I wd. put my five children into panniers & make the best of them. Keeping to the mother-soil for the sake of the children is being "par trop" maternal. May God bless you & dear Mr. Ogilvy say Robert & I. Your ever affectionate EBB.

Address: Mrs. David Ogilvy | Peckham Rye. | Surrey. *Postmarks:* PD MR 15 1855; FP MR 15 1855.

Letter 29

The long lapse of nearly three years in the extant correspondence from Elizabeth to Mrs. Ogilvy indicates the possibility of missing letters, although Elizabeth discloses in the first paragraph of this letter that she had not written for at least a year. The "blows" alluded to are the deaths of her cousin John Kenyon in December 1856 and her father in April 1857. Mrs. Ogilvy had also been under stress, since she had two brothers in India when the mutiny of the Indian army broke out in March 1857.

During these years the Brownings spent the summer of 1855 in London and the winter in Paris, but Elizabeth suffered from the northern climate. Accordingly, after a second summer in England they returned to Florence. With the exception of two months spent at Bagni di Lucca during the summer of 1857, they remained at Casa Guidi, where this letter was written.

From other correspondence, several relevant incidents are known to have occurred in the three-year interim. Mrs. Ogilvy visited Elizabeth in London at least once, on August 23, 1855. She subsequently sent her a copy of her book, *Poems of Ten Years*, care of Arabel Barrett, who in turn gave it to Isa Blagden for delivery to Elizabeth in Paris when she met the Brownings there in January 1856.

It is also known that Mrs. Ogilvy wrote at least two letters to Elizabeth in 1857. One, in January, told Elizabeth that mothers were not allowing their daughters to read *Aurora Leigh*. The other told of the birth of her last child, Violet Isabel, on December 12, 1857.

The "business" Robert agrees to conduct for Mr. Ogilvy derives from the fact that Mr. Ogilvy was anxious to have a painting commissioned in Florence and had asked Robert to enter into negotiations on his behalf. The picture, which remains unidentified, was ultimately executed by G. Mignaty and was sent to Mr. Ogilvy from Florence in May 1858.

In January 1858, Felix Orsini had made an attempt on the life of Louis Napoleon and his empress in Paris. The plot had been planned in England, however, where Orsini had fallen under the influence of a fellow refugee, Giuseppe Mazzini. Mazzini proposed to unify Italy under a republican form of government and as a last resort he advocated the theory of political assassination. When France protested the protection afforded other conspirators, Palmerston remained silent, although he did introduce a bill making conspiracy to murder a felony. The bill's defeat and the fall of the ministry indicate

the growing opposition to the government's apparent acquiescence
to foreign menaces. Elizabeth, as an Napoleonist and a lover of
abstract justice, was greatly offended by England's failure to sympathize with the French position on this issue.

[Florence. c. January 29, 1858]
My dearest Mrs. Ogilvy, I have seemed almost to lose hearing of you in this long silence. You were good to write
first— I know I did not seem to deserve it. For a year past
I have been very slow, nay unwilling to write a line,—and
you and others might well have given me up for what was
less my fault than my misfortune after all. After some
blows, one takes up the burden of life again, but one stag-
gers a little at first, and then creeps. Then the nerves
strengthen, and one walks walks nearly as usual perhaps.
The end is not so far.

You see I mean to behave better in writing; and, to
prove my sincerity, I answer your letter by return of post.
So glad I was to hear what I call a good account of you all,
upon the whole. That you should not have suffered more
from the misfortunes in India, is very pleasant to know:
and since you told me of having two brothers there, I
have been able to measure your anxiety. May God preserve yours for you, & bless you to them.

But dear Mr. Ogilvy should not overwork himself,—
neither should *you*. What would become of me (& of the
house) I wonder, if I had a house to manage! It's a privi-
ledge on my part & an advantage on my husband's, that I
have never ordered dinner once since my marriage. A
positive blessedness is the smooth fashion of continental
life,—yes, I do think so. The two ends meet somehow, by
means chiefly of paying the week's bills & having done
with them. Now, through the kindness of our dear friend,
we are much less pinched & trammelled than in the old
days. We dont increase our establishment & so we have
more money left for pleasures & embroideries of life. I
can remember when I had to think of it, before I bought

gloves. As for you, you pay for the jewels in your caskets, out of the purse in your pocket—& economy with you is a proof of riches. When "your ends meet," you must be overjoyous I should think. Observe how covetous I am of children! Always, always! I shall hanker after little girls to my dying hour. And poor Peni echoes me. When he reads Grimm's story of the "twelve brothers" he sighs, "I wish *I* had twelve brothers." And then he asks how soon he may be "married," in the hope of having "a boy." "Perhaps in twelve years, dear papa & mama?" We answer, "By all means, but that he must get a great deal of wisdom into his head in the course of those years, because so much is necessary in the married & parental state."

He is a funny child. A few nights ago he came in to me in very low spirits—sate down on my knee & threw his arms round my neck & confessed himself "very unhappy"— saw everything 'en ·noir' & was inclined even to perpetual celibacy. "Dear mama, I dont think I shall ever marry myself. If I DO ever, I will take an Italian—(perhaps an Italian princess) but no, I dont think I shall marry myself ever." When I came to enquire tenderly—after the right quantity of kisses administered to spoilt children—why the world looked so black to him, I found that his nurse wanted to hold him by the hand in the carnival, betraying to the whole world, *who* was behind the mask, in the domino. "Dear mama," he repeated, "think what *my position is!!* do think."

He has a rose-coloured domino, &, having got over the difficulties of his position, is enjoying the carnival immensely. I cut the knot, by giving another domino to his attendant. Poor Peni.

He is not, in the least a "young person," but rather quite a young child still,—with the same face & look & ways. His cleverness is a curious contrast to his babynesses of various kinds, & his matrimonial schemes dont tend to mature him. You will cry out perhaps, but he still wears his embroidered short trowsers—high blouses of course, but of a lighter material than cloth—velvet, say, or merino. Even the gastric fever he had at Lucca last summer, which kept him a fortnight in bed, & frightened me out of my wits, did not touch a ringlet of his head, dear darling. But he improves in the power of attention.

March 1 — So far had I written as far back as you see. Alas. Rose-coloured dominos wont decide the colour of life. I broke off there, & before I could begin again, both Robert & Peni were seized with 'grippe,' Peni catching it from his father,—& during the last week of the carnival he was shut up in the house, (domino & all, if he had'nt lent it to a small friend) & so lost the bloom, the bouquet, the glory of the festa time. Poor Pen—he wore it beauti-fully till the last morning dawned, and then he lay in bed & declared his intention (the tears running over the poor eyes) of never getting up again in this world!— The heart which had been getting bigger & bigger with grief, gave way at last.

Never mind. We get over our woes on the earth, in a surprising way. Grippe & despair are alike past; a prom-ise to go to two plays & a piece of five pauls having some-thing to do with it as well as philosophy: and now we are all as well as usual. In a way, too, to be better,—for it is raining,—& I hope we shall soon have our arrears of heat paid up with interest.

In the meanwhile, let me tell dear Mr. Ogilvy, that his business is in a way to be done,—only Robert cant get it well done for less than FORTY *dollars*, and as you mentioned thirty, he waits for instructions from you before he con-cludes the agreement. Write & tell me what you wish.

I wont touch on politics. I too know something of the unfortunate Orsini. I know indeed too much of that party altogether, & of the head of it, Mazzini the unscrupulous, who would crush the world, inclusive of his friends & his enemies, under the chariot wheels of his One Idea, rather than it should swerve an inch. I know of the men, & I have even *loved* the women whom he has mesmerized to the most utter demoralization, . . ready to use the assassin's knife at any moment. These things are hateful to me. Foreigners? Italians? No—Englishmen—English*women*. These things are hideous in my eyes. "Oh Liberty, what deeds are done in thy name!" Oh, Italy, how thou art undone by such deeds!

So I stop myself. I wont talk politics. I know I disagree with you on this French question, as treated in the House. I know perfectly,—so it is better not to write of it. It is certainly glorious for "the French colonels" to have led an English House of Commons to stultify themselves, . . even if it is not glorious for England to have followed the great example of Naples (held up before her by Milner Gibson!) and to refuse to do right because she is asked. For my part I consider the vote & the discussion which threw out Palmerston, dishonored us all. I dont often quote the Times, but really "Brummagem blustering" is the very term for it.— If Lord Derby stands, he must bring forward an equivalent for "the bill"—so it must end,—for what you call "our freedom," dear friend, must'nt be our freedom to murder. The world must'nt point its finger at us as if we were "afraid to do right"— Let me remember to add that in calling Mazzini "head of that party" I dont mean that personally he has been mixed up with the late event in Paris. That may be or may not be. In fact there has been some late coolness between him & Orsini. But indirectly he gives brains & heart to all their conspiracies. He is the apostle of assassination . . *that*, I *know*.

And one word of the "Right of Assylum." What should all we liberals say, if the Church of Rome insisted on exercising her old right of assylum to criminals at the altars?— Civilization has ended such a state of things,—of possibilities even.

My dear friend—do tell me what books your children

read—what, in English, what in French?—and who among them reads French?—what in Italian too? It's most difficult to get Italian books for children,—and Peni is now reading translations from the French of M^dme Guizot. I like to hear all about your dear children. Have you taught any French to Alessandro, or does he keep steadily to Latin? Peni has'nt touched Latin yet. But I should have liked you to hear him read & translate a page of Grimm's German just now in one of his good moods .. which makes an immense difference. He translated quite fluently. In French he has not finished Berquin yet, who is voluminous. —— I myself have done little lately but read German, & have nearly attained to the goal of getting on without a dictionary which is my 'bête noire.' Heaps of M^dme Hahn Hahn's novels have been consumed in this endeavour. Mrs. Jameson who has lived in Casa Guidi all the winter, has read she says, & speaks highly of the 'Christianity without Judaism' you speak of. It seems to *me* that Christianity stripped of its Judaism & its Scholasticism, would be a very different thing from Christianity as generally recognized.

Have you observed an advertisement of a new magazine, the Englishwoman's Magazine, edited by Bessie Parkes. It is chiefly supported by women—& the chief object is to raise the woman's condition. If you liked to contribute I dare say they would be glad & the pay is said to be good. By naming my name to the editor she would give you an immediate reading, I venture to think. Perhaps you might not care. Mrs. Trollope contributes. < . . . >

Letter 30

In July 1858 the Brownings travelled north again to visit family and friends in France, where they remained until mid-October. Because of Elizabeth's previous illness in Florence and her general poor health, the Brownings decided to winter farther south; late in November, accordingly, they settled in their former apartment in Rome and fell into the busy social routine alluded to in the first paragraph.

The letter, which is a fragment, begins with a characteristic statement of their literary activity. It concludes with a reference to the marriage of Prince Napoleon, Louis Napoleon's cousin, to Princess Clotilde of Savoy on January 30, 1859.

[Rome. c. January 30, 1859]

< . . . > But much work cant be done under such circumstances: we must go back to Florence to work. Rome is crowded. Crême de la crême—Duchesses passing as skim milk by the side of crowned heads,—& crowned heads the merest curd by the side of cardinals. Balls, receptions, squeezes in every degree. Meantime Robert is so good (I call it goodness) as never to neglect giving two hours a day to Pen's music. The consequence is that the loss of our Florence master is by no means felt. Little Pen makes great progress, & though I say it who should'nt, *will* play beautifully. There are brilliant points about his execution already, & one wonders to observe the dexterity & activity of the small hands. The sentiment of music is very strong in him. We dont work him hard in other directions—but he reads with me, German French & English, & Italian daily, & writes English & Italian *dictations*, which last I find of excellent use in mending his weak points of spelling. The child is much grown in height of course, but looks so precisely what he was . . with the same delicate infantine features & complexion that you would be surprised perhaps. He wears his blouses somewhat shorter,—and full, *rather* short trowsers of which I got the pattern in Paris . . black fine cloth or velvet for out of doors, white in the house, . . & embroidered collars as usual. I am as fond of "dressing him up" as ever, you see. But there is no want of simplicity in the dress, nor want of fitness for his age, it seems to me. The curls hang naturally—"mamas curls" still—under heavy mortgage to me, though he would fain have them off. But all artists (including my husband, I am glad to

say) applaud me for not translating him into prose before the time of prose comes. By the way, I want you & Mr. Ogilvy, when you are in London with time on your hands, to go to Mr. Monro's studio 6 Upper Belgrave Square, & look at a bust of Peni, in course of production for the next exhibition. The artist was struck by Pen's head this autumn in Florence, & asked to make a clay sketch of it. So successful *that* seemed to me, that I yearned after the marble—& he had the generosity to insist on doing it for us at half price. If you see it, you see Peni—so I want you to see it. Most spiritual, & most like.

Let me tell you what Peni is doing just now. Reading Monte Cristo in an Italian translation. He has entered into it with a passion, a passion! I find him reading it in his bed with a candle propped up in a wash hand basin. "Only one chapter, DEAR mama!"— I hear exclamations, "O Dumas, Dumas, you ARE a great man! I knew by mama you were a great man—but to write a book magnificent like this, I never thought of it"! To tell you the truth, when I let Peni begin the book I did'nt think he would be interested beyond the prison-part—but his interest is alarming, & he is actually at the end of the fourth volume. Of course he has the same facility in reading Italian as English—it's the same thing. The Italian shows itself in his English talk sometimes very amusingly. For instance he told us a few days ago that he had "seen a beautiful bronze in the Corso, which *represented* Romulus & Remus *popping at the wolf.*" And he expresses at dinner a decided liking to "*selvatic* ducks." But his English on the whole is not distressing, while he is always taken for an Italian child by Italians. He speaks French too without any shyness, though of course imperfectly. Latin is in the future for him, & Alexander has an awful advantage there.

Never did a marriage (except my own) please me so well as Prince Napoleon's. Viva la Francia, Viva l'Italia, *Viva Verdi*, as they say at Turin! < . . . >

Letter 31

In the beginning of 1859, diplomatic circles were alarmed at a message Louis Napoleon gave to the Austrian ambassador in Paris, indicating a possible rupture between the two countries. Provoked by Count Cavour, Austria declared war against Piedmont, and Louis Napoleon accordingly supported his ally Cavour, promising a free Italy from the Alps to the Adriatic. The French victories at Magenta and Solferino attested to their military superiority; but Prussia, even though a neutral in this conflict, massed troops on the Rhine, leaving France vulnerable to attack. This threat induced Louis Napoleon to sue for a quick armistice before he had carried out his purpose. The peace terms were hastily concluded at Villafranca on July 8, 1859; Lombardy was ceded to Piedmont, the Venetian state remained in the possession of the Austrian empire, and central Italy was restored to its former rulers.

The Brownings had returned to Florence from Rome at the end of May. Shattered by the news of Villafranca and its impact on the the cause of Italian *Risorgimento*, Elizabeth had a severe attack in her chest (as she mentions in this letter). Once again Siena was chosen for the prescribed change of air. Before leaving, however, the Brownings witnessed the Florentines' rebellion against the Villafranca peace agreement and Leopold II's subsequent abdication in Florence. Tuscany was shortly annexed to Piedmont under the monarchy of Victor-Emmanuel. These fast-moving and revolutionary Italian developments did not leave Elizabeth in a very receptive mood to Tennyson's *Idylls of the King* which began to appear in 1859.

A reference below and one in Letter 34 indicate that Mr. Ogilvy had apparently considered sailing to America via the *Great Eastern*, one of England's early large steam vessels. Her maiden voyage to New York was delayed until 17 June, 1860.

Florence. Monday. [October 31?, 1859]
My dear friend, I *seem* very guilty in having allowed two letters of yours to wait so long for answers. But, instead, I have been very ill—nearly as ill as I could be, to come back again to the natural world: and then the strength was slow in its return, and until the last three weeks, though recovered in appearance, I constantly felt on the edge of a precipice, as if a little too much exertion would plunge me

down. I believe it came from agitation of mind on account of public affairs, combined with a great deal too much talking, and some sort of cold-catching when the body was rendered peculiarly susceptible by the heat of the weather. Lungs & heart were out of order together it seemed. Never have I been so ill in Italy. When able to move, & scarcely able to move, we went to Siena, (nobody here expecting to see me again) & got into a villa in the wilderness for two months, where the good air & absolute seclusion were God's means of restoration. Now I look as usual & *am* as well,—only we are advised to avoid the tramontana & go to Rome for the winter. Perhaps we may be cut up there by the revolution—but the evil of a cold climate is *certain* . . at least for one of us; & we are not afraid of our Italians with swords in their hands, being long used to questo genere. I think I never was so happy in my life as this spring & the early part of the summer—and with such a large, sympathetic, impersonal happiness. It was like the millenium in Florence, as discoursed of by the prophets—lion & lamb lay down together—all classes of persons, & most classes of thinkers, met in one embrace. No, you who read the Times & talk with the English, can have no idea what it was in Italy during the war,—the rapture, the ecstatic union, the gratitude & love. To see such sentiments, beautiful in an individual, flowering in a whole nation, was a sort of miracle. And what was almost stranger was the bearing of the French soldiers, encamped in the Cascine, all apparently penetrated, down to the privates, with the idea of performing a great action for others & getting nothing by it. That was really sublime. It was a true fraternization of the peoples. But the time of the harvest was not yet. Down in the midst of us fell the Peace!—and it was not a millenium peace, and the world was the world still. For a day, two days, there was wrath, anguish, distrust. Then, out everywhere again, came the portraits & busts of Napoleon III, & people took up hope

& faith anew. Only it was no more as before. There were differences of opinion—some were sanguine & some despondent, according to their temperaments: there were discussions on all sides: we were plainly in this natural world. As for me, for weeks afterwards, whenever at nights I caught a little feverish sleep, the dreams which came with it, were of long lists of impracticable conditions of peace,—and eternal transitions of provisionary governments.

Well—it is all past, I thank God. Now, if it were not for Venetia, whose future is not distinct, I should be almost glad for Villafranca. The war could not of itself have solved certain difficulties—and the peace has developed in these Italians the only qualities capable of solving them. How admirable have been the constancy, dignity, & energy of this people. What a ripening since 1848! Afflictions do indeed instruct & mature men.

I am in the highest hopes, and so is my husband. And, in fact, no one here does otherwise than hope, except certain politicians who "see as from a tower the end of all," because they have black in their eyes. The tranquility is profound. We are about to bring out a monumental edition of Macchiavelli (a very Florentine idea) and to erect two equestrian statues of the French emperor & the Piedmontese King in the Piazza dell' Independenza . . that is, "di Maria Antonia." I have found in Penini's journal,—(Peni keeps a journal, you are to know) . . "This is the happiest day of my *hole* life,—for dearest Vittorio Emanuele is really nostro re." Forgive the spelling which is my Pen's weak point (he spells Italian better than English) for the sake of the politics in which he is strong. He was very happy at Siena (apart from public events, poor darling) . . having made friends as usual with all the contadini in the neighbourhood,—keeping sheep with them, catching stray cows for them, driving the grape-carts, & helping to get in the vintage with a knife of his own exactly after the pattern of theirs, & then, at the end of the day, reading Dall' Ongaro's political poems (with occasional expositions) to an admiring circle. Also, to fill up the cup of joy, he once fired off a gun, (for which he was severely reprimanded by papa, & mama in particular)—and every day rode on a pretty Sardinian poney which Robert had the extravagance to give him & which we are positively preparing to take with us to Rome. Think of it!—but an only child! And he rides beautifully & with a most fearless grace, his long curls flying in the wind,—exactly of the same colour as the poney's tail. Do I confess to curls still? Yes— I confess to curls still. Did you see Monro's bust of him in this year's exhibition? If not, do get sight of it at the sculptor's studio, for it is beautiful and *tale quale*. He *is* a very good child, very sweet looking, & childish—not in the least studious . . but forward in many ways, with a facility in fact, which is a disadvantage in certain respects. German he reads & translates currently, and French he understands as he reads,—while as to Italian & English they are the same thing to him,—it is as if he had two native tongues. Latin is still for the future—but we must soon make a beginning. Arithmetic is no where—& spelling at a *rabusso* . . why, I scarcely know. In conversation he is very quick & amusing, with the same musical little voice which must go some day. Robert was very overkind, & heard him all his lessons during the two months of my illness, besides giving in the two hours a day in his own department of music. The child plays a complete sonata of Beethoven, besides some modern German pieces which require still more power of execution. Indeed it's considered quite a wonder how much those small hands can execute, & what a degree of expression the young soul can put into it.

There now— You see I have paid you in kind for your welcome details about your darlings. It seemed to me rather stupendous that you should permit Alexander to "shoot." Pray dont put him into jackets—pray, pray dont! Pen would wear long-tailed coats if I listened to him,—but I resist, I: I am strong-minded on this one point. I dare say your Louisa will be lovely. Oh, I wish I had a daughter.

But, at least, I have an Italy . . or shall have. It will be found that the Emperor Napoleon has been loyal to us from the first to last. Circumstances have been & *are* very difficult, & he has had to walk under the earth as well as over it; but always he has walked in one direction and towards one object. What has surprised me into admiration, is the continued gratitude of the Italians. No disappointment at certain turnings of the road, has hindered the flow of their gratitude. I hear of such men as Garibaldi even, expressing it in public & in private. This is great, on their part.

What am I to say of England & certain other nations?

Are you "satisfied" with the Idylls? So am not I—though there are exquisite things here & there. Perhaps it may be my fault, (surrounded as I have been so long with all this burning, throbbing, anxious life) but the book sounded to me far off, & fell flat & cold. I would rather have written 'Maud' than ten such books. Is it my fault or is it the book's fault, that I should feel so?

Dear Mr. Ogilvy wont go to America this winter in the Great Eastern, & I am glad of it. Write & tell me all about all of you, & give to him & yourself < . . . >

Letter 32

In the eight months that have passed since the previous letter, the Brownings had wintered in Rome and returned to Florence just a week before the present letter was written.

While in Rome Elizabeth decided to issue a slim volume of political verse, *Poems Before Congress,* published by Chapman and Hall on March 12, 1860; shortly before publication she had arranged to have a copy sent to Mrs. Ogilvy. The Congress of major powers, referred to in the title, had been scheduled to meet at Paris in

January to work out an arrangement for the unsettled Italian situation. When Louis Napoleon supported the determination of the central states to accede to Piedmont, the Congress was called off.

Elizabeth speaks of Baron Schleinitz's official statement. It reported that if Louis Napoleon had crossed the river Mincio to battle Austria, that would have induced Prussia to attack France. Such was not the outcome, however, because of the unexpected peace at Villafranca. "I was therefore *literally* right in the poem on Villafranca," she wrote to her sister on the day before this letter.

Prior to the war, Louis Napoleon had arranged with Cavour that as the price of her aid, France should receive Savoy and Nice. After Villafranca he waived his claim to these territories; but the accession of other Italian states to the Piedmontese kingdom so strengthened its position that he reverted to the original arrangement. The final decision was left to the people of Savoy and Nice who ultimately voted for French rule. Garibaldi was upset by this outcome and in anger sailed with a thousand of his supporters to Sicily, determined to overthrow the Kingdom of Naples. By the end of May 1860 he had conquered Sicily and proceeded to sail for the mainland. Elizabeth alludes to all of these developments as well as to the French troops remaining in Rome under General Lamoricière for the protection of the Pope.

In August Elizabeth wrote to her sister Arabel the details concerning Garibaldi's marriage as she understood them. In part the letter reads: "Poor simple Garibaldi was taken in a net like a lion, by her and her father, and he married her last winter . . like an ass . . immediately after the ceremony he discovered, and the wretched girl confessed it on her knees they say, that what she was in instant need of was simply . . a husband . . and a name for an unborn baby. He challenged his father in law and left his wife on the spot."

The photographs Elizabeth enclosed with this letter and which she mentions in her last paragraph have been preserved with the correspondence. They were done by D'Alessandri Frères in Rome and are reproduced in this volume as Plates II to IV.

Florence. June 15. [1860]

My dear friend it did not need your kind letter to remind me that though I send you my book, I owe you the debt of writing & that, instead of sending me a kind letter, you might well have reproached me. For a year past I have had

my life at once so full & so frail that such sins of negligence
or omission have been forced on me here & there. You
said once that as you stepped into life, you felt the calm
of the grave steal on you. I, an unbeliever in the calm of
the grave, may be as sceptical of calms of life—for though
older than you, the further I walk into life, the louder
grows the battle, the quicker beats the drum in my heart.
Never did a year of youth pass to me in a hotter fire &
passion than the last has. Not on personal subjects indeed.
But what difference does it make, if the emotion is personal?—if 'these tears be wet'?

In sending a few copies of my book to you & some
other friends, I felt as if I might be offending unaware.
But you have forgiven me my gift. Thank you. Not so,
have I fared with the English press, by which I am declared renegade & unnatural sinner, in all sorts of type. I
dont know if you have much access to the newspapers &
periodical publications, to be aware with what great feroc-
ity these dogs of war have been up & at my little book.
And now that its pretty well over, I am still alive, & feeling considerably relieved in having spoken out the word
that burnt in me. Whether truth or not, to you, it was truth
to me—& the reception found for it in England simply con-
firms me in the belief that it is God's truth as well as mine.
If the consciences of men had been in a less morbid state,
there would have been less irritation & more temper &
justice towards a writer who could only be disinterested in
her view. At any rate, I have delivered my own soul in
speaking—& if I had destroyed my popularity in the process
I would have spoken out equally. My publisher however
(Chapman) says there will be no injury—& that Aurora
Leigh is in the press for a fifth edition notwithstanding;
& that the B[efore] C[ongress]. poems are selling in spite
of vituperation. Did you read the Saturday Review on me,
& Blackwood? Professor Aytoun of course did the last.

I ask it of your candour to observe that the official

declaration of the Prussian minister (Baron Schleinitz) has settled the question of the Villafranca peace. Only that unexpected conclusion prevented the attack of Prussia, which was definitively fixed for the *passage of the Mincio*. The Emperor's statement therefore, before the Legislative Assembly, as well as his act in Lombardy, are justified beyond objection— . . except to those who saw no drawback in a European war of the largest kind.

You have taken a view of Italy, eminently unItalian, whether right or wrong abstractedly. What you call a "war of aggression" (on what ground?) is to them the "war of independence" for which they thank God. Let Napoleon be the devil twice over, they owe their freedom to him—not only at Milan but at Florence, at Bologna & elsewhere. Only his upraised finger prevents Austrian intervention at this moment—only his troops present in the peninsula, preserved to us the power of choice & the virtue of the vote. He would have "swamped" Tuscany? *Ask the Tuscans!*—who came to the vote with the French flag as well as the Italian. Ask Cavour . . who has been *at one* with the emperor from first to last. He might well say, "Napoleon is in my boat,—& must sink or swim with me." As to the cession of Savoy & Nice, it is'nt to be regarded as an isolated fact. It is'nt the pay for Lombardy. It is the condition (arranged from the beginning) of a reconstituted Italy. It rivets the alliance till the consummation of all things,—& justifies the Head of the French State to the opposing parties in France, & also to posterity, in raising up what in the course of some fifty or a hundred years may be a rival power— France is generous in her foreign policy, but she has like all nations her "interested classes;" and, besides, there are the different factions of the opposition who are using this question of Italy as a weapon against the Empire. For instance . . do you comprehend what is being carried on in Rome by Lamoriciére & M. de Merode & the parties they hang by? It is the

French opposition transported to Rome. Napoleon exposed his life in Lombardy; he is besides risking his dynasty. If you could hear with your ears at Rome the low curses of the clerical party— There was a certain Monsignore who said aloud with significantly ferocious eyes,—"To think, that only *one life* stands betwixt us and prosperity"! Well-instructed persons have said to me, speaking of the emperor,—"I fear for him. He will fail— Forty thousand priests against him!!— They will get their ends by taking his life, if by no other means."

When you come to Florence to "show Marcia her birthplace" (& Alexander's) you will find an equestrian statue of Napoleon side by side with Victor Emmanuels in the Piazza Maria Antonia . . now the Piazza dell' Independenza. You will find a live Tuscany . . an Italy, if it pleases God, restored to herself.

Meanwhile we are living, eating, drinking, dreaming, Garibaldi. His undertaking was pathetic & sublime at once. If he had failed it would have been in the eyes of all, a fault as well as a failure. We must have disclaimed him officially. In fact the danger to Central Italy was great— It was pulling down our house on our heads. More forlorn than any forlorn hope was this enterprise, to which he went, armed with his private grief—the loss of his birthplace, Nice . . and the fact of this miserable marriage of which you probably know the story. If you dont, I will tell you that tragedy. On the subject of Nice, he belonged to the small minority who objected to the annexation to France,—& not having the brain of a Statesman, so as to comprehend certain complications & previdences, he could not be convinced. He's our hero, but not our politician. People whispered, he would break his sword & go to America. No,—he did what was nobler. He avenged his personal suffering upon the enemy of Italy who had permitted the suffering.

We have just returned from Rome, having remained there six months. I had one attack in the course of it, but am well now—though scarcely as strong as before my illness last summer. Early in July we go to a villa near Siena, to avoid the hot season—& there our Abbè (who taught Penini throughout the winter) is to join us, take a lodging hard by & continue his work. He began to teach the child Latin six months ago,—gave him lessons also in French, arithmetic & geography. You may imagine Pen's innocence as to figures when I tell you that before we went to Rome, he never could be "quite sure," he said "which was a 6 & which a 9, as to the tails going up or down." Of course that was my fault. I thought he had enough to do with living languages &c, & I wanted to spare his young brain the fret of even simple addition. Also, I had never put him into Latin. And we wished him to learn according to the Italian vowel system, having a belief in its correctness. Our abbé is a Corsican, & speaks French & Italian with equal purity from his two national relations—not knowing a word of English, of course. He teaches most admirably—, & although an abbè & a priest, is one of the most innocent & amiable of men. Pen likes him extremely, & is'nt afraid of being a little playfully impertinent sometimes (in spite of Robert's lectures) about the Pope's excommunication, & codinism in the Papal states. The child has gone through the Latin grammar, translates the Latin Epitome of Sacred History into Italian, and Italian phrases into Latin, . . & writes parsing lessons, all very fairly—putting to shame my remembrance of the slow creeping classical methods in use in England. But the fact of Pen being a *native* Italian & having the language perfectly, gives him an advantage, which an English child has not, of course. He keeps saying that "Latin is the most beautiful language & *the most easy*, he ever learnt." Oh—but you are not to think he does'nt speak English just as I do. Yes, indeed. Only his Italian is an *Italian's*. Also, I believe I must confess that he writes Italian more correctly & idiomatically. In English idioms, he's astray sometimes—

talks of the "clock *beating* the hour," &c. But this is soon corrected, & in accent & fluency he's as English as the best of us, . . or the worst. Only . . such a politician!— such a Napoleonist! and *"Italianissimo."* I assure you it is'nt my teaching, though you may fancy this. He gets his politics from his friends . . out of the streets & campagne.

After which history of him, I beg you to look at his photograph. It's not *like him*—it's *himself.* We were all executed in our last June days at Rome,—just now; so that you have us as we look at present. Am I simply vain in supposing that you might like to have our shadows, "in memoriam"? I *want* you to see my Peni. As for me, I am "black"—women always suffer by this process,—but my personal vanity takes amends out of the child—I wish I had as much of all of you. Let me <have a let>ter from you at least, & an account of your being & doing? What have you been writing? Why dont you think of making any through the magazines? The Cornhill for instance? Our best love to dear Mr. Ogilvy, & all of you. Your affectionate friend EBB.

Address: Mrs. Ogilvy | Lower Sydenham | London. *Postmark:* LONDON—SW. JU 26 60.

Letter 33

Wilson and Ferdinando had been married in Paris in July 1855. Elizabeth, delighted by their marriage, was greatly shocked two months afterward when Wilson told her that she was expecting a baby in October. The son, Orestes, was born in Nottinghamshire at the home of Wilson's parents, where Wilson left him the following summer when she returned to the Brownings' service. When her second child, Pilade, was born late in 1857, Wilson left the Brownings and set up a boarding house in the Via Nunziatina in Florence. (Her most famous resident was Walter Savage Landor, whom Browning later took under his wing in July 1859. See Letter 35.) Ferdinando went to Rome with the Brownings for the winter of 1858-59; Wilson, listening to false reports sent by her sister (Arabel Barrett's maid), became insanely jealous of her replacement, Annunziata. So severe was her case that upon the Brownings' return to Florence in May, 1859 she alarmed Elizabeth by her delusions: she imagined a local baker was trying to poison her; and she had seen her son Orestes carried past her window by an angel. Ferdinando's return settled her mind and reassurred her, but Wilson wanted Orestes brought to Italy nevertheless. Mrs. Ogilvy offered to help bring this about by having her Italian nurse, Gigia, return to Florence with Orestes. Ultimately, Wilson's parents refused to give the child up and Gigia, accompanied as far as Marseilles by Mr. Ogilvy himself, returned to Florence via Leghorn without him (see Letters 34 and 35).

Despite Elizabeth's optimism, the health of Mrs. Ogilvy's daughter Louisa continued to be delicate. She died in 1870 at the age of 24. This letter also contains Elizabeth's first mention to Mrs. Ogilvy of Henrietta's illness. In June, the Brownings had learned from Taunton that she was in great pain from an internal growth, later diagnosed as cancer.

The meeting between the Emperor of Austria and the Regent of Prussia, held at Töplitz on July 26, 1860 sparked international speculation over its meaning. Although the meeting had no important result and Prussia maintained its position of neutrality, Austria hoped it might anticipate a possible alliance.

> Villa Alberti. Siena.
> August. 24. [1860]

I do thank you, my dear friend, for all the trouble you have taken for Wilson—it is pure goodness both to her & to me. We empower you to insist on the child's being at the ship on the day you shall indicate. Wilson will write to her people by this post. It would be a lamentable thing if such an opportunity were lost through the tenacity or awkwardness of her family. She ought to have her own child—& she ought *not*, moreover, (between you & me) to pay so much for the protection hitherto afforded to him. Also it is time for the Orestes who cant speak Italian, to meet the Pylades who cant speak English & that they should learn to understand one another in a brotherly way.

I am very sorry you should have more care about your

Louisa—but her constitution will steady itself presently. Dear Mrs. Ogilvy too. Yet I sympathize with souls that dont sympathize with bodies—souls that rebel & persist, when the strength cries, 'Past work'. After all there's something not ignoble in it—is it not so?—

Of my own deep anxiety I have not the heart to speak much. My two last accounts have had a shade of improvement in them—which lightened (comparatively) a few days to me—but I know too well, that if there were any reliable *betterness*, I should be told of it distinctly.

There is one cause of suffering which is incidental purely & not dangerous—*piles*. The pressure partly, & partly the opiates & their consequences are the cause of this. May God help us.

I am alive still to public interests. It is a time of grave crisis. We are looking for war—intervention from the enemy Austria. Toeplitz means mischief, if not the special mischief denied by dozens of newspapers. Certainly the Prince of Prussia gave his "parole de gentilhomme" (which I translate to you "word of a rascal") to assist Austria under certain conditions. Dall' Ongaro, the Venetian poet, came over from Florence the day before yesterday & found me sitting under my own figtree outside our windows here. He came full of the gravest news. You should have heard him talk in indignation of "questa canaglia di Germania." Of course its all a coalition against France—only observe what has been said by no unauthentic speaker— "Let Prussia move against Italy, & in that moment "le Rhin commençez à couler dans la France." And for my part I say Amen—well-deserved!

Still . . the fiercer the struggle the sooner over. There is not a simple desire here for the unity of Italy, but a *passion*. The outrageous thing is, that by the fault of Germany, the Italian war should not be allowed to seek its natural issue, without a general war. And I fear much.

Still my friend was very hopeful about Italy. So am I.

As we parted in the sentiment of it, I was carried away to say, "*Vivo* per questo"—to which he answered, his face in a blaze, . . "Vivete dunque."

Our love to dear Mr. Ogilvy when you write or see him. And my love & kisses to the children. Very dear friend, May God bless all of you—

Your most affectionate &

grateful EBB.

Wilson comes to press,—would it be quite impossible for Gigia to go to East Retford Nottinghamshire on her road to Liverpool, and spend two days with the Wilsons. Then she could make friend with the child, & one of them could travel on with her to Liverpool— Of course she would be their visitor at Carrol Gate—no expense. Consider if it be possible.

The address of the Wilsons is Carrol Gate East Retford Notts.

Address: Angleterre via France | Mrs. Ogilvy | Crawford's Lodging | Carnoustie | Forfarshire. | N.B. *Postmarks:* SIENA 25 AGO [1860]; PD.; LONDON AU 29 PAID; CARNOUSTIE AU 30 1860.

Letter 34

After discussing some of the private matters mentioned in the previous letter, Elizabeth turns her attention to commentary on recent developments in the Italian political situation.

Elizabeth's interest in spiritualism was not completely forgotten. In July 1860 a Mr. Howitt printed an article in the *Spiritual Magazine* which suggested that Elizabeth's *Poems Before Congress* was probably inspired by "biologizing infernal 'spirits' " and that for some time she had been under such supernatural influences. Robert found it amusing that spiritualists were making such accusations against his wife. A controversial article, "Stranger than Fiction," in the August issue of the *Cornhill Magazine*, offered a detailed description of the spiritualist craze in London.

Villa Alberti. Siena.

Sept. 12 [1860]

My dear friend, how good you have been & are. I thank you deeply both for my poor Wilson & myself— You have obliged both of us, & made her very very happy—which will be a joy to your kind generous sympathetical nature.

I perfectly agreed with you before, & we both did "right to be angry." The Wilsons were very provoking . . & so was my Wilson here—who being always weak in character showed a peculiar degree of weakness in not being resolute about the child. I do believe, poor thing, she would give up child or husband to anyone who knew how to set about wringing them out of her, & certainly her letters to her family must have encouraged them to assume that attitude of choice & possession . . as if the boy belonged to them & not to his own mother—

Well—it is settled, thank God. Ferdinando will be down at Leghorn to meet Gigia, & if she likes to come back with him here, we shall be very glad to see her. Dont fear about *bibles*— She might bring a bundle of bibles if she pleased, & nobody object. You forget that we are free Italy now. I wish I were as sure that she would have no trouble at the custom-office about her dresses—but I hear great complaints of the vexations heaped upon travellers through an incompleted organization, which is taken advantage of by persons in office. Ferdinando however will be there, & we must hope for the best.

I write at once, when I might wait till over Saturday— but I feel just now as if I *lived* only from day to day (from post to post) and as if I *dared* not put off the duty & desire of thanking you for your goodness to us. Of course you shall hear of Gigia if I am alive enough to write—or indeed she will write herself. Mr. Ogilvy has been *luxuriously* good (I mean to a superfluity) in escorting her to Marseilles. I should not be at all afraid (helpless as I am) to travel across France by myself, & I know young

English girls who do it without a fear.

Dearest Mrs. Ogilvy, my last account from Taunton was slightly improved—but it does not seem to me to amount to more than fluctuation,—though the least breath of a word about diminished pain soothes the burning at the heart which devours me— May God's mercy relieve me & all of us. My anxiety is, on some days, (when letters are expected) DREADFUL— At other times, I feel patient under the weight of a stone—and that is my best state. Oh—most of all, my dear dear friend, I thank you for your prayers.

Let us talk of Italy. You are worthy to know the truth, and yet it seems to me that you are much in the dark. The people are acting admirably, . . miraculously, . . considering their past. There has been some attempted revival of the Mazzinian party, but they were forced to mask to get a hearing, . . & being then unmasked by the government were repudiated by the majority instantly. The sympathy of the nation (even at places like Leghorn & Genoa) goes right against them,—& now that the Government moves openly towards the approaching crisis, their small degree of power is at an end.

Be sure that we have nothing to apologize for in Italy. No people, however educated, could have acted better. I dont speak here of Sicilians & Neapolitans. Things & men were alike rotten in those states—to speak generally, that is. At best, there was a great blind aspiration—but no settled conviction. How could there? The Neapolitans ARE what we remember all the Italians in forty-eight. Garibaldi's progress has been just a triumph. He touched the fruit with a finger, & it fell. There has been no earnest fighting except in Sicily—& even there, the King's troops were not reliable for the King. How could they? Garibaldi is a true hero, & a great military genius. But you are late in England in giving us your sympathy. The Italian question was settled militarily in the north, & civilly in the centre—and the south was only a question of time.

Then . . what can you mean by talking of Lamoricière
on the walls of Rome. Lamoricière has nothing to do
with the walls of Rome. The French keep Rome & have
nothing in common with Lamoricière (so little, that Lamoricière is where he is, only to be in opposition to the
emperor)—and no Italian (not even Mazzini, who in his
late address protested that *he* did not think of it) could
propose to lead Italians against the French— Why, you
would start as at a revelation if you could conceive of the
feeling of the Italians to the French & especially to Napoleon. Count Gori (senatore del regno) said to a friend
of mine yesterday . . "But you dont understand— The
French are at Rome for US— They *must* be there while
Austria holds Venetia." Matteucci (a chief man among
the Tuscan leaders, & who has been a member of Depu-
tations to Paris and of councils in Florence) considers that
the emperor's personal feeling for Italy has been *constant.*
And nothing has been more beautiful & admirable to me
than the stedfast gratitude & faith of this formerly sus-
picious people towards France, notwithstanding the enormous calumnies & misrepresentations sent in upon us on
all sides.

The newspapers are excellently conducted. You would
scarcely believe you were reading Italian newspapers, if you
could see the Nazione of Florence, the Opinione of Turin
& others. There is strength & moderation, largeness &
temper. The *issimo* is in *abeyance.* A great nation is
rising to its feet here, & there is no need of allowances or
of pardon.

But it is a time of crisis— Private cares have been broken
through for me by the press of public events on all sides.
For a week past (for instance) there has been scarcely a
possibility of private travelling on the railroads, (I hope
they may be clear for Gigia) the passage of troops having
been incessant. The King takes Naples from the hands of
Garibaldi—that's certain—but also so is the invasion of the

Pontifical States on the part of the King. Underneath all, there remains a mystery . . . . if it is not the *intervention of Austria* who took heart at Töplitz too much.

There is little doubt that the word *"Finiamo,"* came from Napoleon at Chambery. Farini, straight from his presence, came down into Tuscany. But L. N. is named as little as possible for obvious reasons. It is said to be impossible to make a revolution in white gloves—but at least some official decorum is necessary to avoid the European war which threatens France & Italy, if France helps Italy.

If Austria attacks now, it may be the best for us. Not even Prussia can wonder if France returns to the overt assistance of her ally.

As to Rome . . let Rome remain an independent free municipality in the heart of free Italy, & the Italians would prefer having the pope there than elsewhere. Some of them even venture to speculate on the "santo padre" 's coming to his senses so far as to open the gates of Rome to an Italian parliament, who might find it more convenient to assemble there. This seems to me pure dream-work. The pope will die obstinate—its a matter of martyrdom with him. But time will ripen this question like others,—& time too will open the gates of Rome & end the insulation of the city from the nation. Meanwhile we shall be patient. Violence cannot be applied here either by France or Italy—& only a *protestant* could suppose such an application desireable.

Let me tell you how right *I* think you have been about Gigia. Mrs. Stowe said to me in Rome last spring—"I find it impossible to believe that God *cares* to what church a man belongs." I entirely agreed with her. What IS important is a man's love of truth, & faithfulness to the truth he holds. She is a woman of remarkable largeness of mind & heart, especially considering the sectarian influences she was born & educated under.

For my part, protestants as a body seem to me about as

full of error as the catholics are—the chief difference being that there's a crevice in the protestant box. They hold their errors with a looser hand. Not that even *this* is a difference with all. Talking of "things unseen & eternal" or at least mysterious, do you take in the Cornhill & did you read the article "Stranger than Fiction" by Robert Bell? The subject makes progress with the public, in spite of the ineffable follies of certain believers. There is (for instance) a small controversy going on in the Spiritual Magazine just now as to whether I (EBB) am or am not possessed of the Devil. Mr. Howitt thinks affirmatively. As for me, of course I have not an opinion. Only I should laugh . . if there was a laugh left in me at this point of time.

Oh my silver Penny!— Yes, he's a silver Penny. He goes under no other name but Penini . . declinable (tell Alexander) as *Penini, Peni, Pen* . . all over Florence & Rome, & in among the hills here. We've forgotten him as Wiedemann. He cries out every now & then that he ought to be called "Robert"—but I cant afford two Roberts—and then Peni is grown so dear.

It is kind of you to think of the photographs. I know how black & unfaithful such things can be, so I shall allow for all faults.

My dear little Louisa!— But she will fix steadily on her axle soon, & you will not be too anxious meanwhile. It is very usual for sensitive girls at her age to be not strong. If Mr. Ogilvy had gone to America in your Great Eastern, it might have done her immense good to go with him.

So you let Alexander shoot!— Take care. I think I do much in letting Peni ride.

With kisses to the children, & love to dear Mr. Ogilvy when you see him next, believe me

Your ever affectionate friend

Elizabeth Barrett Browning.

Will Mrs. Ogilvy accept our affectionate remembrances?

Letter 35

Upon reaching the mainland of Italy, Garibaldi drove the King of Naples, Francis II, out of his capital. He fled to Gaeta on September 6, but Louis Napoleon, wishing to stop Garibaldi, stationed his fleet there to protect Francis. The English unexpectedly protested Louis Napoleon's action and likewise supported the advancement of Piedmontese troops from the north. When the troops entered the Papal states (though avoiding Rome), France (in what Elizabeth considered a calculated political gesture) withdrew her ambassador from the Piedmontese court at Turin.

The Italian troops defeated Lamoricière and took Ancona by the end of September. Much to Elizabeth's relief, Garibaldi yielded Naples to Victor-Emmanuel on November 7, being under pressure from Cavour to do so. In January 1861, the French fleet left Gaeta, which fell within the month to the combined Italian forces. The first Italian Parliament met in February and March and proclaimed Victor-Emmanuel King of Italy. The new kingdom thus included Piedmont, Sardinia, Lombardy, Tuscany, Modena, Parma, The Romagna, Naples and Sicily. England immediately gave her formal recognition as did France early in June 1861, a few days before Elizabeth's death. Her dream of Italian unification was not, however, completed until the inclusion of Venetia in 1866 and Rome (later to be the capital) in 1870.

Villa Alberti. Siena

Sept. 20. [1860]

My very dear friend, almost I am ashamed to write to you, and Wilson's letter has been lying here, waiting for my envelope these two days. The Wilsons behaved shamefully . . odiously . . I will say. Ferdinando went down to Leghorn (where he slept) under the full persuasion that he should find the child there with Gigia, . . & when he & she returned alone, his poor wife almost dropped to the ground with the shock & pain of it. Certainly I do blame her a little. She is very weak in character, & has not grown stronger under the responsibilities of her married life: and I feel inward convictions that her letters to her family must have been irresolute and yielding to the point of encouraging them to play the whole trick out. Well—it is over—and everybody must bear their own burden. Ferdinando swears (for which I commend him) that he will send no more money to England, so that all this clinging affection will have to be paid for. Only . . what amends can we offer *you* for the trouble you have taken? Most inadequate thanks indeed. Forgive me for being the innocent occasion of troubling you in vain. You have been very, very good, dearest Mrs. Ogilvy, & I shall not forget it. The only good out of all has been, that poor Gigia had an escort from Leghorn. She came on to our colony here, but I could not persuade her to stay above the one day & night, as she was in haste to get on to Florence. Very well & bright she looked—only melting into tears when I spoke of the children crying as soon as she was out of sight—poor Gigia! I felt sorry at first to have told her—but such proofs of love, though movingly sad at the moment, are soothing to loving hearts —& I am sure that her's is such to you all. When we return to Florence (on the 7th of October) we shall see her very often I think, and whenever I can be useful to her, you may count on me.

Your goodness will make you glad that I have been relieved in some measure from the hardest point of pressure under our anxiety. My precious sister suffers less keenly,—& the acute form of her disease seems falling into the chronic . . so the doctors say, & that it may last many years—which sounds dreadful to *you* perhaps—but if you knew how it strikes me as reprieve, . . and *time* for the healthy habit of her constitution to assert itself . . you will guess what I have suffered lately . . waiting for the post as if for the signal to be shot through the heart. Then she has been carried round the garden, & taken tea out of doors . . which pleased me. Another famous medical man has seen her—& he bids her go out, & even sit up in a chair at intervals. There has been another attack of the flooding, but much less violent. Somehow I am beginning to feel hopeful. It may be illusion perhaps—but for every ray of light let us bless God's sun. It is good as light, even if we dont see quite straight in it. I *am* a little easier.

Dear friend, there is enough here in Italy to devour our selfish griefs, & often I have felt ashamed of mine lately. We were none of us prepared for the intervention from the north. Great is our exultation. Try to understand what the situation is. Difficult, grave, complicated—& as hard for France as for us. The recall of the ambassador from Turin is a *blind*,—articles in the Patrie & Constit[ut]ional in protestation & objection, the same. Napoleon has to face something as like to a European coalition as possible against France, & he has to prevent as far as possible an intervention against Italy. He is suspected on all sides of *wishing* to intervene militarily himself in Italy—which he must actually do (and *will*) if Austria attacks again . . or the honor of France & the liberty of Italy would sink together. His object therefore is to get a settlement here as much by the Italians.as he can, & as quietly, & with his authority as little apparent. At Turin "not the slightest effect" was produced by any of the diplomatical frowning. Nobody doubts that if Austria stirs, France is ready. In fact, here it is hard *not* to see how it is, & that the emperor himself said "Go" at Chambery. Observe Farini (whose relations with the Buonapartes is known) the most energetic of our leaders, came straight from his face to Turin . . & so to Central Italy. The troops swept south at the moment— Pepoli, his own cousin & personal friend, is sent into the Papal States. These men with Cipriani & Mamiani (also accused of Bonaparte relations) have had to do with all our changes—& (except Cipriani) they are with us now. Also it is certain that Cavour *never would* have adopted, against the real will of the emperor, any such line of conduct as the present: . . not that Cavour is a courtier of France, but that he would not run an imprudent risk for his country.

Now, the papal difficulty will be solved, & with the least

scandal, the least pretext offered for the interference of the Catholic powers, possible under the circumstances— If France had done it with her hand, or even officially approved it, the offence would have been double in Europe. Her invitation to England just now for an agreement on the Italian question (patent the English feeling on Popes) is a masterly stroke of fence. As to Rome, Italy would rather keep the pope in Rome than otherwise. Rome may float in a free nation as a free municipality till Time makes "holy fathers" rococo like "holy places."

What we are rather uneasy about just now is Garibaldi. He is an *arm* (with the generous blood of the heart throbbing to the hilt of the sword)—he is not a brain: & Sicily is troubled by that Mazzinian element which has not been resisted enough by the Dictator . . Poor Naples . . I fear for Naples even. Then Garibaldi has mad designs to which he may be encouraged by bad men. He would get no Italian troops of the national party to attack the French at Rome, but he has Mazzinians or foreigners under him—& if such a thing were possible, the complication would be awful for Italy.

Do you know where Mr. Stuart is? Does he write still for the M[orning]. Post, do you suppose?

Our plans for the winter are rendered very uncertain of course by these movements. Rome would not be desireable just now—only, towards the middle of november, things may be settled more.

The photograph, Gigia showed me, was lovely I thought . . only I wanted a sight of the dear elder children, who are nearer to *me* somehow. Still those seemed restored in these. Marcia for instance!—how like. Darlings they all are.

You were very kind, too kind in your gift to Wilson. Her Pylades is a very fine child—does'nt (by the way) *speak a word of English*—a regular Italian—the male element prevailing.

Peni came rushing into the room yesterday . . "Dear

mama, Ancona's taken! Lamoricière's a prisoner. *All Italy's ours*—except Venice!" He was in an ecstasy—but it was false news. Still, Lamoricière is beaten, & shut up in Ancona,—& the rest will come presently, if it shall please God. Yes, even Venice.

Our love to Mrs. Ogilvy—if she will accept it. True love to dear Mr. Ogilvy & the children. Lovingly yours

Elizabeth Barrett Browning

Have I told you anywhere in this letter that we leave Siena for Florence on the 7th of October?

Perhaps you may wonder at Wilson being at Siena with us, . . or in a villino near us . . if you have not heard from me that she is the *padrona* of Mr. Landor (at 86 our adopted son—Robert's peculiar care!) who has passed the summer at Siena to be near us. They go back to Florence when we go. It has been a happy arrangement for Ferdinando (still our servant) and his wife to be together . . at least with a lane separating,—which is not perfectly conjugal, after all, I must allow.

I take Wilson's letter from the envelope to enclose it.

Letter 36

Returning to Florence from Siena on October 11, 1860, the Brownings remained there until around November 18 when they left to be in Rome for the winter. Henrietta died on November 23, the day the Brownings arrived in Rome and the shock of her sister's death undermined Elizabeth's own health severely.

During the months preceeding this letter, Mrs. Ogilvy had also been under stress, since members of her family were involved in the Chinese war. The peace agreement between England and China was signed on October 24, 1860.

To some extent as a reaction against the orthodoxy promulgated by the Oxford Movement of the early 1840's, many spoke out in support of more progressive Church reforms. One example of this appeared in the 1860 publication of *Essays and Reviews*, a volume of essays by six clergymen (including Frederick Temple, later Archbishop of Canterbury) and one layman. The book suggested that study in the areas of natural science and biblical criticism might actually strengthen one's faith rather than the opposite. The book did not attract much attention at first, but having been censured by the Established Church for its heterodox views, it created much excitement in 1861.

Among the Brownings' visitors at Rome was Sir John Bowring, linguist, writer and traveller. He had been plenipotentiary to China, governor, commander-in-chief and vice-admiral of Hong Kong. He was in Italy to investigate possible commercial relations between Britain and Italy.

126. Via Felicè. Rome
Jan. [28, 1861] Tuesday.

My dear dear friend it has not been easy for me to write— I never can write or speak. I am congealed by grief always, & the tears which come to nearly everybody will not come to me.

If the touch of a tender hand could help me . . . oh, I know all your goodness. But I have sate here through two heavy months in the silence which was best for me, & have not doubted that you, when you knew the whole, would not think hardly of me for not answering your letter.

Now let us talk of other things. Dear—I put the past not behind me but *before*, where I shall find it again after— perhaps not many days. I believe I am without excuse, in suffering *more than I ought* in these apparent separations,— knowing, as I seem to do, that they are only apparent, that what we call *death*, does not change the personality or the individuality even, & that even on this earth there is union & access. I have a distinct persuasion on these points,— and yet when a shock comes, it shakes,—I catch out at a forsaken garment & get bewildered between the Seen & Unseen. Only the Divine stands steadily with one foot on the sea & one on the land—and we placed suddenly between the natural & the spiritual, seem to slip & lose our Beloveds . . whom we do not lose, as Christ lives.

Forgive me—I am always trying to explain to myself & others how it is that I do not believe in loss & yet am overwhelmed as if by loss. But I am inconsistent & very weak . . "*without excuse*," as I began by saying just now.

Now you will write me another letter all about yourselves. I want to hear that you are easy at last about those dear to you. The Chinese situation must have been painful—but I do hope that you are not anxious, & that the arrival from India has brought you freedom from uneasy thoughts. Tell me too of the children—of dear Louisa & of Mrs. Ogilvy who had not been well when you wrote this letter.

We are in sunny rooms, too high up, but it is quiet . . which I care for chiefly. Robert has been very good in keeping people off, so that I have had repose, & have learnt to live again, as we all must. To break out of the narrow personal life into the larger & higher, is the only secret of satisfaction in this world—and I have begun again to do it & to work a little in the healthy way.

There has been & is some cause for anxiety in the Neapolitan states, through the inferiority of the population & the virulence of parties: Mazzini stayed there too long. With all this, however, the evils have been exaggerated, and the principle of union will be strong enough to triumph. The French fleet at Gaeta did far less harm than has been supposed. If Francis II had fallen under the first shock of revolution, there was imminent danger of North & South Italy falling in two. This I have heard from intelligent thinkers who had opportunities of observation at Naples.

In Rome the intention plainly is to let the rotten fruit hang till it drops. The papacy is being starved out financially. Presently the French will go out & the Piedmontese come in: both quietly too. Within these few days I have seen Sir John Bowring, (who was in China—& began life as a disciple of Bentham—very liberal accordingly, & learned in

governments) & he assures us, having intimate knowledge
of the Emperor Napoleon, that never for a moment has he
faltered in his good intentions towards Italy, & that whatever has seemed equivocal has been either misapprehended,
or caused by a misapprehension, his difficulties both in
clerical France & Europe being immense. I did not require this testimony, but I give it to you for what it is
worth.

The dry bones shake throughout the world—& even in
America, see how things are. My only fear is that the
north will *compromise*—which will be fatal to the moral
life of the nation, only threatened so far in her natural
life. When the burden of slavery is thrown off, she will
arise up & go forward.

Tell me if you comprehend the Oxford movement (expressed in the ["] Essays &c") & what you think of it. We
want a blast of free air through the churches, & a sweeping away of traditional forms—but I am afraid, from what
I can catch & understand, (I have not read the book) that
the thinkers there have let go *too* much to hold *so* much.

I have not seen Gibson yet—but Robert says he looks
well. Penini has his poney here & his abbé. I am weak
in body & in spirits—but one must bear on—at least the
spring will come. May the bitter weather in England not
have hurt you & yours. What of the hooping-cough? May
God bless you. Robert's love—with that of your
ever affectionate & grateful
EBB.

Ah, dearest friend!—*the children*! You will understand how
I have seen my own child's face through a mist, since then!

No. Arabel pleaded hard for the little girl . . one lonely
little girl—but she was refused by the poor father. He could
not, he said. I mean to try again presently, both for the
child's sake & Arabel's who longs to have it. There is a
governess at present.

Letter 37

Mrs. Marcia Anne Symson Ogilvy, Mrs. Ogilvy's mother-in-law, whom the Brownings had known well at Florence and Bagni di Lucca in 1849 (see Letters 1-4) died in Perth on April 1, 1861 at the age of 78.

The author of *Agnes Tremorne* was Isa Blagden. Elizabeth was aware of its shortcomings, but nevertheless recommended it to all her friends, in part because one of the characters was modeled on Pen (a detailed description of the character, Giacinto, can be found in Maisie Ward's *The Tragi-Comedy of Pen Browning*, page 156).

This is Elizabeth's last letter to Mrs. Ogilvy. In it she recognizes to a considerable extent the proportions of her weakened physical condition, which led to her death on June 29, 1861.

> Rome. 126. Via Felicè.
>
> May. [12? 1861] Saturday.

My very dear friend,

If I have not written before, it was not that we were ignorant of your loss or careless of your pain, but that, from an idiosyncrasy of mine, I am always unwilling to write letters of condolence, through a consciousness of my own terrible unwillingness to receive such. Only *that* is not a common feeling—and certainly even I could & did value your sympathy when it came to me so kindly. Well. We have felt indeed for dear Mr. Ogilvy. You have had, of course, heaps of letters to receive & answer, & when the last is done with, let me have a line to say that he has quite turned his face to the light, & is reconciled after the manner of the good & brave, to the course of God's natural providences. A woman of so long & pure & conscientious a life, leaves her children the inheritance of golden peace in the things relating to her. She has lived well, died well—it is well with [her] for ever. And their grief does not come to them separate from Thanksgiving.

Robert saw it in the newspaper—'Perth' left no doubt. We were thrown back in cordial regard to the times at Florence & Lucca, when we were younger, & some of us richer in loving hopes for this earth. Now the ranks here are thinned, the angels there stand thicker, . . the babies which were round us, are growing up into men. My Penini, who was an infant, reads in Latin about "Illustrious men of the city of Rome," and I dream of those on whom I shall not look again in this world, & who are learning higher lessons with God, than any to be learnt below by the young or the old. Your Alexander . . where is he? You had sent him from you when you wrote before. Tell me if he is contented,—& if you are not otherwise. Tell me too of Louisa's health, & of the other darlings. And I should so much like to know what your plans are—if there is any modification of plan. Shall you remain at Sydenham?

We are at Rome till the end of May. We have had some chilly wind out of season, to pay for the singularly mild winter, and I have not taken a general licence to go out & get my strength back for the summer's uses. Our intention is to go to Florence for a week or two on our way to the neighbourhood of Paris, where we shall spend three months with Robert's family & my sister Arabel who will meet us there. I am very little "up" to this effort, either in my body or my soul, & am most averse to it. Only the *duty* of it is clear, . . seeing that my husband's father is not young, & I have already been the cause of the meeting being put off a year—so I shall eschew farther responsibility, & shut my eyes & leap. Oh—how deeply my inclination is, . . never to set foot out of Italy again! I have grown to the soil. Everywhere else seems too loud & too light. I can live here my own way, & work my own work, & enjoy my own silence.

The world is in an hour of great crisis. Is it the time of the "restitution of all things"? I read in a private letter from Francis Newman the other day that "for years he had looked in vain for the finger of God in the fate of nations,—but that within the last *two years he had seen it!*" That was striking, was it not? . . coming from such a man.

America is passing through a tragic crisis. She will either be lost,—or be greater than ever, I hope, for my part.

Italy will do well. Our Garibaldi, that grand child, has turned good again,—& the danger of his setting the house on fire is hindered for the moment. The Neapolitan States present difficulties, but they are much exaggerated.

The war question is still in suspence: depending much upon Hungary, but not all. I scarcely believe in the possibility of prolonging the actual position (between Austria & Italy) throughout this summer & autumn. Reasons of finance seem against it still more than reasons of passion.

The egotism of England illustrates itself in Syria & Turkey, not to name the Ionian islands—Poveri noi! The nationalities meanwhile are burning their way out into the air, & we shall have flames, for all the repressive & cautious policy. It is understood that the French are here now simply to prevent the Austrians from coming. The queen of Naples (the young one) wanders about with her lovely sorrowful face,—another ruin added to the rest.

If you ever read novels, read 'Agnes Tremorne,' written by a female friend of mine. It is a first book, & has its faults—but you will like certain things in it—and the scene is in Rome. The writer has a very active mind & considerable talent—besides being one of the < . . . >

Letter 38

Before the Brownings left Rome, it had already been decided that Elizabeth was in no condition to travel to Paris to visit family and friends. The unexpected news of the death of Cavour on June 6, 1861 (the day following their return to Florence) was a great shock to Elizabeth. Furthermore, on Thursday, June 20 Elizabeth opened the windows at Casa Guidi, leaving herself vulnerable to the draft. By the next day she had developed a severe cold which worsened over the next several days. On June 29, at half past four in the morning, she died in her husband's arms.

Robert decided to leave Florence. As a memento of his happy years in Florence he attempted to have the rooms at Casa Guidi photographed. Since this proved unsuccessful he commissioned George Mignaty to paint the Salon (see frontispiece). When this was completed, he had those furnishings he wanted to keep stored for shipment later.

Three days before Robert left Florence for ever he wrote the Ogilvys the following letter. Preserved with it is the promised photograph of Elizabeth (see Plate V). He perhaps sent the photograph when he presented Mrs. Ogilvy with a copy of Elizabeth's *Last Poems*, inscribed and dated "May 11, '62." That date marks the last known communication between the families.

Florence, July 29. '61.

Dear Friends, Thank you from my heart for your goodness and sympathy— I can hardly say more, but this, as I mean it, says something.

I go away from Florence—next Thursday—for many a year. I pass only a day or two at London with Arabel Barrett, then return to France for some quiet months with my family—eventually I shall reside in London, I suppose, but my plans are very rough—only consistent in their main purpose: I shall devote myself to Peni, & do what I can to make my own work less unworthy of its old advantages: do not believe I am "prostrated" or unmindful of the alleviations which I thank God for. There was no pain,—above all, no least expectation of the parting which to her would have been the cruelest of pains. She was sure up to the last that the attack differed in nothing from the many she had recovered from. I believed this to a certain degree, but (as it now seems to me) disbelieved it at the bottom of my soul. Your old acquaintance Dr. Wilson was called in for the first time,—he looked gravely at the symptoms,— she reassured me—"The way with them all,—so I was told all those years ago,—what is there new in hearing that my lungs are affected? You will see!" And Wilson confessed she was better, that the case was exceptional, & so on— till the end. She told me smilingly "This *is* exaggerating the case!"—when I was warming her feet a few minutes before she died, but I can't tell you now. This much I ought to trust to your affectionateness, as it is my own chief comfort. She went into the presence of God fearless as his own child, that she was. I could have wished no better for her or myself, if the end *was* to be.

During my two or three days stay with Arabel B. I may hardly see anybody else—there will be an aftertime when I shall be happy indeed to see *you*—you know it must be so. I am to be heard of in Paris, 151. Rue de Grenelle, Faubourg St. Germain.—or at Chapman's.

Pen is her very child, with something of her spirit in him —he tries hard to "comfort me," he says—& finds his own comfort in that: he is changed,—so considerate & dear. He is very well in health & so am I.

God bless you both, & keep you for each other: how your children must be grown! I shall see them one day. I will give you a photograph—perfect, the one likeness that exists, taken just before we left Rome.

Ever yours affectionately,
Robert Browning.

Appendices

Appendix A

The following curious letter, written by Mr. David Ogilvy to his aunt Mrs. Yorke on March 27, 1844, includes a poem written by his wife celebrating the birth of their first child, Rose Theresa Charlotte Ogilvy on March 19, 1844. Mrs. Ogilvy's obvious joy over this event was shattered by Rose's death early in July of the following year. In *Rose Leaves*, which was privately printed later in 1845, she collected a number of happy lyrics written during her daughter's lifetime. But in this slim volume she also included verses which attempt to place the immediate personal tragedy within the framework of Christian Salvation. Despite her assurance about Rose's happy immortal state in the last poem of the collection—

> Yet recalling how on earth
>   Love was in each tone and glance—
> Love presiding o'er thy birth,
>   Struggling through thy death-bed trance:
> Something then we dimly guess
> Of thy unknown happiness.

—such later poems as "Newly Dead and Newly Born" and "A Family Picture" evidence the mother's fear for the health of her other children or her imagination of Rose's reappearance in the family circle (see Appendix B, pages 190 and 195). The poem included with the present letter shows by contrast how "the Muse ran away with her" in a more whimsical fashion.

The Browning Institute is grateful to Mrs. Ogilvy's grandson, Lt.-Col. Herbert F. Collingridge, for the gift of this letter to its manuscript collection.

13 Montagu Sq.
Wednesday 27th

My dear Auntie M.

You will be glad to hear that my dear Wife's recovery has gone on steadily from the first hour to this—and that the Baby is also in great force, being a little less yellow than it was a few days ago, and the hair getting a little darker more like Mamas than *Papa's*. Yes I have really—it is no dream—attained that dignity. I trust I may prove worthy of the blessing. As for eloquence I am sure I never could have been more vociferous at the same tender age than my daughter is. Such a Pipe! The elegant stanzas in the opposite page were composed on the day of the Child's birth (really!) by the incorrigible Poetess, my Wifie. I think they will amuse you—they were begun in a serious mood, she says, but the Muse ran away with her. I doubt if such good verses were ever composed at so extraordinary a time!

Have you heard any thing from Nottingham? If not I can easily apply to the Author who has a living now in this neighbourhood.

My, or rather both our loves, to Mʳ Yorke, and accept the same yourself from Eliza and

Your affecᵗ Nephew
David Ogilvy

A Natal Address to My
Child. March 19ᵗʰ 1844.

———————

Hail to thy puggy nose, my Darling,
Fair womankind's last added scrap,
That, callow as an unfledg'd starling,
Liest screaming in the Nurse's lap.

No locks they tender cranium boasteth,
No lashes veil thy gummy eye
And, like some steak gridiron toasteth,
Thy skin is red and crisp and dry.

Thy mouth is swollen past describing
Its corners twisted as in scorn
Of all the Leech is now prescribing
To doctor thee, the newly born.

Sweet little lump of flannel binding,
Thou perfect cataract of clothes,
Thy many folds there's no unwinding
Small mummy without arms or toes!

And am I really then thy Mother?
My very child I cannot doubt thee,
Rememb'ring all the fuss and bother
And moans and groans I made about thee!

'Tis now thy turn to groan and grumble,
As if afraid to enter life,
To dare each whipping scar and tumble
And task and toil with which 'tis rife.

O Baby of the wise round forehead,
Be not too thoughtful ere thy time;
Life is not truly quite so horrid—
Oh! how she squalls!— she can't bear rhyme!

E. A. H. O.

Appendix B

The following poems have been selected from Mrs. Ogilvy's published and unpublished works to acquaint the reader of these letters with the quality of her literary productivity in general and those poems Elizabeth alludes to in the correspondence in particular (see Letters 18 and 25). Several of the poems have been selected because they represent Mrs. Ogilvy's treatment of events or ideas referred to during the period of the correspondence. The contents of the Appendix are as follows:

From *A Book of Highland Minstrelsy* (1846):
  "The Vigil of the Dead"

From *Traditions of Tuscany, In Verse* (1851):
  "Alla Giornata"
  "A December Day in the Campagna, Rome"

From *Poems of Ten Years, 1846-1855* (1856):
  "Despondency" (1850)
  "Newly Dead and Newly Born" (1850)
  "The Austrian Night Patrol, Florence" (1851)
  "The End of 1851" (1851)
  "A Family Picture" (1852)
  "Farewell to Florence" (1852)
  "The Death of Eliot Warburton" (1852)
  "Charon's Ferry" (1853)

From manuscript book of verses for the years
    1884-1887:
  "Grannie's Birthday" (January 6, 1885)
  "Allan Water, August 27th, 1887)

THE VIGIL OF THE DEAD.

The Highlanders believed that when a burial took place in their mountain churchyard the spirit of the deceased was compelled by some mysterious law to keep watch there by night until relieved by another interment, when the ghost of the newly-arrived corpse assumed his unwelcome duties, and the weary wraith passed to its ultimate destination whether of happiness or woe.

It must have been an irksome duty to be thus excluded from earth's interests without being admitted to participate in the joys of heaven.

The successor was obliged in his turn to await another interment, and the advent of another ghost to give him liberty.

If we can fancy this bodiless watcher to preserve any consciousness of the doings on that earthly scene, in which he could no longer take an active part, we may picture the irritation and eagerness which would impel him to wish that all sickness among his old companions might end in death, that all accidents among the dangerous crags and morasses might prove fatal to life as well as limb.

Far from an improving preparation for the holiness of heaven was this detention below, when the unhappy ghost, shivering in the frosty moonlight, counted over the chances of mortality among his former friends, no doubt complaining fretfully of a delay which retarded his own release and prolonged his own discomfort.

Yet to those who felt themselves by the verdict of their consciences to be destined for eternal retribution, how awful must have been this breathing-time between the sins and the avengement! How dreadful the retrospect! how far, far more dreadful the anticipation! In the awful solitude of the desolate graveyard how active would memory be, how mighty remorse! The mind turns shuddering from an idea of so much horror.

The "Dreeng," or meteor, on which the souls of the blessed arose to heaven, was a remnant of the ancient Druidical faith.

It was probably derived from the aurora borealis, seen most resplendently in the clear nights of a Highland autumn or winter.

Its dazzling coruscations and rapidly changing evolutions, wheeling and darting among the thickly-sown stars of the northern firmament, might readily suggest to the imaginative the ecstatic raptures of the freed spirits of the redeemed.

When the night-mist is swathing the mountain's gray head,
When the night-dews are bathing the graves of the dead,

When the soft breath of slumber ascendeth from men,
And the torch of the watcher burns low in the glen,
When the peace of forgetting, sole peace of this life,
Hath deadened each sorrow and silenced each strife,
A bodiless spirit out-thrust from my corse,
Excluded from heaven and dogged by remorse,
I stand here and shiver, so bloodless and thin,
Recalling past pleasure, bewailing past sin;
By the cold dyke that circles the mounds of the dead,
I wait for another to watch in my stead.
But clear is the winter and healthful the frost;
Since the last night of summer no life has been lost:
That last night of summer! long, long shall they tell
How Allan, the herdsman, was killed on the fell.
'Twixt the hill and the precipice scant was the road,
The eagles flew near him as heedless he trode;
He slipped on the wet moss, the rock-face was bare,
The heather-roots crumbled—he clutched in despair;
And at morn when the shepherds went by with the flock
Dead Allan lay crushed at the foot of the rock!
'Twas the last night of summer, now Yule is at hand,
Yet still by the grave-stones alone I must stand
And watch the blue doors of the adamant sky
That ope not to shelter when humbly I cry;
'Tis my doom to keep sentinel over the dead
Till the soul of another shall come in my stead,
Till the corse of another be laid in the sod,
And I float on the meteor to heaven and God.

But hale are the clansmen; the patriarch of all,
No staff doth support him, so sturdy and tall;
Each Sabbath I've marked him stride under the trees,
His white hairs flow freely to welcome the breeze;
His children attend him with reverence and pride,
And the wife of his youth moveth slow at his side:
Yes, long have I marked him my soul to release,
But long shall he linger when I am at peace.
It is not the oldest who first are laid low,
It is not the ripest who drop from the bough;
For Death will be dainty when choosing his prey,
And the best and the choicest he sweepeth away;

A younger, and dearer, and lovelier sprite
Shall replace in this churchyard my watching by night.

Oh fair was the maiden I wedded in spring,
And fondly my Morag around me would cling;
The balm of her kisses, the warmth of her breath,—
Dear wife of my bosom!—they cheer me in death.
Now widowed is Morag, in sadness she sits
While the wind through her hovel goes howling by fits,
Till the babe in his cradle is wakened to hear.
To her bosom she strains him, all sobbing with fear;
His forehead is buring, and red with disease,
His breathing comes broken in gusts like the breeze.
Ah! hush him to slumber, ah! soothe him with song;
Ah! call him thine Allan, not thine is he long,
For there's death in his gasping, there's death in his eye;
Pale widow, pale mother, too soon shall he die!
The fatherless infant is drooping his head,
To lie in the churchyard, to watch in my stead:
Unborn at my dying, his death sets me free,
And his soul in departing opes heaven for me!
The meteor approacheth, it burns on my sight,
It quickens the dawn with its tremulous light;
The dawn that revealeth the baby's damp cheek,
Which the dark hues of dying so fearfully streak.
Sore weepeth my Morag, she thinks not of me,
As she bends o'er that fast changing face on her knee;
Her heart with her nursling goes down to the tomb,
While the sire he hath ransomed is freed from his doom.

That fair little stranger! they'll bring him at morn,
By the dust will they lay him from which he was born—
His face white and tranquil close nestled beside,
With the smile still upon it he smiled as he died.
And his spirit at evening shall come to our grave
As the dews are thick falling, and loud the winds rave.
When the meteor down-shooting shall bear me on high,
Shall the baby-soul speed me with farewell and sigh;
For then shall he know me, and then will he love,
As I float on that flickering radiance above.
Haste, Death! take another, nor long leave the child

To watch by the graves in the midnight so wild;
No evil hath stained him such penance to need,
For the soul of the infant hath love for its creed;
Give his charge to another, and lift him with me,
That the babe and the father in bliss may be free.

ALLA GIORNATA.
(Written Above the Lanfreducci Palace, Pisa.)

Over the entrance of a yellow marble palace on the beautiful quay at Pisa, called Lungo l'Arno, is the inscription, "Alla Giornata." A fragment of iron chain hangs down the lintels of the door. This has always been a puzzle to travellers, none of whom have satisfactorily accounted for it. Murray's Handbook, however, hints at an origin which I have since heard confirmed more in detail by that learned and courteous antiquary, the discoverer of Giotto's fresco portrait of Dante, Mr. Kirkup. The story had been related to him by a sexagenarian lady, the last of the noble family of the Lanfreducci.

A certain Count Lanfreducci was taken prisoner by the Algerines, and endured long and grievous slavery. He escaped at last, and made his way back to his native city. With some difficulty he obtained restitution of his lands, which, by his supposed death, had lapsed to legal heirs. In grateful memory of his escape, he built this palace, hanging thereon a chain, emblem of his weary bondage, and carving this dedicatory line, "To the day" of his recovered freedom.

I must own that a difficulty lies in the exact rendering of the term "Alla Giornata." Giornata is used to express the space of a day, the French journée. Also the workman uses this term to distinguish that he is to be paid "by the Day" instead of "by the Piece." But also it might, as is here supposed, refer to the contents of the Day, the events included in its round, which events the framer of the motto desired thus eternally to commemorate.

The architecture of this palace is simple, and reminded me in its rich material and pure style of the elegant design of Raphael in the Palazzo Pandolfini at Florence. It has been ascribed to Michael Angelo, but is actually the work of a certain Cosmo Pagliano, of whose other performances I know nothing, but I bear him all due honour for the beauty and good taste of this, the only one I have heard imputed to him.

There stands a Palace by the Arno's flow,
    Built in the days when Pisa to herself
Sufficed for King and Kingdom, white as snow
    Its marble masses glittered to the Guelph.
Now they are yellow as a jonquil flower,
    Dull and deserted, and above the gate
A half-forgotten mystery doth lower,
    Which no conclusions learned can abate.
There this strange motto fastens on your sight,
"Unto the Day," which none can read aright.

Unto what Day canst thou be dedicate,
    Pile, solemnly impressive to the last!
And keeping up a show of princely state
    In this abandoned region of the Past.
This mute cold effigy of Pisa dead,
    This monumental corse, whereon our glance
Asks if indeed the vital flame be fled,
    Or only choked in temporary trance.
Dost thou with Italy's fond hopes connive?
"Unto the Day" when Pisa shall revive.

Unto what Day? Thou hast outlived the name
    Of thy first founder, and the last is gone
Of his posterity—henceforth thy fame
    Rests for support on this device alone;
Some incoherent fragments yet remain
    Of His eventful story, who compiled
Thy chiselled walls—when he had snapped the chain
    Of Moorish captors o'er the billows wild
He carved this pious offering that ye see,
Unto The Day when he again was free.

The Blessed Day that filled his soul once more
    When fierce Algeria missed him from her slaves,
And far before him stretched the Tuscan shore,
    And Monte Nero's crest, and Arno's yellow waves.
And restituted wealth profusely poured
    On him the long-thought dead, and this new home
Grew at his bidding, of the costliest hoard
    Carrara keeps for statue or for dome.

Right grateful was the Heart that did record
Unto The Day remembered of the Lord!

We all have such a temple in our soul,
   Enchased with richest jewels of the mind;
Set in Imagination is the whole,
   Gilded with Feelings seven times refined.
And by that shrine we do commemorate
   Some epoch in our being, whose great force
Doth every moment after dominate,
   Glassing itself in all our future course.
And though not visible, 'tis understood
This motto—"To the Day!" or be it bad or good!

Unto the Day when suddenly alit
   Our happy eyes on the Beloved Face;
The Day of Youthful Passion's frenzy fit,
   Or our Last Love, and firmest—or in case
Grief rule the House of Life amid the stars,
   The day of our first sorrow,—when our ear
Strained the dumb void of absence—or the jars
   Of alienation rasped lips too sincere
Unto the Day—the merry or the sad,
Which hath most skill to make us wise or mad.

Each hath this Altar dedicate within;
   Some to a Power they willingly obey,
Some to dark memory of repented sin
   Which yet o'errules them with repugnant sway;
Look back on life, and tell me, is't not so?
   One day, one hour more salient than the rest
Stands prominently forth—the joy or woe—
   The pride or torment of the subject breast;
Which must, per force, its high place consecrate
Unto That Day—the crisis of its fate.

A DECEMBER DAY IN THE CAMPAGNA,
ROME.

On Scottish graves the snow is thick,
　　Its flakes of wintry foliage cling
Along the planetree's withered stick,
　　That querulously moans for Spring.
But round the Roman Lady's Tomb
　　That looks upon the Appian Way,
Geraniums scatter wilding bloom,
　　And sunshine-loving lizards play.

The mountains of my Scottish home
　　Are labouring in December's storms,
The driving mists, in wreaths of foam,
　　Like vapory mantles, wrap their forms,
But here Soracte pales the rose,
　　The reddest rose that tempts the bee,
And gleam the high Abruzzi snows,
　　Like frigate-sails far out at sea.

In Scottish Town from murky skies,
　　The shiverer to his hearth repairs,
Heaps up the blaze, the flagon plies,
　　Forgets the cold and all his cares.
Far different our December joy
　　In the long heathy grass to muse,
Until our ravished soul we cloy,
　　Drinking the Noon's delicious hues.

A dreamy and reflective mood,
　　It gendereth our eyes to cast
Here on the Peasant's cabin rude
　　There on the Relics of the Past.
The antechamber and the hall,
　　Vaster than palaces—to lave
A Cæsar's luxury, and the small,
　　Low niches where they tombed the slave.

Crumbling together. Over both
　　The Daisy's round bright eyeballs stare;

A kitten basks in sunny sloth,
    Where once the bathers smoothed their hair;
For garlands and for myrtle wreath,
    For unguents in a womanish store,
I hail the gentian's fragrant breath,
    Swept o'er the Bath-room's inlaid floor.

O Path of Tombs! O Appian Way!
    Based where the Lava Torrent burned.
Where the great Scipio's kindred lay,
    And sweet Cecilia was inurned;
Death's aspect more severely broods
    Upon thy line of burial towers,
Since vanished in Mediæval feuds
    Their ashes of immortal powers.

It is as if a second flight
    Of man's remembrance happened here;
First the great souls to sink in night,
    And then their dust to disappear,
Cleft is the water-bearing Arch,
    Whose range the broad Campagna spanned;
O centuries in your fateful march,
    Ye build and break with either hand.

Lo, glittering by the Tiber's side,
    The Christian city's domes and towers;
Nought boasts she of Barbaric pride,
    Who in the Campus Martius cowers;
She crouches in a narrow space,
    A corner fits her mean desires,
A puny and a pauper face
    Belies the glory of her sires.

And livid-eyed Disease is free
    Within her father's halls to mope,
The King of antique Rome is he,
    Thrice more respected than the Pope.
Slowly a long, long sigh we fetch,
    And turn away our saddened eyes
To where the Volscian mountains stretch,
    Like violets budding in the skies.

To where the nearer Sabine hills
 Reflect the Amethystine ray,
And Alba with red life-blood fills
 At the last kisses of the Day.
This man changed never—cannot change,
 The wolf-nursed Twins beheld it too,
In their fierce eyes yon mountain range
 Wore the same rich exhaustless hue.

Trampled beneath the victor's hoof,
 No widow-weeds can Rome assume,
Her raiment must be sunbeam woof,
 Her cheek hath everlasting bloom;
Girdled she is with cestus rare,
 That must bewitch us through all time,
Through all her misery and despair,
 Meet for the canvas and the rhyme!

DESPONDENCY.

Yon ebon cloud that overcharged and weary
Labours from rock to rock along the hill,
Shadows a likeness, in its progress dreary
   To my exhausted will.

Yon ebon cloud with gathering tempests heavy,
And my repressed and overladen heart!
Each step of my existence seems to levy
   More strength than I impart.

I am worn out by this incessant travel
Over rough tracks, where never rest I win,
The snake that crawls across the gritty gravel
   Bruiseth her tender skin.

I am too weakly fibred, thinly coated
For this rude clambouring, surely I was made,
In some green covert silent and unnoted,
   To glide from blade to blade.

I was not meant to tack for days together,
My sails are rent, my masts go by the board,
I, like a yacht, was launched for summer weather,
      With flowers and music stored.

Let stronger hearts set out for Arctic oceans,
Let them find glory, I desire but peace,
I am too sick of fluctuating motions
      And pining for release.

O brothers, sisters, of earth's strifeful kindred!
How would I love you, did ye let me love,
But by unnatural dissensions hind'red,
      I lift my hopes above.

NEWLY DEAD AND NEWLY BORN.

The mother lies in travail bed,
    The babe beside her sleepeth,
When, hark! a chaunting for the dead
    Below her window creepeth.

It swelleth nearer, filling loud
    That vast Florentian palace,
Deaf is the corpse within its shroud
    To sympathy or malice.

Deaf as the little babe above
    To all its kindred's praises,
Both child and corpse are shut from love
    In mystery's awful mazes.

Hard by with round Etruscan arch
    Expands the church's portal,
'Mid smoking brands the funeral march
    Leads in those relics mortal.

As if 'twere round her infant's head
    The mother hears them singing,
While from the bier up to the bed
    Rise fumes of censers swinging.

Herself yet trembling on the verge
    Of scarce escapèd danger,
A shudder takes her at this dirge
    From Death, the great all-changer.

And when the requiem's failing sighs
    Expire along the distance,
She turneth where her new-born lies
    To test its warm existence.

By touch, and sight, and fine-edged ear,
    To certify its thriving,
Then cry "O Death, go with that bier,
    And leave this life surviving."

Poor mother! look for higher things!
    To warnings rest beholden:
All human souls are born with wings
    Which but awhile are folden.

They sink or soar as God sees right
    When grown to full extension,
Pray, when arrives her hour of flight,
    The summons be ascension.

Casa Guidi, Florence.

THE AUSTRIAN NIGHT PATROL.
FLORENCE.

In the guise of conquerors,
    Harnessed with their guns and glaives,
March the Austrian patrols
    Through the city of their slaves.

From the fastened jalousies
    Greeted with indignant groans,
As their hoofs from street to street
    Ring metallic on the stones.

When these bats do fly abroad
  By the stately palace-eaves,
Florentines, like timorous birds,
  Nestle close among their leaves:

For that clash and clang proclaim
  Insolently night and day,
Tuscans! ye are prisoners!
  Florence! thou'rt the German's prey!

I remember of a time
  When the night was glad and boon,
Children sang of liberty
  Unrebuked beneath the moon.

Then the sovereign's name was sweet
  To his people's loving ear,
Hark the foreign troopers' beat!
  He has brought those bloodhounds here.

When his Tuscans cried "Come back
  We repent, we were too bold,"
With his mouth he promised fair,
  With his hand their freedom sold.

So some petty Afric chief
  Sells his negroes on the strand,
Yielded to the slaver's grip
  Chained together foot and hand.

Ah, that savage cannot see
  What his victims undergo,
But this nation-seller lives
  Present to his people's woe.

And content? he who was hymned
  By his country's grateful verse?
Now despised, his honour dimmed,
  Every blessing changed to curse.

Every subject for his foe,
  Christendom's contempt and blame,

Go with Pope, with Bourbon go
    To the pit of endless shame!

Hark, again the stern patrol
    Drowns the holy midnight bells,
Up, Italia! can'st thou sleep
    With thy foes for sentinels?

THE END OF 1851.

A sinner lies on his death-bed
    And groans his last confession,
The bells ring out ere he is dead,
    His heir has seized possession.

He sighs, "My youth had promise fair,
    My middle age renown,
Earth's multitudes I bid repair
    Unto one single town.

One city in an island small,
    Washed by nor'-western tide,
Became the centre of them all,
    The summit of their pride.

From every land that has a sense
    However vaguely stirred,
Of honour and intelligence,
    I led a pilgrim herd.

And festal banquetings I made
    Through my short summer time,
And my fair crystal bower arrayed
    In beams like southern clime.

Then was I praised in speech and book
    With prophecies of fame,
I should have died while men could look
    On my unsullied name.

I die now, but alas, too late!
    For with this aged hand
I have struck down a vigorous state
    And fettered a free land.

I've added to the lists of slaves
    And to the tyrants' scrolls,
I've heaped up more of patriot graves,
    And damned more perjured souls.

O France! I leave thee in the dust
    Under the despot's heel,
Thou wert unworthy of thy trust
    Of Freedom's charter-seal.

I saw thee try its wax at flame
    To prove the fastening true,
It holds no longer, but the name
    Stands mockingly to view.

Irate, I snatched from such a grasp
    A signet so abused,
I gave it to the tyrant's clasp—
    I cannot be excused.

Forgive me, France, forgive me, man!
    This outrage on thy right,
I have contracted wisdom's span,
    And clouded hope with night;

Men, by my madness, are driven back
    On the old life of brutes,
I see red war upon his track,
    I taste of thraldom's fruits.

O Crystal Palace, clear as day,
    Would I had fallen with thee,
The good I did has passed away,
    The ill begins to be!"

A FAMILY PICTURE.

Her cottage is a noisy place,
 Where healthy children romping play,
Now shouting in a mimic chase,
 Now shrieking in a short-lived fray.
Their cup of life runs o'er its brim,
 It froths and foams from morn to night,
They are as fish who happiest swim
 When most the waves are lashed to white.

At evening they come laughing in,
 And cluster round their father's chair,
The eldest with her waxen skin,
 Her slender shape and yellow hair,
Her eager eyes that wondering scan
 The narrow world within her reach,
Her thoughts that brood on God and man
 And overflow in artless speech.

Few thoughts hath he, the next in age,
 A winsome wight, a gleeful boy,
He never asks a question sage,
 His large blue eyes are round with joy;
So fearless, frank, and debonair,
 So trustful of his bright to-day,
He spreads a sunshine on the air,
 And strangers stop him on the way.

Next, twinkles in a shining head,
 Crowned with a classic Roman name
On parted tresses burnished red,
 Like sunset slanting into flame.
Imperious as that name befits,
 Yet tender in her wildest ways,
And fashioning her baby wits
 To many a soft Ausonian phrase.

Last closing this domestic row
 The newly born, a tiny mite,
Whose soul, like lichens under snow,
 Grows unperceived by human sight.

He liveth but for food and sleep,
 An inarticulate atom, we
Know not what ray may pierce the deep
 Of his unfathomed entity.

Lo, these are all that in the flesh
 Are present entering at the door,
But to the mother's eye afresh
 Her first-born riseth with the four.
A spirit form, that year by year
 Takes new proportions e'en as they,
That duly foremost will appear,
 And as her birthright lead the way.

She dwarfs them by her elder height,
 She dims them by her angel smile,
They are of clay and she of light,
 No passion-storms her brow defile.
When strangers greet the mother proud
 Of children four, she inly sighs,
"There was one fairer in her shroud,
 Yea, now is fairer in the skies."

FAREWELL TO FLORENCE.

Veil thy blue radiance, Tuscan sky,
 Draw near in likeness to those gray
Low hanging vaults, all sough and sigh,
 Which shall o'erarch me from to-day.

Rain down strange vapours, intercept
 The wonted clearness of thy dome,
A clammier mist will soon have crept
 Around me in mine island home.

I needed this to brace my slack
 Weak courage for farewell, this dense
Uncustomed darkness presses back
 My fond reluctance to go hence.

Yet, give me one last glittering eve
    From Fiesole's enamouring bowers,
Let me behold before I leave
    Valdarno from Saint Margaret's towers,

Far Pagni Peaks like blocks of gold
    Slow melting in the western blaze,
White towns and hamlets manifold
    Swimming like foam bells on the haze.

And thou, dear Florence, rainbow girt,
    With purple domes and ruby spires,
The very dust upon thy skirt
    Transfigured to prismatic fires.

Cruel, thou scorn'st this love of mine!
    Thou shut'st me out with rainy door,
Saying, "To-morrow I will shine
    When thou can'st see my face no more.

"Again I'll light up every range
    Of palace windows, every roof
I'll plate with silver, but this change
    I'll work when thou must roam aloof.

"Aha! in London streets recall
    How I am bright as newmade star,
The jaspers of my mountain wall
    Seek thou in smoke-dried bricks afar."

Ungenerous! yet despite thy frowns
    Except in love we cannot part,
Armida of all earthly towns!
    Thy beauty lives within my heart.

Can I forget for this day's wrath
    Long years of sweetness? 'twere ingrate,
I needs must own the pleasant path
    Wherein thou smoothly leddest fate.

I bless thee, Florence, for each hour
    Of fair imaginative peace,

Ah, let their memory keep its power
    Though to my sense thy beauties cease.

Where'er I sojourn, east or west,
    Exuberant France or Albion grave,
My Florence days for ever blest
    I'll count, because of light they gave.

THE DEATH OF ELIOT WARBURTON.

Strange dreams had lately haunted him
    While yet he dwelt upon the land,
Of shipwrecked sailors as they swim
    And strike out vainly for the strand.

Of boats beneath a vessel's lee
    Swamping unnumbered leagues from shore,
Of drowning wretches' agony,
    And outcries choked by ocean's roar.

Of helmless bark whose masts are gone,
    Whose crew is fled, whose timbers strain,
Where some lost passenger alone
    Drifts starving o'er the naked main.

Or haply, with foreboding light,
    The death by which he was to die
Flung its red horror o'er the night,
    A burning ship 'twixt sea and sky.

Until he was contrained to tell,
    By pressure he could not resist,
What perils indescribable
    Lurked for him in the raw sea mist.

But as when to the morning bright
    We tell what sleep uneasy showed
And feel at once our burden light,
    Perchance he writing eased his load.

Now when in truth the ponderous wheel
　　His vessel o'er the sand-bar drave,
When the great steamer's maiden keel
　　Shore proudly the Atlantic wave,

Did it return that well known dread,
　　And change the foam sparks' frosty blue
To eyes of comrades floating dead,
　　And he himself among them too?

Or did the cordage slack at night,
　　That creaked outside his cabin door,
Wake him with suddenness of fright
　　Like voice prophetic, "sleep no more?"

Not long for sleep, not long for fear,
　　The second night they passed at sea
Brought rage of winds and waters near
　　With certain sense of jeopardy.

And yet unwarned, O God of love!
　　In careless peace they sank to rest,
Clouds whirled across the moon above,
　　Below, the billows reared their crest.

They slept a sleep, whence some should wake
　　To spring bewildered from their pyre,
And some a shorter path must take
　　To God, through martyrdom of fire.

Realization of his thought
　　Burst thus on him when he awoke,
And scarce surprised the deck he sought
　　Across a bridge of blazing smoke.

Beyond the yellow wreaths of flame
　　He saw them launching boats in haste,
They may have called him by his name,
　　May have forgot him, danger-chased.

Though by the helm one saw him stand,
　　Who through sore perils safety gained

And told this story on the land,
  But him the sea and fire retained.

Forewarned he died, how, none can say;
  With him an hundred others sank,
The ship pursued her furious way
  Lashed on by piston and by crank.

No human hand the engines touched,
  But swift the monster wheels kept pace,
As if Sathanas' self had clutched
  The red-hot lever for that race.

Wildly she drove with groaning cry;
  Erect, her chimney's iron frame
Like furnace glass against the sky
  Rose crimson through the clear white flame.

Till with a loud explosive roar,
  One burst of shivered stars she fell,
And the flushed seething deep once more
  Grew pallid o'er that dying yell.

O'er his warm heart who at the helm
  By fleeing sailors last was seen,
Expectant till the waves o'erwhelm
  His pregnant thought and fearless mien.

He struggled not, resigned to fate
  He seemed to recognize his doom;
Perhaps beyond the burning gate
  He saw the flowers of Eden bloom.

Perhaps through raging seas and gales
  He heard the heavenly harpers' strings;
What others took for shrivelling sails
  To him were angels' ready wings.

We hope it, Lord! thy realm extends
  O'er faithless ocean, steadfast land;
What comfort else have we for friends
  Whose bodies cumber up the strand.

The rain drips slowly as I sit,
　　The sky is lowering, dark, and dree,
It is a day of all most fit
　　To think of them who died at sea.

Winds are abated, and the thick
　　Wet stagnant airs upon us brood,
Our souls turn wearied from the quick
　　To lean on death in morbid mood.

The strife is stilled, the calm is come,
　　A heavy opiate dulls our woe,
Flat waters obstinately dumb
　　Beneath our questions darkly flow.

No jar, no sigh, lethargic peace
　　O'ercomes us as we sadly pore,
And whispers "death was their release,
　　The fire-sword waves at Eden's door."

CHARON'S FERRY.

The tide runs up the estuary,
The fog-wind rises from the sea,
And damp and chill with driving spray
Soaks the loose sandhills of the bay,
Till their reed grasses, stiff as spears,
Bow down beneath his silent tears,
While wails and sighs around them float:
　　　"Charon! Charon! loose thy boat;
　　　Shift thy helm and take us in;
　　　We are sick with cold and sin—
　　　　　Charon! Charon!"

There is a hazy helpless moon:
She cannot light the vast lagoon,
Nor daunt the marsh-fire wandering wild
Like some belated orphan child,
Nor pierce the sea-fog's misty curls,
As on the sandy marge it swirls
In vapoury wreaths and folds of shrouds,

All shifting like aërial clouds,
All wailing, wailing evermore:
> "Charon! Charon! lift thine oar;
> Haste to help us; urge thy bark;
> We are waiting in the dark—
> > Charon! Charon!"

Then from behind a jutting cape
Steered out a boat of ghastly shape.
With coffined ridge it blackly glides,
Like those that brush San Marco's sides,
And shoot below Venetian walls
Their rapid, noiseless, funeral palls.
Her prow hangs forth a single lamp,
That flares and flickers in the damp;
A single boatman tugs the oar,
And, stoutly pulling, nears the shore,
Whence issue sighs and dreary wails:
> "Charon! Charon! spread thy sails!
> We have watched the midnight through,
> Dawn approaches, cold and blue—
> > Charon! Charon!"

But lo! the boatman stern replied:
"O ye who haunt this fatal tide,
Remember, he who sails with me
Must buy his place and pay his fee,
Since I account to gods below
For souls that o'er their ferry go."
Then sad and sadder down the gale
Outrang the spirits' woful wail:
> "Charon! Charon! grant us grace;
> We were slaves of wretched race,
> Lived with brutes, man's serf and hind,
> Died deserted by our kind—
> > Charon! Charon!"

Inexorable still, he said:
"I judge you not, ye hapless dead;
Your life was hard, your road was rough,
Of stripes and plagues you felt enough;

Howe'er, this word abideth true,
The Elysian fields are not for you:
Without my token none may cross;
Ye should have friends to save your loss."
Then rose a shriek of men and maids,
Of aged ghosts and infant shades:
      "Charon! Charon! we were poor;
      Must the punishment endure?
      Are the gods like men, who hate
      Those who are abused by Fate?
            Charon! Charon!"

Lo! fables these of ancient times—
They only live in poets' rhymes;
Yet still, methinks, there are to-day
Who would the churlish Charon play,
And standing by Salvation's shore
Forbid the Outcast's passage o'er,
Pressing the mockery of a claim
On some neglected child of shame,
And crying out: "The fee, the fee!"
While spirits wail in jeopardy:
      "Charon! Charon! we were slaves,
      Tossed on Misery's barren waves,
      Want, despair, and crime our lot,
      We can give but what we got—
            Charon! Charon!"

GRANNIE'S BIRTHDAY.

1
Happy Returns! the children say
Grannie is Sixty-three today
Her hair is white and her eyes are bleared
But she is'nt the sort that grows a beard!
You ca'nt expect to be "Fair to see"
When you reach the age of *63*.

2

She lives by herself on her own small hoard
She asks no tendance, so no one's bored
The young are busy at work and play
Grannie might find herself in the way
So she trots down hill with a lonely glee
Thank Heaven, I'm hale at 63.

3

The day must come when her legs will fail
When a cough will lurk in the winter gale
When Grannie must sit in the ingle nook
With a bit of work, and a bit of book
But she hopes she never a fash may be
E'en if she lives to 73!

Jan. 6th, 1885

ALLAN WATER AUGUST 27th, 1887.
(On the death of Alexander Ogilvy.)

River, river, cruel river, give me give me back my Dead
Then the Allan voice made answer, I have done e'en as thou said
O thou mocking wicked water, Was't my Son thou gavest again
Stressed by years of evil fortune hampered with a clouded brain
Yet brimful of loving-kindness smiling in the face of pain
What was that among thy shadows which with strong indignant force
Neighbours wrenched from thy black eddies, and thy swift and
     treacherous course
That which lay all cold and silent on the greensward stretching stark
Lips for ever unresponsive, eyes that stared out on the dark
River, fierce remorseless river, give me back the Living Man—
Then the Allan laughed derisive to the ocean as she ran
Blame not me thou foolish woman, me, the instrument of Fate
Twas foredoomed thy Son should perish and assistance come too late
This is not the first occasion I have kissed a dying face
Every year it is my mission to send forth a soul in space
If they seek me I must slay them carrying out High Heaven's decree
Go thy way, thou foolish woman, blame is not twixt Me and Thee—

Appendix C

The following letter from Elizabeth Barrett Browning was written to her sister Arabel during the visit the Brownings and Ogilvys made to Venice in May of 1851.

Venice. May 16. [1851]

I send you a note this time, my beloved Arabel, to keep you up in information about us. We are all well, you see, and at Venice! The place is exquisite—& though my fancy had of course been brim-full of floating sea-pavements, marble palaces with sea-weed on their marble steps, & black gondolas sweeping through sunlit & moonlit silence, . . though I had fancied these things all my life, (my "eyes making pictures while they were shut.") the real *sight* exceeded the imagination . . oh, by far & far! I have been in a sort of rapture ever since we arrived. It is wonderful, enchanting . . nothing seems to me equal to it in the world. For the sake of it, I would give up Florence, & twenty Parises besides—only I cant quite give up *you*. Do you know what Wiedeman did? He is very sensible to beauty at all times. When he saw for the first time the church of St Mark, (as he was carried out of the gondola in Wilson's arms across the great piazza) he threw up his little hands with a shriek of joy, & then turning round suddenly, he kissed her, to show how delighted he was. This after a long tiring journey from Mantua, when most other children would have been cross & perfectly indifferent to architecture, to say the least. Again, at the sight of the Dogana del Mare, with the great golden ball at the summit, he threw his hands out east & west & clasped them together, crying "Oh, mamma,—oh, papa." He generally invokes us when he is in any particular ecstasy. The child has enjoyed everything in the journey as much as anybody, & instead of suffering, as I feared he might, from fatigue & change of diet & hours, has visibly grown & improved—his cheeks are redder & fatter than when we set out. I should not be nervous now to take him a voyage round the world. Mrs. Ogilvy says that her children would have been laid up, all three of them, with the same amount of fatigue— she laughs at me when I call him "delicate." But he has a delicate organization, notwithstanding, & we must be careful of him in certain ways. I have made a great fuss, for instance, about the apartment we took here, & insisted on airy rooms at a somewhat higher price, to avoid the risk of close ones. I think Mrs. Ogilvy thought me fanciful . . but Robert let me have my way, & we have only paid eight pence a day more for very evident advantages. To stay at the hotel, you see, was impossible—we had to find private rooms. We have taken four . . two bedrooms, a large dressingroom for Robert, and a delightful sitting room with four windows & balconies upon the Canal Grande, the best situation in Venice, & in a noble palazzo, at the rate of thirty shillings a week. We call this immensely dear . . because Florence spoils us for prices . . but considering that Venice is not Florence, & that we have taken the apartment only for a short time, I have begun to incline to think that our outcry is rather unreasonable. Mr. & Mrs. Ogilvy have a bedroom down stairs . . & she comes up to join us at breakfast. *She*, . . not he, I am sorry to say . . we have all been in trouble about him. Probably he caught cold, somehow, . . in the railway . . in the gondola . . one does'nt know how—but on the night of our arrival in Venice he was siezed with fever & affection of the throat, & has been in bed ever since. The day before yesterday a physician was called in, & yesterday (the fever not yielding) he was bled. You may suppose how anxious & pained his poor wife has been, & that indeed it was painful in different degrees to every one of us. At one time I felt quite frightened—for he seemed stupified, Robert said. Today however he is better, & he will probably be up in a day or two. There is nothing infectious—it is just fever from cold, he being what is called a "highly inflammatory subject." The physician never apprehended anything bad, but thought it should be "taken in time." This illness may make some difference in their plans, as they intended to remain here only ten days & then hasten on to England by Munich. Most agreeable fellow-travellers they have been to us—full of intelligence & good humour . . really clever in their knowledge & apprehension of pictures & churches . . and yet, and yet, . . Robert & I agree sometimes that being alone is a good thing. The whole day, for instance, he was outside & I inside, travelling . . and I had to talk . . talk— Now I like to receive impressions quietly & deeply, without so much talk of this & that. Still, it seems ungrateful to write down any drawback to a delightful journey,—& to really delightful persons. She is both good & charming . . only a little wanting in repose & concentration of character . . *too* sensitive to all manner of impressions . . omni-sensitive, rather than intense. We have taken our apartment for a fortnight certain, & mean to stay a month at least. If it were not for you, I could stay here all my life.

The *aspectable* reason, however, is our wish to wait & hear something of the ship-money, as travelling is very expensive. We left poor dear Florence in the rain— I am glad it rained . . I was very sorrowful. The poor balia we took leave of the evening before, that Wiedeman might not be distressed by leaving her behind. She cried dreadfully. I promised to write to her, & not to let Wiedeman forget her, & that when we came back, he should bring her a 'regalo' from Paris. It was a heartbreaking business. For Alessandro, he almost squeezed my hand off as he helped me into the carriage—*he* cried too: but as himself & the balia hate one another intensely, there is some hope that the pleasure of separating may console them by degrees. We escaped the banditti on the mountains, . . Mrs. Ogilvy holding the probability of them in great dread, . . & slept at Pietra Mala a mountain station between Florence & Bologna, where it was so cold that I lighted a great heap of faggots in Wiedeman's room & mine with my own hand. When we travel, I generally get a double bedded room & sleep with Wilson & the baby . . sending Robert away by himself . . because it is so convenient to have Wilson at dressing time, & to have our night things in one carpet bag. On the second day we were at Bologna, . . spent two days there among the pictures—then to Modena . . spent half a day there—then to Parma, to which we gave a whole day. Correggio, Arabel, is divine—he is the Venice of painters. From Mantua we took the railroad, & swept through Verona, past Vicenza, past Padua, along the glittering snow Alps, as in a vision—then shot into the heart of Venice. The air is not too hot—indeed it is cool & fresh & most enjoyable. I cant describe what the scene is—the mixture of intricate beauty & open glory, . . the mystery of the rippling streets & soundless gondolas. I could be content to live out my life here. I never saw a place which I could be so glad to live a life in. It fitted my desires in a moment. If Paris turned out ill, & Florence failed us, here would be Venice, ready! Robert & I were sitting outside the caffè in the piazza of St Mark last night at nearly ten, taking our coffee & listening to music, & watching the soundless crowd drift backwards & forwards through that grand square, as if swept by the airs they were listening to. I say 'soundless'—for the absence of carriage or horse removed all ordinary noises. You heard nothing but the music. It was a phantom-sight altogether.

We go to the traiteur to dine—even Wiedeman does. By which you may judge what a good *adaptable* child he really is. He has made friends with the "holy pigeons," & they were surrounding him like a cloud today for the sake of his piece of bread, . . he stamping & crying out for rapture in the grand piazza. You have read perhaps about these pigeons, & remember how the whole people of Venice protect them, & how to kill one of them is a crime against the nations. In consequence of which, they are so tame that they mix with the crowd, having no fear of man. You may fancy that Wiedeman is enchanted with the holy pigeons. Also, he has gone with Wilson, to see all the churches on our route. He shook his head at those of Parma, when I asked him if he thought them beautiful, & said "No, no." But nothing has pleased him so much as Venice, & St Mark's—& the gondolas. Only he always wants to get into the water, "per fare bagno." We enquired of him how long he would stay here, and he answered *"Due"*—by which he meant "a long while," *'Due'* being his idea of more than one .. in fact of the infinite.

Here I must end, Robert says. Oh Arabel—do let me have a letter directly. God bless you my beloved. I dont wait to read this over, & it has been written in *course of conversation.*

Your own Ba—

Best love to dearest Trippy & everyone.

Appendix D

The following clipping from a contemporary periodical quotes passages relating to Elizabeth Barrett Browning which originally appeared in *Recollections of a Literary Life* (1852) by M. R. Mitford. This clipping was preserved with the manuscripts of Elizabeth's letters to Mrs. Ogilvy.

ELIZABETH BARRETT BROWNING, THE POETESS.

My first acquaintance with Elizabeth Barrett commenced about fifteen years ago. She was certainly one of the most interesting persons that I had ever seen. Everybody who then saw her said the same ; so that it is not merely the impression of my partiality or my enthusiasm. Of a slight delicate figure, with a shower of dark curls falling on either side of a most expressive face, large tender eyes, richly fringed with dark eyelashes, a smile like a sunbeam, and such a look of youthfulness, that I had some difficulty in persuading a friend, in whose carriage we went together to Chiswick, that the translatress of the " Prometheus" of Æschylus, the authoress of the " Essay on Mind," was old enough to be introduced into company, in technical language was *out*. Through the kindness of another invaluable friend, to whom I owe many obligations, but none so great as this, I saw much of her during my stay in town. We met so constantly and so familiarly, that in spite of the difference of age intimacy ripened into friendship, and after my return into the country, we corresponded freely and frequently, her letters being just what letters ought to be—her own talk put upon paper. The next year was a painful one to herself and to all who loved her. She broke a blood vessel upon the lungs, which did not heal. If there had been consumption in the family, that disease would have intervened. There were no seeds of the fatal English malady in her constitution, and she escaped. Still, however, the vessel did not heal, and after attending her above a twelvemonth at her father's house in Wimpole-street, Dr. Chambers, on the approach of winter, ordered her to a milder climate. Her eldest brother, a brother in heart and in talent worthy of such a sister, together with other devoted relatives, accompanied her to Torquay, and *there* occurred the fatal event which saddened her bloom of youth, and gave a deeper hue of thought and feeling, especially of devotional feeling, to her poetry. I have so often been asked what could have been the shadow that passed over that young heart, that now that time has softened the first agony, it seems to me right that the world should hear the story of an accident in which there was much sorrow but no blame. Nearly a twelvemonth had passed, and the invalid, still attended by her affectionate companions, had

[209]

derived much benefit from the mild sea breezes of Devonshire. One fine summer morning, her favourite brother, together with two other fine young men, his friends, embarked on board of a small sailing-vessel for a trip of a few hours. Excellent sailors all, and familiar with the coast, they sent back the boatmen, and undertook themselves the management of the little craft. Danger was not dreamt of by any one ; after the catastrophe no one could divine the cause, but in a few minutes after their embarkation, and in sight of their very windows, just as they were crossing the bar, the boat went down, and all who were in her perished. Even the bodies were never found. I was told by a party who were travelling that year in Devonshire and Cornwall, that it was most affecting to see on the corner houses of every village street, on every churc'. door, and almost on every cliff for miles along the coa.; handbills offering large rewards for linen cast ashore marked with the initials of the beloved dead ; for it so chanced that all the three were of the dearest and the best; one, I believe, an only son, the other the son of a widow. This tragedy nearly killed Elizabeth Barrett. She was utterly prostrated by the horror and grief, and by a natural but a most unjust feeling that she had been in some sort the cause of this great misery. It was not until the following year that she could be removed in an invalid carriage, and by journeys of twenty miles a day, to her afflicted family and her London home. The house that she occupied at Torquay had been chosen as one of the most sheltered in the place. It stood at the bottom of the cliffs almost close to the sea ; and she told me herself that during that whole winter the sound of the waves rang in her ears like the moans of one dying. Still she clung to literature and to Greek ; in all probability she would have died without that wholesome diversion to her thoughts. Her medical attendant did not always understand this. To prevent the remonstrances of her friendly physician, Dr Barry, she caused a small edition of Plato to be so bound as to resemble a novel. He did not know, skilful and kind though he were, that to her such books were not an arduous and painful study, but a consolation and delight. Returned to London, she began the life which she continued for so many years, confined to one large and commodious but darkened chamber, admitting only her own affectionate family and a few devoted friends (I, myself, have often joyfully travelled five-and-forty miles to see her, and returned the same evening, without entering another house) ; reading almost every book worth reading in almost every language, and giving herself, heart and soul, to that poetry of which she seemed born to be the priestess. Gradually her health improved. About four years ago she married Mr Browning, and immediately accompanied him to Pisa. They then settled at Florence; and this summer I have had the exquisite pleasure of seeing her once more in London, with a lovely boy at her knee, almost as well as ever, and telling tales of Italian rambles, of losing herself in chestnut forests, and scrambling on muleback up the sources of extinct volcanoes. May heaven continue to her such health and such happiness.—*Recollections of a Literary Life, by Miss Mitford.*

Appendix E

The Ogilvy Family – Abridged Genealogical Table

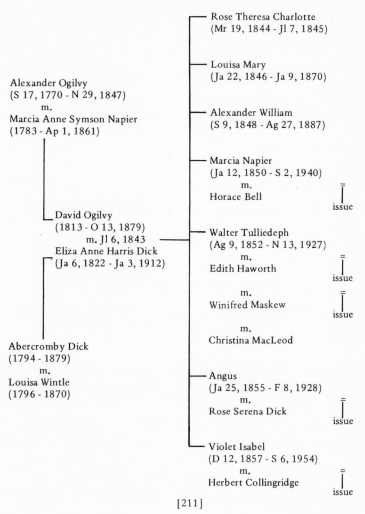

Alexander Ogilvy
(S 17, 1770 - N 29, 1847)
m.
Marcia Anne Symson Napier
(1783 - Ap 1, 1861)

David Ogilvy
(1813 - O 13, 1879)
m. Jl 6, 1843
Eliza Anne Harris Dick
(Ja 6, 1822 - Ja 3, 1912)

Abercromby Dick
(1794 - 1879)
m.
Louisa Wintle
(1796 - 1870)

Rose Theresa Charlotte
(Mr 19, 1844 - Jl 7, 1845)

Louisa Mary
(Ja 22, 1846 - Ja 9, 1870)

Alexander William
(S 9, 1848 - Ag 27, 1887)

Marcia Napier
(Ja 12, 1850 - S 2, 1940)
m.
Horace Bell
issue

Walter Tulliedeph
(Ag 9, 1852 - N 13, 1927)
m.
Edith Haworth
issue

m.
Winifred Maskew
issue

m.
Christina MacLeod

Angus
(Ja 25, 1855 - F 8, 1928)
m.
Rose Serena Dick
issue

Violet Isabel
(D 12, 1857 - S 6, 1954)
m.
Herbert Collingridge
issue

Index